The Indian Ocean

A History of People and The Sea

Kenneth McPherson

DELHI
OXFORD UNIVERSITY PRESS
OXFORD NEW YORK
1993

Oxford University Press, Walton Street, Oxford OX2 6DP

Oxford   New York   Toronto
Delhi Bombay Calcutta Madras Karachi
Kuala Lumpur Singapore Hong Kong Tokyo
Nairobi Dar es Salaam Cape Town
Melbourne Auckland Madrid
and associates in
Berlin   Ibadan

SBN 0 19 563374 1

Typeset by Resodyn, New Delhi 110070
Printed in India at Rekha Printers Pvt. Ltd., New Delhi 110020
and published by Neil O'Brien, Oxford University Press
YMCA Library Building, Jai Singh Road, New Delhi 110001

*For my mother, Joan McPherson,
and for my grandfather, William Robert Nicoll
(Madras, 1885–London, 1948)*

Contents

Maps

Preface

This volume evolved out of fifteen years of teaching under-graduate courses in South Asian and Indian Ocean history at Curtin University in Western Australia. But while its structure was formed by that experience, my interest in the region was shaped by living on the shores of the Ocean and my family's involvement with India.

Until recently there was virtually no interest in the Indian Ocean region in Australia. The teaching of Indian Ocean history provided many challenges in establishing the concept of the region and present-ing it to fellow Australians as part of their world. In practical terms, such a course raised many problems, not the least of which was the absence of suitable texts dealing with the region as a whole. My students' reading lists comprised works dealing with the component parts of the region (East Africa, the Middle East, South and South East Asia and Australia), structured around topics which brought together the history of those disparate parts.

In recent years the tasks of teachers and students of Indian Ocean history have been made easier by the work of historians such as Holden Furber, Charles Boxer, Ashin Das Gupta, Tapan Raychaudhuri, Om Prakash, Michael Pearson, K.N. Chaudhuri, Sinnappah Arasaratnam and Sanjay Subrahmanyam, all of whom have produced studies which have begun the tortuous process of exploring links between various parts of the Indian Ocean littoral. In addition, I have been strongly influenced by the work of Alan Villiers whose studies of the living maritime world of the Indian Ocean confirmed my fascination with the story of people and the sea. This book is built upon their work, and the work of many others, and is a synthetic, interpretive essay offering an introduction to the human history of the Indian Ocean. I have not written an encyclopaedic survey, but have attempted a broad analysis which deals with the whole Indian Ocean region rather than with its parts. The parts are obviously deserving of far more detailed treatment than can be offered in a book of this size. But there is a place for such a survey, to locate existing studies of the parts within a regional context highlighting commonalities and interactions which reveal yet another face of human history.

Some experts on the history of the component parts of the Indian Ocean region will no doubt question my selection of events and trends. Such processes of selection reflect one's imperfect attempts to achieve the nirvana of perfect objectivity and I hope that they will bear with me. This history is unashamedly impressionistic, using a broad canvas to suggest a new way of viewing the peoples who shaped the human history of the Indian Ocean.

Many friends have contributed to this history. My family, along with Hugh and Terry Owen, introduced me to the history of South Asia; Margaret Steven, Geoffrey Bolton, Ashin Das Gupta and Ravinder Kumar have probably forgotten that they fired my interest in an 'Indian Ocean region', while Peter Reeves has been a constant and constructive critic and source of inspiration. Susan Maushart, Sanjay Subrahmanyam, Joan Wardrop, Frank Broeze, Lotika Varadarajan, Brian Stoddart, Scott MacWilliam, John McGuire, Will Christensen, Phil Moore, Geoff Kay, Bob Pokrant and my students have commented on, and encouraged, the writing of some or all of the manuscript. Terry Richards and Peter Gadsden introduced me to the arcane world of the word processor and Viv Forbes and Greg Baxter prepared the maps.

My mother and her family inherited my exiled grandfather's gloriously exaggerated and embroidered tales of the India of his youth and of his ancestors. They, with my sailor father, are ultimately responsible for my fascination with the romance of Indian Ocean history.

Indian Ocean Centre for Peace Studies   Kenneth McPherson
Perth, October 1992

Introduction

Aims

This book is about the Indian Ocean region, whose boundaries and history have been determined by waters which provided a great highway for cargoes of people, goods and ideas. The Indian Ocean enabled the peoples on its shores to share a range of cultural values and economic activities which set them apart from peoples of regions around the Mediterranean, the Atlantic and the Pacific. The Mediterranean, like the Indian Ocean, linked the peoples on its shores over thousands of years in a web of cultural and economic commonalities; whereas the peoples on the opposite shores of the Pacific and the Atlantic were divided by great stretches of ocean not crossed regularly until the sixteenth century.

Any history of the Indian Ocean region must focus on the people who have used that ocean, and on the forces which shaped their relationship with the sea, if it is to have validity as a regional history and not dissolve into a collection of histories about separate peoples, civilizations and nations. The Indian Ocean region was the home of the world's first urban civilization, and centre of the first sophisticated commercial and maritime activities. This Ocean—as a great highway and source of food and raw materials—was a vital force moulding the many societies on its shores long before people maintained written records.

The central assertion of this book is that the history of the modern world can only be understood by examining the component parts from which it is constructed and not by separating human history into studies of 'them' and 'us'. Such a history proposes the view that regional histories are the foundation of global history and provide yet another means of discovering how our ancestors interacted with one another and shaped the world in which they lived.

The manner in which this history has been written obviously reflects the influence of a range of historians. Most notable among these are the French historian of the Mediterranean, Fernand Braudel, who created a new model for the exploration of regional history; and the historians of the Indian Ocean region, Holden Furber, Auguste Toussaint and K.N. Chaudhuri.

Braudel's endeavour to grasp the terrestrial and maritime characteristics of the Mediterranean region, and of the rise of world civilization and capitalism, by dissecting history into different planes had a profound effect upon my own approach.[1] His consideration of the story of human interaction with the natural environment, and the impact of short-term human and natural events which scar the surface of more enduring types of human activity (such as food production and social and cultural organization), have given shape to this history, though I make no claim to the breadth and depth of his vision.

Furber, Toussaint and Chaudhuri prefigured this present work by writing histories that examined some of the forces which, at various times, shaped human activity across the Indian Ocean.[2] Furber led me into the exciting and complex economic history of the Indian Ocean at a time when Europeans were jostling with one another and locals for a slice of maritime trade; Toussaint and Chaudhuri painted the history of the Indian Ocean region on a broad canvas: they too left me with a sense that there was something missing in their approaches, or something that needed expansion.

Furber's vision is essentially Eurocentric, in that he limits his works to the period after the arrival of the Portuguese in 1498 and concentrates on the history of the European trading companies. Toussaint and Chaudhuri delve into the centuries before this event. However, Toussaint merely sketches in very broad outline some of the forces at work shaping the world of the Indian Ocean, while Chaudhuri in his latest work (1990) is primarily concerned with 'an exercise in the comparative history of the regions around the Indian Ocean from the rise of Islam to the mid-eighteenth century'.[3]

No historian has successfully argued for a regional identity for the Indian Ocean beyond a commonality of essentially economic practices

---

[1] Fernand Braudel, 1972, 1973 & 1986.
[2] Holden Furber, 1948 & 1976; Auguste Toussaint, 1968; K.N. Chaudhuri, 1978, 1985 & 1990.
[3] K.N. Chaudhuri, 1990, 19.

which, it could be claimed, are universal, even if their external forms vary from one civilization to another. The essential unity of the Indian Ocean 'world' was determined by the rhythms of long-distance maritime trade until major changes in this trade occurred in the eighteenth century. It was this trade which enabled people and ideas to cross the Indian Ocean, leading to the spread of three great world religions—Hinduism, Buddhism and Islam—and the growth of cosmopolitan civilizations in Asia and Africa which drew their inspiration from a great range of cultures along the shores of the Ocean.

Nor have Furber, Toussaint and Chaudhuri addressed another issue which is central to any understanding of the history of people and the sea: the relationship between maritime trade and processes of cultural diffusion and interaction. It is common to admit that there was an association between maritime trade and cultural interaction; the mechanics of this process, which are central to our understanding of how economic activity and social change are related, are not adequately explored.

There is a wealth of literature relating to the history of the disparate parts of the Indian Ocean region. Historians, economists, anthropologists and other scholars have produced an enormous body of research relating to specific parts of the region, but as yet there has been no satisfactory attempt to see if there was in fact a discrete Indian Ocean region or 'world'. There are many histories of East Africa, the Middle East, South Asia, South East Asia and Australia, but these have not been integrated into a regional history based upon the human working of the Ocean which links these areas. There is value in constructing a regional history out of these fragments to reveal more about the history of human endeavour and the interlocked nature of human history, and to counter the Eurocentrism of many modern historical writings.

Terms of Reference

The specific purpose of this book is to offer new perspectives on the lives and experiences of the people who used the Indian Ocean from prehistoric to modern times, and who were participants in a rich and vibrant history which helped shape the modern world. Before Europeans came into direct and frequent contact with them in the sixteenth century, they developed a remarkably self-sustaining economic and cultural 'world' which was set apart from other 'worlds' such as the Mediterranean and East Asia. The Indian Ocean 'world' had its own set of human and natural rhythms which dictated the patterns of human activity. It had its own natural and fluctuating human boundaries which varied over time, and until the fifteenth century AD it was remarkably self-contained. By the eighteenth century the boundaries of this world were crumbling as it was overwhelmed, physically and economically, by European merchants and soldiers.

Although I have used the term 'Indian Ocean world' to describe a physical arena used by civilizations which had direct access to the Indian Ocean, it was not a unitary 'cultural area'. It was an area which included an enormous range of cultural and economic practices, bonded and defined by its unique maritime trading system, which provided the peoples of that 'world' with an economic unity and *certain* cultural commonalities which set them apart from the peoples of contiguous 'worlds' such as the Mediterranean and East Asia. Cultural commonalities were made possible by trade linkages which facilitated the diffusion of religious and cultural systems such as Hinduism, Buddhism and Islam across the Ocean.

Among the great oceans of the world, the Indian Ocean is exceptional in its geographic dimensions. Unlike the Atlantic and Pacific, which stretch from pole to pole across the northern and southern hemispheres, it is bounded on the north by the landmass of Asia and great chains of mountains which separate the Ocean from the climatic forces of Central Asia. The major consequence of this particular geographic configuration is its system of seasonal monsoons which determine patterns of rainfall, winds and ocean currents. Blowing in opposite directions during alternating seasons, these winds made possible and dominated the rhythms of agricultural and maritime activity in Asia. For millennia, maritime activity operated along a wide arc stretching from south-east Africa and Madagascar to South East Asia and northern Australia, enabling people to travel the Ocean, leading to a constant intermingling of cultures, races, religions and trading goods. The lands of the littoral possessed plentiful supplies of raw materials and, in the pre-modern world, produced an astonishing range of processed and manufactured goods. The distances travelled by traders could be formidable, but the wealth that could be extracted made the journeys worthwhile.

The Indian Ocean provides a highway linking a great variety of peoples, cultures and economies. It forms the eastern boundary of the African continent; is almost linked to the Mediterranean through the Red Sea; penetrates the central lands of the Middle East via the Persian Gulf; washes both shores of the Indian subcontinent; and across the Bay of Bengal links up with the South China Sea, beyond which is the Pacific. Ancient civilizations in Egypt, Arabia, Mesopotamia, the Persian highlands, the Indian subcontinent and mainland and insular South East Asia had ready access to the Ocean and used it to develop their first maritime trading links. These sea routes were linked in turn to overland trade routes which bound sea and land in a tight economic relationship, in which the rhythms of agricultural life interacted with the rhythms of the seasonal monsoons to set the pace of maritime activity.

Seaborne trade across the Indian Ocean was primarily determined by what Braudel called the *longue durée* or long term rhythms of the natural and human environment. In the short term, random political and natural events affected rhythms of human activity, but the major rhythms were set in the long term by climate and agriculture which determined basic social attitudes towards food, clothing, architecture and trade. The cultures and economies of the Indian Ocean before the arrival of Europeans were essentially self-sufficient within the geographic boundaries of the Indian Ocean, and were only marginally determined in the *longue durée* by influences from outside the region. To this extent it is possible to argue that the peoples, cultures and economies of the Indian Ocean region formed a distinctive 'world' until it was integrated into a global economy in the eighteenth and nineteenth centuries.

The boundaries of this Indian Ocean world were rarely constant. There was of course a fixed geographic boundary determined by the limits of the Ocean, but in human and economic terms this was a porous frontier. The human and economic limits of the Indian Ocean world constantly fluctuated in response to changing patterns of human activity on land and sea. I have used general terms—East Africa, the

Middle East, South Asia, South East Asia—mainly as terms of convenience, but the boundaries of each of these areas changed over the centuries. Two examples will suffice here.

In this book, the term 'East Africa' refers in the early historical period to the area now covered by Somalia, with an extension into modern Ethiopia, but in the following centuries its boundaries expanded to cover the African seaboard as far south as modern Mozambique. At no stage in the pre-modern period, however, did the culture and economic activity peculiar to the coast stretch very far inland. Beyond a narrow coastal belt, the peoples, cultures and economies of eastern Africa were only loosely linked to the coast and were separated as much by different physical environments as by economic activity. In the short-term there are instances—the establishment of the gold-rich Shona kingdoms from the twelfth and thirteenth centuries AD, and the construction of the city of Zimbabwe with its monumental architecture[4]—where it might be argued that a temporary strengthening of economic linkages between inland and coastal peoples drew the former into the world of the Indian Ocean; but in general the *longue durée* rhythm was one of relative isolation from one another.

The usage of the term 'Middle East' presents even more problems. At the beginning of the period under review the term refers simply to the early civilizations of Mesopotamia and the Nile valley, with some reference to parts of the Arabian peninsula. By the beginning of the present era—that is the period dating from the beginning of the Christian calendar—the term encompassed all the lands stretching from Egypt to Persia and northward to the Black Sea. From the period of Alexander the Great in the fourth century BC, to the rise of Islam in the seventh century AD, this entire area provided a hinterland for ports on the Red Sea, Arabia and the Persian Gulf which were linked by caravan routes to ports on the Mediterranean Sea.

From the seventh to the nineteenth centuries, however, the depth of this porous frontier fluctuated. From the seventh to the thirteenth centuries, under the Islamic Empire or Khilafat which was centred upon the great city of Baghdad in Mesopotamia, links with the Mediterranean weakened in favour of links with Central Asia and

[4] D.N. Beach, 1980.

Africa; from the thirteenth to the sixteenth centuries, internal economic and political chaos within the Middle East fragmented local economic systems, reducing the Middle East, for the purposes of this book, essentially to Egypt and Persia plus the Levant with its linkages into the Mediterranean; from the sixteenth century there was some recovery in Middle Eastern economic and political fortunes, leading to a revival of the trading links of the Ottoman and Safavid empires with the Indian Ocean. But even given these improvements in fortune, Egypt had been reduced to an economic backwater, the wealth and culture of the Safavid empire peaked in the seventeenth century, and the great trade routes into Central Asia had collapsed, reducing the hinterland linkages of Red Sea and Persian Gulf ports to a geographically restricted range of markets in the decaying Ottoman and Safavid empires.

Australia stands apart from the above discussion. From earliest times the peoples of Australia have had marginal contacts with the Indian Ocean. Until the nineteenth century AD, the western part of the continent was only rarely visited by outsiders, while its aboriginal peoples seldom ventured beyond shallow coastal waters.

Throughout history the lands of the Indian Ocean have been influenced by extra-regional civilizations in the Mediterranean and East Asia. The Persians, Greeks, Romans and Arabs ruled empires which stretched from the Mediterranean to the Indian Ocean, but the linkages created between the two seas were short term and their effects were marginal until new linkages were created from the eighteenth century. Closer and more extended economic linkages certainly existed between the lands of the Indian Ocean and East Asia—most particularly the great Chinese empire—but these were subject to enormous fluctuations in intensity. They were never of central importance to the economies of East Asia, and did not lead to marked cultural interaction between the civilizations involved in the economic exchange.

In a less tangible sense, the boundaries of the Indian Ocean world were also set by cultural and religious linkages. By the fifteenth century, Islam stretched across the Indian Ocean from East Africa to insular South East Asia, providing yet another integrating bond within the Indian Ocean world. But Islam had also spread into Central Asia, the Mediterranean and Africa as far west as the Atlantic. Muslims in the Indian Ocean had a worldview which stretched beyond narrow geographic and economic boundaries to encompass much of Asia and Africa, and some of Europe. To an extent, the same was true of Buddhism, which penetrated as far east as Japan, and was certainly true for the small number of Christians and Jews who inhabited the Indian Ocean world before the arrival of Europeans in the late fifteenth century.

With the arrival of Europeans the economic boundaries of the Indian Ocean world expanded to encompass direct linkages with European and American markets. Until the late seventeenth century, however, these extra-regional linkages did not fundamentally alter the long-term rhythms of life in the Indian Ocean world. But from the eighteenth century European capitalism, first commercial and then industrial, began to drastically alter patterns of indigenous economic, cultural and political life. The indigenous long-term forces which had shaped the history and cultures of the Indian Ocean world were overwhelmed, and it was integrated as a region into a global system whose long-term cultural and economic rhythms were fundamentally influenced by the industrialized nations of Europe and North America.

A study of the Indian Ocean region as a discrete 'world' has much to tell us about the history of its inhabitants beyond the narrow confines of a particular culture and state; about more universal issues such as cultural diffusion and adaptation; and about the development of commerce, imperialism and capitalism. The modern world is the product of the integration of a range of cultures and economies which gathered pace in the eighteenth century. To understand this world it is not sufficient to study its component parts based upon modern states; rather, we need to explore the economic and cultural networks which existed beyond Europe, which were eventually integrated into a global capitalist system.

The Setting

The Indian Ocean region comprises an enormous variety of physical settings for all forms of life. One particular physical event, however, binds many of the lands around the Indian Ocean into a distinctive environment: the monsoons.

From the shores of the Arabian Sea, across the Bay of Bengal and into the South China Sea there are two distinctive seasons of winds. For about six months of the year these winds blow as northeasterlies and for another six months as southwesterlies. The Arabs first coined the expression *mausim* to mean a season of winds, and across monsoon Asia the two distinctive seasons of winds are also associated with rainfall and the cycles of agricultural activity. The seasonal reversal of monsoons means alternate dry and wet seasons from northern India to South East Asia, and in the age before steamships the monsoon winds facilitated a seasonal movement of sailing ships across the Arabian Sea, the Bay of Bengal and the South China Sea.

Although the monsoons set the basic rhythms for life across much of tropical and equatorial Asia, there are vast tracts of territory in the Middle East, East Africa and Australia where the monsoon system has no impact. The lands of the Indian Ocean region exhibit a spectrum of climates, landscapes, and animal and vegetable life, providing a range of environments for human survival and the evolution of human societies.

The monsoon rains sustain agriculture in a swathe of land stretching from the semi-arid plains of the Indus valley to the equatorial lands of insular South East Asia. Within this area rainfall patterns are both seasonal and erratic, creating pockets of arid land cheek by jowl with semi-tropical, tropical and equatorial scrubland and forest. Except for the equatorial belt, rainfall is strictly seasonal, so that even in areas where the monsoons are a regular event there is a long dry season during which agriculture can only be sustained by using water stored in tanks and dams. In parts of the monsoon belt, in South Asia and mainland South East Asia, great rivers provide another source of water during the dry season, but to sustain agriculture their waters too must be diverted through irrigation systems (See Map 1).

In other parts of the Indian Ocean the monsoons have no impact. Australia, apart from its northern reaches, is the driest continent in the world. In the pre-modern world it was largely unsuitable for agriculture, but a bountiful land for the hunter-gatherers who first populated the continent. East Africa has erratic rainfall, which encouraged its indigenous inhabitants to develop mixed economies comprising hunter-gathering, pastoralism and agriculture. In the Ethiopian

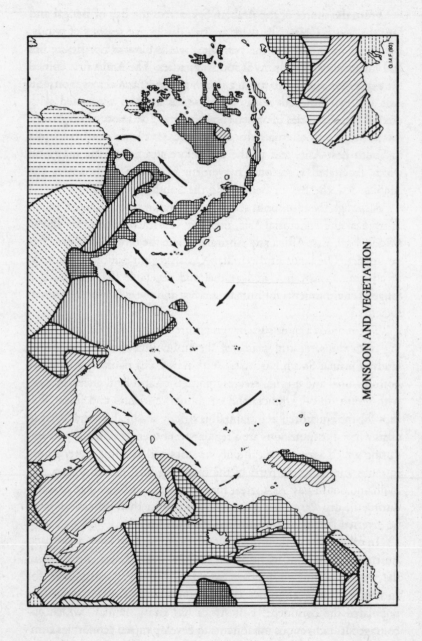

MONSOON AND VEGETATION

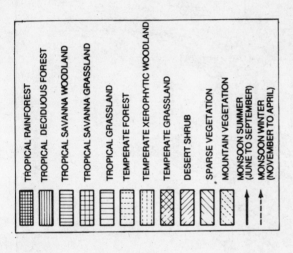

Map 1: Monsoon and Vegetation

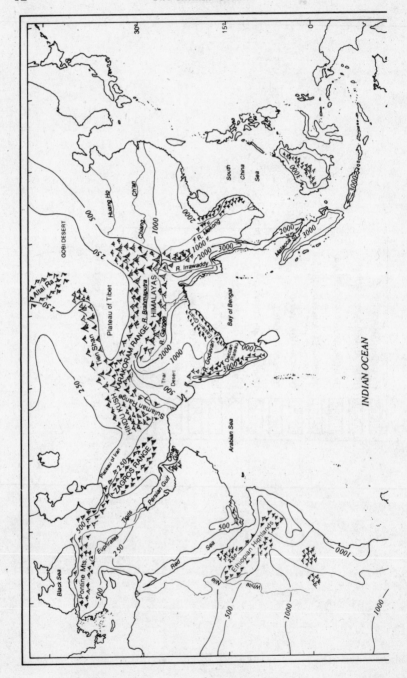

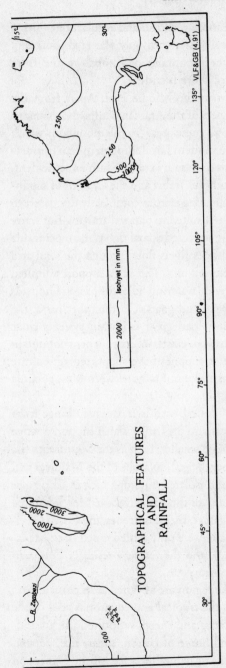

Map 2: Topographical Features and Rainfall

highlands rainfall tends to be more plentiful and regular, but further south the coastal belt is generally dry, with only scattered sources of water along rivers rising in the mountains of Zimbabwe and from wells along the coast and on offshore islands.

Rainfall is also a problem in the Middle East. Apart from the south-west and south-east corners of the Arabian peninsula, the monsoons have little impact. Beyond these areas, to the mountains which form a crescent stretching from modern Israel through to Iran (formerly Persia), rainfall is insufficient to sustain extensive human settlement. Between the mountains of southern Arabia and the crescent of mountains to the north, the landscape ranges from completely dry desert to semi-arid scrub-covered land best suited to pastoral activity. But water is not entirely absent. Oases are scattered across the Arabian peninsula and the great Tigris and Euphrates rivers flow through the semi-arid lands of Iraq, the ancient Mesopotamia. The oases support a limited amount of agriculture and provide watering holes for pastoral nomads with their herds of camels, sheep and goats. On the other hand, the Tigris and Euphrates have sustained great irrigation systems since ancient times. A similar situation exists in Iran, where mountain streams and underground water supplies have supported agriculture in the midst of semi-arid plains and mountains between Mesopotamia and the Indus valley (See Map 2).

The Indian Ocean is also dotted with islands which range from the largest—such as Madagascar and Sri Lanka which support a range of micro-environments—through smaller, such as the Mascarenes (La Réunion, Mauritius and the Seychelles), to atolls of the Maldives and the Cocos (Keeling) Islands, and isolated outcrops such as Christmas Island to the south of Java. Many of these islands have been inhabited since ancient times, but Madagascar, the Mascarenes, the Cocos (Keeling) Islands and Christmas Island were only settled much later: Madagascar in the early centuries AD, and the rest as a result of European activity from the eighteenth century AD.

The natural products of the region are as varied as its climates and landscapes. Until this century the tropical and equatorial belts, while unsuitable for domesticated cattle and sheep, supported thick stands of timber and were the natural home of cotton, sugar, rice, pepper, spices, the pig and the chicken, to name but a few of the plants and animals native to the region; the semi-arid savannas supported great herds of wild animals, such as the elephant, which was found in monsoon Asia as well as in Africa and the Middle East, and domesticated cattle; and the region was rich in most minerals ranging from gemstones and gold to tin and iron ore. Some minerals—notably copper, gold and silver were in short supply (it was not until the nineteenth century AD that suitable technology was available to mine gold in South Africa and Australia) and the pursuit of such minerals led traders to distant lands where they were more readily available. Rivers and seas also returned a bounty. Fish were abundant in rivers and coastal waters, while parts of the Ocean were also rich in valuable and rare goods such as ambergris, pearls, shells and coral.

The lands of the Indian Ocean provided a range of environments for human settlement in the pre-historic period. Wide savannas full of game and plant life were ideal for hunter-gatherers and nomadic pastoralists; arid plains bisected by great rivers were the home of irrigation technology developed by settled communities of farmers; while in monsoon Asia heavy seasonal rains stimulated similar patterns of technological development as farming societies evolved. Throughout the region, with the exception of dry Australia (the exclusive domain of the hunter-gatherer), human beings followed different means of economic activity and coexisted within easy reach of one another: the nomadic pastoralist and settled farmer coexisted in the Middle East and South Asia; the nomadic pastoralist, hunter-gatherer and farmer in East Africa; and the hunter-gatherer and farmer in South East Asia. All these different occupational groups on the shores of the Indian Ocean formed an interlocked human world joined by the common highway of the Ocean.

1

The Early Maritime Trade of the Indian Ocean

Overview

Thousands of years ago sailors and traders from many lands began to travel the Indian Ocean. They created the first of a web of maritime linkages which, in succeeding centuries, would bind the peoples of the Indian Ocean into a largely self-contained world.

Before the advent of modern communication technology, trade across the high seas and land was the major means of contact between peoples living around the Ocean. Sailing ships, pack animals, sailors and traders were the carriers of invisible cargoes of ideas, cultures and technologies which bound different peoples and cultures into a unique Indian Ocean world. Without trade the extent of human communication would have been greatly restricted, so too would the cross-fertilization of ideas which precipitated the flowering of many brilliant cultures. Cultures could indeed evolve even with only limited trade, as, for example, did the complex cultures of Aboriginal Australia. However, where trade was extensive and complex, there were spectacular examples of cultural interaction, giving rise to some of the world's greatest civilizations.

By the beginning of the present era, merchants and sailors from Egypt, the Red Sea, the Persian Gulf and South Asia thronged ports around the Arabian Sea from the Horn of Africa to the west coast of India; others had navigated past the Horn of Africa to sail as far south as the Tanzanian coast; and, if we accept Phoenician claims, had rounded the Cape of Good Hope. Mastery of the monsoon winds provided such travellers with regular passage across the Arabian Sea, enabling the growth of international trade networks based upon the growing prosperity and wealth of great states in the Mediterranean, the fertile heartland of the Middle East, and South Asia.

The eastern half of the Indian Ocean, centred upon the Bay of Bengal, was the exclusive domain of merchants and mariners from South and South East Asia. South Asian sailing vessels and large outriggers from South East Asia carried cargoes of South East Asian and Chinese commodities to markets around the Bay of Bengal, and to entrepôts in southern India and Sri Lanka, where their cargoes were trans-shipped in Arab and Persian craft to ports in the Persian Gulf, Arabia and the Red Sea.

The eastward movement of South Asian merchants and mariners was marked by the dispersion of South Asian culture and religion into South East Asia. Throughout this area, from the Irrawaddy valley of Burma to coastal Vietnam, where the spread of settled farming communities was giving rise to more complex social and economic organization, South Asian cultural and religious forms were adopted.

The Origins of Maritime Skills and Trade

To understand the maritime trade network of the Indian Ocean is to understand how the majority of pre-modern societies on the shores of the Indian Ocean integrated into a unique world. To do so, we need to examine the conditions which made it possible, including the evolution of maritime skills, as well as the impact of trade upon the societies it linked.

The enabling conditions of maritime trade were numerous: shipbuilding and navigational techniques had to be developed and refined; and the patterns of wind, ocean currents and stars observed. Further, for the sea to assume the function of a highway there had to be markets for foreign goods. These are the universal preconditions of maritime trade. But at the same time it needs to be recognized that each of them is subject to the constraints of specific geographic, climatic, ecological and economic contexts; and the Indian Ocean is no exception.

Certain parts of the region obviously possess a greater degree of natural intimacy with the Ocean than others. The islands of the Ocean, for example, are bonded to it in a way that the continental landmasses are not. But in other areas too, geographic considerations encouraged an early use of the Ocean by humans. Around the shores of the South China Sea and in the South East Asian archipelagos, stretching from Sumatra to Luzon, the sea was from very early times the common highway. It was a major source of food and material resources, and a powerful factor which moulded economic and cultural forms.

In East Africa the rugged terrain—and often the arid and disease-ridden interior—encouraged the use of the sea for local communication by the first-settled coastal peoples. The off-shore fringe of islands from Kenya to Somalia were a bonus which provided sheltered passage for boats between the open sea and shore.

The intrusion of the Red Sea and the Persian Gulf into the Middle Eastern landmass linked the Ocean with the populous 'Fertile Crescent', which stretched from Egypt and Palestine in a great curve through Syria, encompassing Mesopotamia and the Zagros mountains. Elsewhere, the inhabitants of narrow coastal plains hemmed in by mountains often found the pull of the sea greater than that of the land: for example, the rich tropical seaboard of Kerala in south-western India, separated from the rest of the subcontinent by the mountain barrier of the Ghats; the coastal lands of Oman and the Hadhramaut; and the narrow coastal plains of Burma.

In areas which favoured the Ocean as a means of livelihood and communication there was an early development of maritime skills. For their inhabitants the Ocean was a major source of food which was worked for its resources as land is worked by farmers. But, given certain conditions, the Ocean returned other bounties, providing a highway for the exchange of goods. Thus, the Ocean could facilitate communication and economic expansion, and while fishing provided some rewards, trade provided others.

If the history of humanity is a seamless garment, then we must search for the origins of human maritime interest back beyond the period when coastal people first took to local seas. The skills and technology required for deep-sea trade did not spring fully formed to the mind of some ancient navigator but were learned in localized nurseries. In these, over generations, the lore of the sea was refined in response to local economic and environmental imperatives. There is, therefore, no single maritime tradition or technology which encompasses the Indian Ocean. In place of a single maritime heritage there are series of local traditions and histories, of local technologies and techniques, each suited to a particular maritime environment and set of human needs.

The beginnings of this grand maritime venture lay with small communities of fisherfolk on the shores of the Ocean and on the banks of the great rivers which flowed into it. From Mesopotamia to South East Asia, while some fisherfolk remained seasonal nomads, others formed what were among the first sedentary human settlements, utilizing both land and Ocean to survive, particularly where there were limited land-based resources. The 'farming' of the sea parallels the farming of the land as a sedentary occupation which led to the first permanent human settlements some 12,000 years ago. The seasons of the sea were frequently more reliable than the vagaries of climate which dominated agricultural life, and provided many early communities with a more reliable food supply than the land.

The need to survive encouraged as many different responses as there were different physical environments on the shores of the Ocean. In some areas, most notably insular South East Asia, coastal East Africa and the Persian Gulf, where the bounty of the sea was greater than that of the land, the relationship between humans and the sea matured early. In areas such as Australia, however, after initial seaborne settlement, exploitation of marine resources and the development of navigational skills remained marginal to survival. The land, riverine and coastal resources of the continent were sufficient to maintain the majority of the population without any significant recourse to the sea. Compare this with insular South East Asia, encompassing shallow seas, where land and sea were almost indivisible in terms of human survival. Here there was an early and rapid development of maritime skills as seas rose 12,000 years ago, when the icecaps shrank, creating myriad islands, where once there had been a great landmass. The early development of maritime skills in this area were evidenced not only by the great seaborne migrations of Austronesian-speaking peoples throughout South East Asia, and later into the Pacific and to Madagascar across the Indian Ocean, but also by the constant movement of peoples such as the Orang Laut (the Sea Gipsies of the Strait of Melaka), and the Bugis from Sulawesi, within maritime South East Asia, up to the nineteenth century AD.

In East Africa, the Fertile Crescent, and South and South East Asia too, the needs and resources of particular societies shaped the first approaches to the sea, including the design of sailing vessels. Over the centuries, technological innovation and contact with other maritime technologies led to increasing sophistication in design and materials, but elements of the early differentiation are reflected in the distinctive shapes of East African, Middle Eastern and South and South East Asian sailing craft. Given that a variety of maritime technologies evolved around the Indian Ocean in response to different environmental and social imperatives, what was the nature of the earliest maritime trade?

In areas such as East Africa and insular South East Asia, many communities engaged in fishing and casual seaborne barter or exchange for survival (given the poor return they could obtain from farming). Their cargoes, comprising basic commodities such as foodstuffs and raw materials—and the odd rare item such as trochus shell used to make arm rings and other forms of jewellery in many parts of South East Asia—were exchanged with other coastal and island communities for goods which were locally in short supply. In contrast, across the northern reaches of the Arabian Sea, maritime trade evolved initially as a response to the growth of urban civilizations in Egypt, Mesopotamia and the Indus valley, which produced manufactured items such as cloth and metal goods, traded for luxury goods sought by the warrior groups and priests who ruled these civilizations.

At least 5000 years ago, complex civilizations had evolved in the Nile, Tigris-Euphrates and Indus river valleys. Cities, writing, mathematics and engineering skills, sophisticated pottery and weaving techniques, metallurgy and a great range of craft activities flourished. All these developments were based upon the large agricultural systems made possible by the harnessing of river waters. In these areas, ruling groups of warriors and priests drew their wealth from the labour of peasant farmers and used that wealth to develop complex urban civilizations with an insatiable desire for exotic imported raw materials and luxuries. The growth of great cities, temple complexes and palaces in the valleys of the Nile and the Indus and across the plains of Mesopotamia stimulated the development of both land- and sea-based trade and the technologies required to sustain such trade.

The result of urbanization and the growth of trade was the establishment of occupational groups such as merchants, sailors, artisans and moneylenders around the marketplace who, in time, would forge wider land and sea contacts linking the disparate economies and cultures of the Indian Ocean.

Regional Variations

As we have seen, the evolution of maritime trade was not uniform around the Indian Ocean. It began where the sea was a more attractive communication route than the land. In insular South East Asia the sea provided the only highway linking thousands of islands, and even on mainland South East Asia the many north-south spurs of mountains discouraged land transport between the great river valleys, encouraging transport down rivers and across coastal waters. In mainland South East Asia too—as in South Asia, Mesopotamia and Egypt—the presence of great navigable rivers gave a fillip to the early development of maritime skills to take advantage of a means of swift and regular travel.

Perhaps 100,000 years ago humans crossed the shallow seas which divide South East Asia. As hunter-gatherers they settled what is now Indonesia, New Guinea and Australia, giving earliest expression of the close nexus between humans and the sea in the history of the area. In succeeding millennia different groups of people moved through mainland and insular South East Asia, developing their maritime skills as they tackled the seas which fragmented the area: the most famous of these maritime peoples were undoubtedly the Austronesian-speaking 'Malayo-Polynesians' whose descendants settled islands as far distant as Madagascar off the coast of East Africa and Easter Island on the eastern rim of the Pacific. Such groups of people criss-crossed the South China Sea as they moved through South East Asia, utilizing the seas of the area as a great corridor which linked the Indian Ocean with the waters of the western and central Pacific.

By at least the third millennium BC, long-distance voyaging in double- and single hulled outriggers and plank built boats was increas-

[1] I.C. Glover, 1990.

ingly common in South East Asia.[1] Such voyages were more than
simply a matter of transporting human passengers: voyages for which
trade was the major objective were probably as equally important.
Initially such voyages probably comprised vital cargoes of foodstuffs,
particularly rice, fish and salt. The rainfall and soils of South East Asia
have always varied enormously in quantity and fertility, and consequently rice was a surplus crop only in certain areas. This led to the
early development of seaborne barter in rice between different parts
of South East Asia. Fermented fish paste formed a traditional comp-
lement to rice, and the two provided the staple diet for many of the
inhabitants of mainland and insular South East Asia. This ensured a
lasting relationship between land and sea resources, and an enduring
dependence upon maritime skills.[2]

The earliest of these long-distance voyages probably linked the
rich deltaic areas of South East Asia. The lower Irrawaddy and the
Menam and Mekong river valleys in what is now Burma, Thailand
and Cambodia, and lesser river systems in Java, Borneo and Sumatra,
were early sites of agricultural activity and of maritime trade in South
East Asia. Given the wealth they derived both from agriculture and
trade, these sites were to sustain the earliest civilizations in South East
Asia.

The intimacy between land and sea which is such a feature of
much of South East Asian history was not mirrored in the history of
East Africa beyond a narrow strip of littoral lands. The physical
environment of the East African coast is markedly different from that
of much of the Asian coast of the Indian Ocean. Apart from the lower
reaches of the Zambezi, there are no navigable rivers linking the shore
to the interior. Nor, along much of the seaboard, was the immediate
hinterland in the pre-modern period ideal for intensive agriculture
needed to sustain complex trading networks linking the coast and the
interior. From Somalia to Mombasa, the coastal lands form a distinctive ecological zone marked off from the interior by the harsh, parched
wilderness of the *nyika* which gives way to dry savanna country and
increasing fringes of mangrove swamps further south. For these reasons
the strongest exchange and communication linkages did not develop

[2] P.Y. Manguin, 1986.

initially on an east–west axis between the coast and the interior, but on a north–south coastal axis between pockets of land where intensive human settlement was possible.

The shallow, island-protected waterways of the coast provided an ideal communication route for scattered coastal agricultural communities. Coral reefs and a series of archipelagos stretching from Somalia to Mozambique formed a protected coastal passageway. Favourable ocean currents and regular coastal winds to the south of the Kenya coast were further incentives to regular use of the coastal passage, in preference to any land route.

In comparison with South East Asia, the peoples of coastal East Africa were slow to develop extensive systems of maritime trade, though there is plentiful evidence of early farming activity in pockets of fertile, well-watered land along the coast. From Mozambique to Somalia, the relics of earliest human habitation point to the evolution of particular localised maritime skills 2000–3000 years ago, as scattered farming communities began the dual exploitation of land and sea resources.[3] Although the anonymous author of *The Periplus of the Erythraean Sea*, an Egyptian Romano-Greek merchants' guide to the western Indian Ocean compiled about 2000 years ago, commented upon this coastal trading network, we know little of the peoples and economies which supported this trade until the fifth and sixth centuries AD.

At the time *The Periplus* was written the external maritime trade south of the Horn comprised exotic goods, primarily raw materials, collected by local peoples for barter with occasional foreign traders. Various wild spices, slaves and tortoiseshell were bartered along the Somali coast at small markets, each under its own chief, for Egyptian cloth and foodstuffs such as wheat, rice, ghee and sesame oil from the Indian port of Broach (Barugaza) in Gujarat. Further south, along the coast of what is now Tanzania and Kenya, past isolated farming and fishing settlements and pirates, there were more shore markets. The greatest of these was Rhapta (probably on the delta of the Rufiji river) which was regularly visited by Arabs who traded metal weapons, glassware and some wine and corn in exchange for ivory, rhinoceros horn and coconut.

[3] G.W.B. Huntingford (ed.), 1980; A.M. Sheriff, 1981, 554–556.

The beginnings of sustained and significant East African maritime trade are undoubtedly associated with the spread of iron-working into East Africa some 2000 years ago, and the arrival of the Austronesian-speaking ancestors of the Malagache from South East Asia. They appeared in East Africa during the first millennium BC as traders, and then, sometime in the early centuries of the present era, as settlers.

Iron technology, spreading from the north-west into eastern Africa along with Bantu-speaking peoples as they migrated eastward from western and central Africa, made it easier to clear forest and scrub lands for agriculture. The Austronesians, who sailed from the Indonesian archipelago in great outriggers, introduced a range of new foodstuffs from South East Asia—the breadfruit, the taro root, the coconut, and the banana—which increased farming activity along the coast. Rice and sugar cane were later added to this list, most probably coming from South Asia.

When *The Periplus* was compiled, the maritime trade of East Africa was little more than a minor traffic engaging a small number of foreign visitors, with little evidence of trade along the coast between Africans. But the conditions for the growth of such trade were provided by the spread of metallurgical technology and the diversification and intensification of agriculture.

In the centuries following the compilation of *The Periplus*, farming spread throughout eastern Africa and there was an increase in the number of more substantial coastal settlements as far south as Mozambique, the Comoros and Madagascar. A growing number of these settlements not only produced surplus food but additionally collected exotic goods locally—ivory, tortoiseshell and timber—which laid the foundations for the earliest trade between the coast and the interior and sustained a growing maritime trade with the Red Sea, Arabia, the Persian Gulf and northern India.

In neither the Fertile Crescent nor South Asia was the exploitation of the sea vital to the survival of the major local societies. Fishing and maritime trade were important, but only as adjuncts to agriculture, except on the arid shores of the Persian Gulf and the Red Sea or in the island chains of the Lakshadweep and the Maldives. Generally, land-based trade networks played a more vital role in the distribution of goods in the Middle East and South Asia than in South East Asia or along the East African coast, where major societies were shaped more frequently by the dual exploitation of land and sea resources.

In South Asia there were regular coastal trading links between the urban civilization of the Indus valley and that of Mesopotamia, at least 5000 years ago.[4]

In the Indus valley, as in the Nile valley and in Mesopotamia, by the third millennium BC a flourishing civilization existed whose wealth came from agricultural lands watered by a great river. Large and complex urban centres, such as Mohenjo-daro and Harappa, built around great temple complexes flourished as did ports strung along more than 1000 kilometres of coast between Sutkagen-gor on the Gulf of Oman and Lothal on the Gulf of Cambay. Such ports were served by the immediate hinterland of the fertile Indus valley and by overland trade routes linking the valley to Baluchistan, Afghanistan and central India which supplied timber, metal and gemstones.

While some of the goods traded out of the Indus valley may have comprised raw materials such as timber, semi-precious stones and ivory, exports also comprised manufactured goods. The weaving of cotton cloth was pioneered in the Indus valley and traders from its cities sold cotton cloth and worked glass and shell beads in the markets of Mesopotamia, travelling in coastal vessels via Oman and Dilmun (Bahrain) from where copper and pearls were obtained. Return cargoes may have included woollen cloth and similar perishable manufactures produced by the skilled artisans of the many cities sustained by the waters of the Tigris and the Euphrates.[5]

The two great river systems were also linked by land routes, although these crossed difficult mountain and desert terrain and it seems doubtful that the volume of goods moving along these routes could match that moving by sea. Even after the collapse of the Indus valley civilization some 3500 years ago, maritime skills survived, as evident from oral traditions preserved in later literary works, and the migration to Sri Lanka and the Maldives of Indo-European speakers from northern India. No doubt elsewhere in South Asia the exploitation of riverine food resources helped to refine skills in river and coastal

---

[4] Nayanjot Lahiri, 1990.
[5] S. Ratnagar, 1981; M.K. Dhavalikar, 1991.

fishing, navigational techniques and boat building. In the north, the
Indus and Ganges river systems provided a nursery for the learning
of boating skills, but elsewhere in the subcontinent, and in Sri Lanka,
the mountainous terrain made most rivers unfit for navigation and
encouraged an early emphasis on coastal navigation.

The earliest trade between South Asia and the Middle East did
not lead to any marked cultural diffusion and interaction. At a very
refined level there may have been some borrowing of artistic forms
and technological processes, but in terms of religion and major cultural
forms the civilizations of Mesopotamia and the Indus valley remained
singularly distinct, apart from their common dependence upon river
valley farming.

Trade links were more intimate between the civilizations of Mesopotamia and Egypt. Physical proximity led to the early development
of overland trade routes through the copper-rich Sinai peninsula, Palestine and Syria, along which also moved great armies, as various dynasties in both Egypt and Mesopotamia struggled for control of these
resource-rich areas. In Egypt the Nile, with its annual inundation,
supported a complex civilization which, although distinctive in many
of its external characteristics, absorbed much of the technology of
Mesopotamia. Proximity and more intensive physical contact through
trade and warfare encouraged closer cultural interaction between
Egypt and Mesopotamia than it did between Mesopotamia and the
Indus valley.

However, in this early stage of contact between Egypt and Mesopotamia there is no evidence of seaborne trade linking the Red Sea
and the Persian Gulf. Egyptian trade down the Red Sea, although as
ancient as the trade between Mesopotamia and the Indus valley, was
limited to contacts with less sophisticated peoples of the Ethiopian,
Somali and Yemenite coastal lands. This trade—based on the exchange
of Egyptian manufactured goods at temporary beach markets for slaves
and exotic raw materials such as wild spices and resins—continued
for thousands of years but was not intensive and led to no obvious
cultural interaction between the various peoples involved until the
first millennium BC.

In the Persian Gulf maritime trade was under way at least 7000
years ago, based on links between the pre-urban Ubaid culture of

southern Mesopotamia and the peoples of eastern Arabia, at a time when the area was undergoing a relatively moist interval in the growing aridity of the Arabian peninsula. As maritime trade developed in the Gulf substantial ports evolved along the western side of the Gulf at Bahrain (Dilmun) and Failaka, sustained initially by the lure of the rich copper mines of Oman. Sharing a common culture, the Barbar culture, the inhabitants of these ports serviced both the Arabian and Mesopotamian hinterlands, with Bahrain also functioning as an entrepôt for the Mesopotamia-Oman-Indus trade and as a source of pearls and coral.[6] The ancient Mesopotamian states of Sumer, Ur, Lagash and Assyria—and neighbouring states such as Elam which bordered on the Iranian highlands—supplied the ports of the Gulf with food-stuffs, silver and manufactured goods, sustaining a maritime trade which supplied them with valuable raw materials and exotic luxuries which were locally unavailable.

In the period when this first trade linking the Gulf and South Asia took shape the maritime trade of the Red Sea evolved quite separately. The foci for the Red Sea trade were Yemen, which produced aromatic resins such as frankincense and myrrh, used liberally in Middle Eastern and Mediterranean religious rituals; and Ethiopia and Somalia, rich in ivory, resins and gold. Initially, these areas lay on the southern limits of Middle Eastern maritime enterprise; however, as trade networks expanded, they evolved important entrepôts serving even more distant areas such as the northernmost coast of East Africa and South Asia.

In the Red Sea during the fourth millennium BC, the pharaohs of the fifth Egyptian dynasty (*c.*3100 BC) inaugurated state trading voyages down the Red Sea to the exotic land of Punt, stretching from Ethiopia to Somalia. Their ships carried cargoes of manufactured goods such as copperware, faience objects, beads and worked alabaster. At seashore markets these cargoes were bartered for gold, ivory, timber, slaves, rare animals, and frankincense and myrrh trees to grace temples and royal palaces. Such official trade contacts were maintained inter-mittently for more than 2000 years. In the days of the twentieth Egyptian dynasty, 3000 years ago, Egyptian voyagers in the Red Sea

[6] Henry Innes Macadam, 1990.

were joined by Israelites and Phoenicians when Solomon, ruler of the fledgling state of Israel, joined forces with Hiram of Phoenician Tyre, to send expeditions from the Red Sea port of Tharshish (Ezion Geber) to the land of Ophir (India?) and to East Africa, which were recorded in the Book of Kings of the Old Testament as 'bringing gold and silver, ivory, and apes, and peacocks'.

In contrast to the maritime trade between the Indus valley and Mesopotamia, none of these expeditions heralded the beginnings of a strong and regular maritime trading linkage. Most were simply occasional forays to beach markets in remote lands, where items were bartered for exotic goods to adorn Egyptian palaces and temples. While these Egyptian expeditions continued for a millennium or more, they were never based on regular markets, and tended to peak at various times in Egyptian history when conquest had filled the coffers of the pharaohs and the temples with disposable goods and bullion.

Such maritime trade was insufficiently intensive to become a major preoccupation for the peoples of Punt and consequently had little impact upon their traditional lifestyles. Irregular contact with Egyptian voyagers did not encourage the growth of port settlements or promote sustained economic activity, which might have led to more complex social organization and the adaptation of sophisticated Egyptian cultural values.

From earliest times land-based trading networks developed more rapidly than sea-based trading networks within the Middle East. Land routes, thronged with merchant caravans, linked cities of the Fertile Crescent with the mineral-rich Iranian and Turkish highlands, while relatively few Middle Eastern merchants and mariners travelled the Arabian Sea to South Asia. Such land-based routes facilitated greater economic and cultural integration across the Middle East, leading to an intermingling of Mesopotamian culture and technology with local cultures, from the shores of the Mediterranean to the mountains of Turkey and Iran. Competition for control of such routes also led to almost endless wars between the rulers of Egypt and Mesopotamia from the second millennium BC. The borders of the two great civilizations overlapped in the Levant and Syria and their rulers fought for control of rich agricultural lands and the seaborne trade of the eastern Mediterranean. But by the second millennium BC, more extensive and sustained maritime trade had developed along the Red Sea, linking Egypt with Yemen, Ethiopia and South Asia.

In Yemen, highly sophisticated states developed, based on complex irrigated agricultural systems and the very profitable export of frankincense and myrrh. Initially Egypt was the main customer for the precious resins of the area and links were maintained by sea. However, after the dromedary camel was domesticated about 4000 years ago, these aromatic resins were also exported northwards along land routes to Egypt and other states in the Middle East where they were valued as vital components in religious rituals. Many a covetous royal eye in the Middle East was turned to the rich lands of distant Yemen, which maintained its independence, guarded by the wastes of Arabia.

During the first millennium BC, when maritime links were established between the Red Sea and northern India, state formation gathered pace in Yemen. The resin trade was joined by rich luxury goods from Ethiopia, Somalia and India, and by levying taxes and tolls, agrarian states and tribes astride caravan routes grew wealthy. Petty states still fought one another for control of the main trade routes and ports but increasingly the encouragement of trade was seen as more remunerative than chaotic piracy and the robbing of caravans. gradually ports such as Aden and Qana' ('Eudaimon Arabia' and 'Kane' of *The Periplus*) became entrepôts whose lifeblood was long-distance commerce. By the late fifth century BC the kingdom of Saba' dominated most of Yemen and, seeking trade commodities such as gold and ivory, established a trading colony across the Red Sea on the coast of Ethiopia (modern Eritrea), where interaction with local peoples helped develop the Aksumite state, and the first urban African civilization south of the Nile valley.

This migration established a still-extant linkage with the Red Sea which shaped the classical civilization of Ethiopia. In architectural and religious forms this civilization exhibited a mixed Afro-Asian heritage, and maintained close links with the Middle East, leading to the adoption of Christianity in the fifth century AD, the presence of a substantial Jewish community which survived into the twentieth century AD, and the penetration of Islam from the seventh century AD. In both Yemen and Ethiopia urban centres flourished as more intensive farming systems spread and as regular foreign trade developed.

Complex technologies from Mesopotamia and Egypt were borrowed and adapted, first by the civilizations of Yemen, and then in Ethiopia, where rich agricultural lands and valuable export commodities sustained new forms of economic and social organization and thriving urban centres.

In Yemen, Sabaean power was replaced, first by the kingdom of Qataban and in succeeding centuries by a host of states all with a confirmed interest in both the caravan and maritime trade. In Ethiopia the kingdom of Aksum established its own great entrepôt at Adulis on the Red Sea from where ivory and gold were exported directly to Egyptian ports such as Bernike and Arsinoe, and textiles, spices and semi-precious stones were imported from Indian ports such as Broach (Barugaza) on the Gulf of Cambay. The establishment of Adulis undermined the monopoly of Yemenite ports over the Egyptian and Indian trade, heightening a vicious rivalry which lead to devastating wars from the third to the seventh centuries AD.

Along the Persian Gulf, maritime trade appears to have declined between *c.*1500 and 800 BC, in response to the collapse of the Indus civilization and political fragmentation in Mesopotamia, when both areas were subject to invasions of vigorous pastoral peoples. The recovery of Persian Gulf trade from about 800 BC was associated with the rise of a new empire in the Fertile Crescent, Assyria, and the renewal of urban and political life across the Indo-Gangetic plain.

The invasions of pastoral peoples, which caused political chaos across the Middle East and a decline in its external trade, did not, however, destroy urban civilization. The invaders eventually merged with the older inhabitants, but not before they had reinvigorated political and military life by the introduction of new ideas and technologies which laid the foundations for the rise of powerful new states. In contrast, in the Indus valley, the arrival of invaders from Central Asia and Persia coincided with the decline of urban civilization, the abandonment and destruction of cities and towns as a result of environmental changes and warfare, and the collapse of more sophisticated economic activity. Urban civilization vanished, to be replaced by village cultures in which basic crafts and popular religious ideas survived. The new rulers were tribal pastoral people who only slowly absorbed the remnants of the old civilization preserved by isolated farming communities. A thousand years would pass before a new civilization would emerge in South Asia, as urban life and trade began to spread across the Indo-Gangetic plain from the Indus valley to Bengal.

Shipping Technologies

Just as there are great variations between the cultural, economic, geographic and climatic environments of the Indian Ocean region, there was an early and distinctive differentiation of shipping technologies in the age of sail. There was no single or dominant maritime technology, but rather, sub-regional technological traditions formed by local imperatives and the selective adaptation of other technological traditions.

Local materials, environmental conditions—the depth of coastal waters, the strength of winds, the direction of ocean currents—and the weight and volume of the most common cargoes were all factors which influenced the design of sailing craft around the Indian Ocean. Politics and war were possibly other factors in encouraging new maritime technologies.

In general terms, the shipping technology of the Indian Ocean region can be divided into four zones: East Africa, the Middle East, and South and South East Asia. Each of these zones developed distinctive shipping technologies. But such technologies did not remain discrete; rather they evolved similarities over time as maritime contact helped diffuse technology from one sub-region to another.

Zonal variations aside, there were certain commonalities which underlay the various shipping technologies of the Indian Ocean. For example, the earliest craft, from East Africa to South East Asia, seem to have been dugout log canoes and raft-type vessels made of materials ranging from papyrus reeds on the rivers of the Fertile Crescent to bundles of bamboo in South East Asia. In some areas, dugout log canoes represented the next stage in evolution; in others, the first primitive sewn-plank boats represented this stage. In general, canoes and rafts were essentially intended for use as inshore craft, while more complex vessels were designed for travel between islands or on comparable voyages. But beyond these commonalities, local initiatives and needs evolved myriad variations of basic types.

The earliest Middle Eastern shipping technology evolved out of reed-built rafts which plied the Nile and the rivers of Mesopotamia. Such craft, waterproofed with bitumen, were adapted to sailing the shallow coastal waters of the Red Sea and Persian Gulf, and for coast-hugging forays along the southern coast of Persia to the mouth of the Indus by 3000 BC. Four thousand years ago, sewn plank-boats were in use in the Gulf and as far east as the Indus river, and were in evidence along the coast of East Africa 2000 years ago.

With the recognition of the monsoon wind systems in the first millennium BC, there were undoubtedly major changes in shipping technology across the Indian Ocean. Strong winds and deep-sea sailing called for more solid timber construction, larger hulls and more complex rigging, such as the lateen sail. In the Arabian Sea, sewn plank boats with lateen sails—ancestors of the ubiquitous dhow—became the dominant type, while across the Bay of Bengal double-outrigger canoe technology was developed to produce much larger ships which could sail directly between the eastern coast of India and Sri Lanka to the Malay peninsula, Sumatra and Java.

Until recently, Middle Eastern shipping technology—epitomized by the dhow, a term used only by Europeans—has been portrayed as dominant in the Indian Ocean, just as Middle Eastern merchants have been cast as the major mercantile players around whom lesser groups of indigenous merchants orbited. But South and South East Asians were at least as important as their Middle Eastern counterparts in maritime trade, as were South and South East Asian shipping technologies.

The sewn plank dhow, in some instances from the seventh century AD also built with iron nails, represented the dominant type of shipping technology in the western Indian Ocean. But it existed in a variety of forms, ranging from the large two masted *baghla* to the small *zaruk* which could be easily beached by a couple of men. Such variations reflected sub-systems of technology dictated by local environmental conditions, the availability of building materials and the requirements of local trade. On some routes, large deep-sea dhows were necessary to cope with the strong monsoon winds across the Arabian Sea, while smaller shallow-draught vessels were better suited to coastal routes and in shallow seas.

Middle Eastern shipping exhibited similarities with that of East Africa and South Asia, but not to the exclusion of local shipping peculiarities. It is not clear if technological similarities reflect a diffusion of technology from east to west or west to east, or is simply the result of independent inspiration driven by the same imperatives. The double-outrigger canoe and log-craft technology in all these areas indicated the influence of local needs and inventiveness, and perhaps of technological influences of the sailors from the shallow seas of insular South East Asia.

Along the coast of East Africa, at least 2000 years ago, the author of *The Periplus* noted an indigenous sewn plank shipbuilding tradition, which eventually evolved the distinctive *mtepe*, built on the coast up until the twentieth century. Small craft were designed for fishing and navigation in shallow coastal waters, creek inlets and for beaching. In the succeeding centuries South East Asian double-outrigger canoe technology and the Middle Eastern technology of shallow-draught dhows influenced the design of larger local craft. But the essentially African technology of the small indigenous *mtepe* survived, especially among coastal fishing communities.

Coastal environmental variations in South Asia led to the development of a range of subtly different shipping technologies. In addition, navigable river systems, most notably the Indus and the Ganges, provided early testing grounds for the development of boats: just as the Nile and the rivers of Mesopotamia did for Middle Eastern shipping technology in its earliest stages. Later technological innovations indicate Middle Eastern influence along the west coast of India and in the Lakshadweep islands, and South East Asian influence in the Maldives, Sri Lanka and along the eastern coast of India. The particular genius of South Asian shipping technologies was derived from the requirements of coastal and river fishing and navigation, but its deep-sea technologies were the outgrowth of the selective adaptation of various external technologies, prompted by the development of long-distance maritime trade.

The mixed origins of South Asian shipping technologies can be seen in the various types of sailing craft which survived into the twentieth century. This is true in both north-west and southern India. In Gujarat, nearly 2000 years ago, *The Periplus* described 'fully-manned long ships' called *trappaga* and *kotumba* which have been identified with the modern *kotia*: two-masted vessels sharing similarities with Arab vessels and described as 'the oceanic tramps of Indian craft'.[7] Southern India and Sri Lanka have a greater diversity in shipping technology than any other part of South Asia; shipping types here range from crude rafts designed for fishing in shallow waters, to the distinctive deep-sea two-masted *dhoni* which was used both for extended fishing voyages and for long-distance trade.[8]

The true catamaran (the *kattumaram*), a bundle of several logs lashed together with coconut fibre to form a raft, and not the popular double canoe of today, was the traditional fishing craft of southern India and Sri Lanka. Dugout canoes probably originated later than the catamaran. Some, like the *padavu* and *paru* of southern Tamilnad and northern Sri Lanka, had added refinements such as sails, thwarts and hull ribs, while others were fitted with outriggers to give greater stability. Known as *oru* in Sri Lanka, they may have been an indigenous evolution, or they may represent the influence of Indonesia double-outrigger canoe technology. In *The Periplus* there is reference to the *sangara* of southern India which were coastal lashed-log craft perhaps related to the outriggers of South East Asia. *The Periplus* also recorded the presence of the ocean-going two-masted *kolandiophonta* (probably equipped with a stout outrigger) which sailed between the Coromandel coast, Bengal and Burma and which later evolved in Sri Lanka into the sewn-plank *yathra dhoni*, which sailed the waters between Sri Lanka, southern India and the Maldives, carrying rice, salted fish, cloth and coir products such as rope and matting.

Elsewhere in South Asia, the *pedar* of southern India and Sri Lanka, the *odam* of the Lakshadweep islands, and the *masula* boat of the Coromandel coast, appear to represent local evolutions of sewn-plank craft before Arab shipbuilding technology spread across the Arabian Sea. Such boats evolved on coasts with few natural harbours where they ferried goods and passengers from larger vessels anchored off shore. Larger boats in the area—the *pattamar* of the Konkan coast

[7] G.W.B. Huntingford, 1980, 162–163.
[8] V. Vitharana, 1992.

and some types of *dhoni* from the Malabar coast and Sri Lanka—appear to be local variations of the Middle Eastern dhow, with rigging and hull design adapted to very specific local conditions.

South East Asian shipping technology had its own peculiarities defined by local conditions and needs. The migration of peoples by sea from southern China and within South East Asia, at least 12,000 years ago, stimulated a precocious development of maritime skills and technology. The plentiful bamboo of the area provided a light, tough and tensile shipbuilding material ideally suited for craft crossing the shallow stormy seas of South East Asia. The earliest of these craft, which may have even carried the first Australians some 50,000 years ago, were probably simple rafts.

As in other parts of the Indian Ocean, there was also a development of dugout canoes. It seems likely that the combination of bamboo raft and log canoe gave shape to the earliest double-outrigger canoes, whose technology spread across the Indian Ocean as far west as Madagascar and the Comoros with migrating peoples from South East Asia during the first millennium AD. Similar technology was carried by other South East Asian migrants into the Pacific. Refinements such as the rudder support post and the fixed sail, which are found in the Indonesian outrigger canoe, are clues to technological influences between east and west, and indicate technological interactions which probably occurred as maritime trade links developed in the first millennium of the present era. However, sewn plank technology seems to have developed quite independently in insular South East Asia, where the outrigger dugout canoe was developed into a single-hulled sewn-plank outrigger which reached its most refined form in the *kora kora* of Sulawesi and the Moluccas, capable of carrying up to 300 fighting men.

Just as Europeans coined the word dhow as a collective term for Middle Eastern seagoing vessels, they coined the word prahu to collectively describe the traditional shipping of South East Asia. But just as the term dhow does not do justice to the type and variety of Middle Eastern shipping, the term prahu simply means a ship and obscures the variety of South East Asian shipping types.

South East Asian shipping technology was the product of shallow seas, strong winds, frequent inter-island traffic, and the attractiveness of the sea, compared with land routes, for the movement of peoples and goods. Variations in needs produced different types of shipping technology, ranging from the log-based double-outrigger canoe, through various types of sewn-plank craft, to the large seagoing South East Asian vessels of the eighth century AD depicted in stone at Borobodur in Java. Its later version, the *jong*, was made of sheaths of planks secured by wooden dowels with vestigial sewn plank construction and had fore-and-aft rig. As in South Asia, these various types of shipping technology coexisted over the centuries. Along the coasts of Malaya, for example, there are at least three distinctive traditional boat-building technologies determined by local beach and sea conditions, ranging from exposed beaches and heavy swells on the east coast to sheltered beaches and shallow seas on the west coast.[9]

Paralleling the development of the jong, the Chinese appeared with their great multi-masted junks, the leviathans of the South China Sea and, briefly, of the Indian Ocean, between the thirteenth and fifteenth centuries. Chinese shipbuilding technology was marked by its wide use of iron nails. Iron nails were also used in ship construction around the Arabian Sea, but only commonly along the west coast of India before the sixteenth century.[10] This technology permitted the construction of large multi-decked vessels: perhaps the largest in the world before the great Spanish Manila galleons of the seventeenth century.

Within all these very broad technological traditions there was great variation in the size of shipping. Small ships were best suited to minor roadsteads, but larger ships could get around this problem by carrying or trailing smaller boats to offload and pick up cargoes and passengers. On some routes, passenger traffic was of considerable importance and dictated the use of larger ships. This was particularly true of pilgrim routes. By the fifth century AD there was a steady flow of Buddhist pilgrims on the run between China, the Strait of Melaka and South Asia, which was to last until the twelfth and thirteenth centuries when the great Buddhist sites of northern India were destroyed by Muslim armies. Even more spectacular was the hajj run from Gujarat to the Red Sea, which by the sixteenth century involved thousands of pious Muslims annually on pilgrimage to the Holy Cities of Islam in Arabia.

[9] G.L. Kesteven, 1949.
[10] Jeremy Green, 1990.

The nature of cargoes could also define shape and size. On runs where bulk cargoes of timber, metals, grain, dates, cheap cloth or ceramics were carried, tonnage was of a higher premium than on routes where the principal cargoes comprised low-bulk costly goods, such as gold or ivory.

Where ruling groups were involved in maritime trade or warfare, as in Mughal India from the sixteenth to eighteenth centuries, the indications are that there were some very large ships ranging from 800 to 1000 tonnes. Similarly, some merchant magnates owned large ships, but in general, few merchants possessed sufficient capital to invest in them, or, given the great risks associated with maritime trade, were inclined towards such investment. But whatever the availability of local capital for shipbuilding, the technology adopted reflected local needs.

As we have seen from earliest times, different shipping technologies developed across the Indian Ocean. Most were evolved for the construction of boats no bigger than 1000 tonnes, as late as the eighteenth century. With the development of long-distance trade, there was a considerable amount of technological interaction and adaptation in the technology of long-distance craft, reflecting the common sailing conditions and challenges imposed by the monsoon winds which dominate both the Arabian Sea and the Bay of Bengal.

Empires, States and Monsoons

During the first millennium BC, there was a quickening of passenger traffic and maritime trade across the Indian Ocean. In part, this was due to the establishment of new states and empires, underpinned by large-scale agricultural systems in South Asia and the Mesopotamian heartland of the Middle East. Another important factor was the rise in the production of trade goods in other, politically less complex, areas of the Indian Ocean world.

Political consolidation in South Asia and the Middle East went hand-in-hand with increasing economic activity and technological innovation. In the heartland of the Middle East the period *c*.1500 BC–*c*.800 BC was one of political fragmentation, invasions from Central Asia and a general decline in long-distance trade. At the end of this period the establishment of a large state which encompassed the Middle East from Egypt to Iran under the Assyrians gave a fillip to local and international trade. Similarly in South Asia, the rise of the Assyrians to power in the Middle East was matched by the re-emergence of urban life and large states across the plains of northern India and the development of ports along the west coast of the subcontinent, from Gujarat to the Malabar coast and beyond to Sri Lanka, which once more linked South Asia with the Middle East.

In both the Middle East and South Asia the spread of iron-working provided a plentiful supply of cheap and tough agricultural equipment which made it much easier to bring more land under cultivation, to plough more deeply and hence produce larger crop yields. Greater and more intensive farming activity led to larger populations and agricultural surpluses which were used by new ruling classes to construct cities, palaces and temples, as well as to maintain armies as instruments of defence and aggression. The spread of urban life was intimately associated with the spread of trade, which broke down the barriers between localized economies, forming much larger conglomerations of marketplaces linked by an increasing number of travelling merchants.

In both South Asia and the Middle East, travelling merchants were vital to the spread of urban life; not only did they perform a vital economic function but they were the carriers of new ideas, technologies, fashions and religions as they moved from one area to another. Merchants were the most mobile and cosmopolitan members of any pre-modern society and their activity was vital to the prosperity of any state. But the impact of these new technological and economic developments was felt beyond the boundaries of expanding core civilizations, as expanding maritime trade encouraged the spread of urban life, centred upon hinterland and coastal marketplaces on the periphery of the great civilizations of the Middle East and South Asia.

The creation of larger states and markets is not, however, sufficient to explain the very rapid expansion of maritime trade on the eve of the present era. A third and decisive factor was the breaking of the code of the monsoons. It was this breakthrough that enabled sailors and merchants to shrug off the constraints of coastal trading and undertake regular long-distance voyages across the high seas. The mastery of the monsoons—perhaps an instance of a need providing the stimulus for the acquisition of knowledge—coincided with an increase in farming activity and urban life. This combination of circumstances enabled an increasing number of communities, once they had acquired the maritime technology appropriate for transoceanic voyages, to utilize the ocean as a means of gaining regular access to a greater number of outlets for their products. In South Asia, a thousand years after the severing of regular external maritime trade links, following the disintegration of the Indus civilization, a resurgence of maritime trade paralleled the spread of settled farming and the development of urban life in the Ganges valley and the Dry Zone of northern Sri Lanka. By about 500 BC, the spread of rice cropping and iron technology had led to an increase in agricultural production in the Ganges valley, and then in pockets across the rest of the subcontinent and Sri Lanka. Marketplaces, towns and ports reemerged with the growth of inland and coastal trade, and in these markets agricultural goods, often augmented by hunter-gathering and mining activities, were sold for imported goods.

By about the seventh century BC small kingdoms and republics were beginning to emerge across northern India in the Ganges valley and the Himalayan foothills. In the next century these small states consolidated into *mahajanapadas*, or great realms, which after a further series of wars were to form the single kingdom of Magadha with its great capital at Pataliputra (Patna), strategically located astride the Ganges trade route. Paralleling these political developments north Indian religious and social ideas penetrated south to central and southern India where minor states began to emerge in the shadow of the more sophisticated political world of northern India. Magadha and its precursors were oriented, in terms of its external contacts, firmly towards the complex civilizations of the Middle East which, under the Assyrians, once more became a major market for the exports of South Asia.

South Asia was a merchant's paradise. Topographically diverse, it contained a range of economies which produced an astounding variety of raw materials and manufactured items, eagerly sought after in markets from the Maldives to the high valleys of the Himalayas. By the middle of the first millennium BC, peninsular India, Sri Lanka and the Maldives were linked into an extensive coastal trading network.

The expansion of markets across South Asia not only led to a quickening of the pace of economic activity but also encouraged the expansion of technological and cultural practices. Throughout South Asia ruling groups absorbed and adapted aspects of the urban civilization which was re-emerging in the Ganges valley. Regional cultural variations remain a feature of South Asian civilization, but, during the first millennium BC, urbanized groups throughout South Asia adapted religious practices which had originated with the Indo-European settlers in the second millennium BC. Such practices, most notably the hierarchical caste system which included the idea of ritual social organization, and their widespread adoption reflected the emergence of a subcontinental wide form of early Hinduism. Hinduism evolved from the merging of the beliefs and practices of the Indo-European invaders of the Indo-Gangetic plains and older indigenous social and religious forms. During the first millennium BC it spread across South Asia, subtly blending with local traditions as trade began to undermine the insularity of previously isolated communities.

Paralleling the re-emergence and spreading of urban life in South Asia was a quickening of processes of political and economic integration across the Middle East. The core area of urban civilization in the Fertile Crescent was encompassed by a succession of great empires. The merging of these ancient city states and small kingdoms into larger territorial states both strengthened internal trade links and expanded Middle Eastern connections with the Mediterranean and the Indian Ocean worlds.

The first of these great empires in the Middle East was created by the Assyrian people of northern Mesopotamia, after they gained control of the Tigris-Euphrates plain during the first millennium BC. The Assyrians fatally undermined Egypt as a great power in the eastern Mediterranean and the Levant, and they created the first Middle Eastern state whose borders matched those of the natural limits of settled farming: the Nile, the mountains of Anatolia, the semi-arid plains of Arabia, and the Zagros mountains bordering the Iranian uplands. Although the imperial authorities showed little direct interest in the Persian Gulf trade, such trade nevertheless responded to the wealth of the empire by once more pushing out tentacles in search of rare and exotic items. Regular links were re-established with the Indo-Gangetic plain, via the Makran coast of southern Persia and Baluchistan. Trade also intensified along the Red Sea, linking Egypt more closely to the markets of Ethiopia (See Map 3).

The major incentive to this extension of maritime trade was ivory, after the Middle Eastern elephant was hunted to extinction in the eighth century BC. Ivory was imported from western India and north-east Africa to satisfy the insatiable demand of the Assyrian nobility, and of Mediterranean élites as far west as the Iberian peninsula, for ivory jewellery, ornaments and inlaid furniture.

While maritime links between the Middle East and other parts of the Indian Ocean world may have grown slowly during the first millennium BC, overland trade grew rapidly within the Assyrian empire. Merchants from Mesopotamia, Egypt, Phoenecia and many other lands of the empire moved along routes which stretched from one imperial city to another, expanding trading boundaries and forging closer economic connections between the Mediterranean, Mesopotamia and through to the Arabian Sea.

During the centuries of Assyrian rule, closer trading links were also forged between the Middle East and the rapidly growing maritime systems of the Mediterranean, stretching as far west as the Iberian peninsula. To the east, the trade routes of the Assyrian empire linked into the economies of petty states, which stretched from the Zagros mountains into the Iranian highlands and beyond to the Indo-Gangetic plain and to the edge of the steppes of Central Asia.

No ruler could remain indifferent to the economic rewards offered by the promotion of trade, or ignore the importance of merchants. Merchants were frequently the only members of any society who had access to capital, usually precious metals which represented their profits, which was often drawn upon by rulers to finance their states and armies. Merchants doubled as moneylenders and bankers and no ruler could afford to neglect their interests. But while land-based trade was universally important to ruling classes, maritime trade was not. Inland markets were always of concern to rulers; the port marketplace, on the other hand, would have a chequered history wherever its economic activities were not vital to ruling class interests. But where

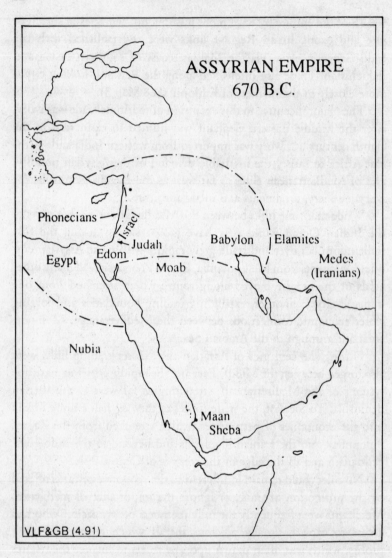

Map 3: Assyrian Empire 670 BC

the port marketplace was of importance to the ruling class, considerable efforts were taken to protect merchant's interests. Foreign merchant groups were frequently allowed to govern themselves according to their own traditions, merchant and craft guilds wielded much power in the councils of state, marketplaces were closely policed to ensure standardized weights and measures, and strict rules governed the quality and content of coins.

As overland and maritime trade in the Middle East began to expand to the west and east under Assyrian rule, trade began to provide an alternative to agriculture as a livelihood for an increasing number of people.

Pre-eminent among the maritime peoples of the Middle East were the Phoenicians of the eastern Mediterranean, who created a mercantile empire stretching from Cadiz on the Atlantic to Sidon and Tyre on the Levant coast, and who may have circumnavigated Africa. Their seaborne empire was sustained by a string of trading colonies around the Mediterranean, the most famous of which was Carthage. Similar communities evolved among the Arab and Persian peoples of the Persian Gulf, coastal Oman and the Hadhramaut, who acted as middlemen in the expanding maritime trade between the Middle East, South Asia and the northern reaches of coastal East Africa.

The economic legacy of Assyria was the greater integration of the Middle Eastern economy and the expansion of its trading links with the larger Mediterranean and Asian world. This resulted in a revival of maritime trade between the Persian Gulf and South Asia, and the development of more regular trade between the Red Sea, South Asia and East Africa. Ancient ports of the Persian Gulf, most notably Bahrain (Dilmun) and probably Failaka, or at least ports in the same area such as Pasinou Kharax and Apologou on the Tigris-Euphrates delta, revived to link with newly emerging ports on the Gujarat coast and the Gulf of Cambay which tapped the expanding agricultural frontiers of northern and central India. In the Red Sea, Egyptian mariners and traders established more regular links with the lands astride the junction of the Red Sea and the main body of the Indian Ocean. Egyptian ports on the Gulf of Suez such as Arsinoe and Clysma, and on the Red Sea coast such as Muos Hormos and Bernike, traded more regularly with Leucecome on the Arabian shore of the

Red Sea and nascent ports on the coast of Ethiopia, Yemen, Somalia and the Hadhramaut. These minor ports—for example, Aden—on the periphery of the Middle East were, in coming centuries, to evolve as great entrepôts for the maritime trade between the Red Sea, East Africa and South Asia.

It was probably sometime during the twilight years of Assyrian rule, or perhaps during the early years of their successors, the Persian people of the Iranian plateau, that the secrets of the monsoon wind systems were unravelled in the Indian Ocean. This dramatically extended the range of human movement across the Ocean, making possible increased direct contact between the Middle East, South Asia and South East Asia from at least the seventh century BC. The growth of South Asian trading diasporas at places such as the island of Suqutra in the Arabian Sea, and the earliest regular maritime trading contacts between South and South East Asia were consequences of such interaction, as was the growing knowledge in the Mediterranean and the Middle East of the world beyond the Red Sea and the Persian Gulf. Use of the monsoons also gave long-distance trade a temporal regularity which was a vital prerequisite for establishing a system of sustained maritime trade between producers of commodities and their markets.

The cycles of the monsoons provided the basic rhythms of long-distance voyaging across the Indian Ocean. These winds gave regular and swift passage across the great distances of ocean separating East Africa, the Middle East, South Asia and South East Asia, enabling sailors and merchants to break the confines of these areas. But the monsoon cycles also imposed a tyranny of time, for their direction and duration was seasonal. They set sailing seasons, imposed several months of dormancy on all ports, and dictated timetables for the sale and movement of export commodities. Eventually, sailors would learn to limit this tyranny by developing suitable maritime technologies, but they remained its captives until the steam engine left sail and monsoon behind. Until this happened, voyages and mercantile decisions, the life of ports, the building of ships, the collection of excise duties, the communication of ideas . . . a myriad decisions and processes concerned with time and distance were imprisoned in cycles set by the rhythms of the seasonal monsoons. To this extent, Man and the sea were as closely bonded to the seasons as Man and the land in monsoon Asia.

The long-haul maritime trade which evolved with the discovery of the monsoon system was a mixture of the rare and the common, of staples and luxuries. From East Africa—most likely from the coastal lands of modern Eritrea and Somalia, and particularly through the great Aksumite port of Adulis—came ivory, gold, ambergris, coral, tortoise shell, rhinoceros horn, foodstuffs, spices, minerals and timber in Arab and Persian vessels to Middle Eastern entrepôts such as Aden and Suqutra, where South Asian merchants arrived with gemstones, pearls, pepper, spices, foodstuffs and cotton textiles. Middle Eastern merchants contributed frankincense and myrrh, metal goods, glassware, ceramics, pearls, wine, gold and silver coins and a range of exotic manufactured items. South East Asian sailors added gold, aromatic timbers and spices. Participants in this trade were Middle Eastern, South Asian and South East Asian sailors and merchants, with a sprinkling of Greeks, Romans and Africans by the beginning of the present era.

Although the monsoon system offered great potential for enhancing maritime trade, it was the growth of two increasingly powerful imperial systems that ensured its realization. One centred upon the Middle East and the Mediterranean, the other on South Asia. In both areas, by the latter half of the first millennium BC, great and wealthy empires had evolved underpinned by flourishing farming communities and thriving towns and cities.

The Markets of the Middle East and South Asia

From about 2500 years ago the lands of the Middle East, stretching from Egypt to Persia, traded regularly with the Mediterranean, the Black Sea, the Caucasus, the southern reaches of Central Asia, Afghanistan and the Indus valley. In South Asia during the same period, there was a rapid expansion of trade linking previously isolated farming communities.

In the sixth century BC Assyrian power gave way to that of the vigorous people of the Zagros mountains and the Iranian plateau, the Persians. Under the Achaemenid dynasty, the Persians expanded the imperial boundaries known to the Assyrians, to incorporate new agricultural and trade frontiers in Thrace on the eastern fringe of Europe, and Anatolia, Central Asia and the Indus valley in Asia. Great Royal Roads crossed the empire for thousands of kilometres, linking Ephesus on the Mediterranean coast of Turkey with Babylon in Mesopotamia, the port of Charax on the Persian Gulf, Ecbatana in northern Iran and ultimately Kabul (Ortospana). Garrisons guarded these roads indicating that trade and safe transportation were central imperial concerns. In this way, the Persians gained new supplies of rich natural resources and extended the trade routes developed under Assyrian rule. Encouraged by the imperial authorities, trade flourished within the empire and across its borders into adjoining areas, particularly Central and South Asia. Before it fell to the armies of the Greek conqueror, Alexander the Great, in the fourth century BC, the Persian empire promoted more intensive economic and cultural contact between east and west, as merchants from many lands moved along its highways (See Map 4).

During the Achaemenid period the marketplaces of the Indo-Gangetic plain and Sri Lanka were linked to those of the Middle East by merchants from the Persian heartland, and from the Mediterranean provinces of the empire. The most notable of these were the Ionian Greeks, or Yavanas as they were known in South Asia. There was also an expansion of Egyptian maritime trade down the Red Sea into the Indian Ocean through ports such as Bernike and Arsinoe, which by the time *The Periplus* was written were flourishing way stations linking Egypt with Adulis and beyond to the ports of western India. This began in the sixth century BC, when Egypt briefly regained its freedom between the decline of Assyria and the rise of Persia. Egyptian rulers of this period attempted to build the forerunner of the Suez canal to link the Mediterranean and the Red Sea, to better tap the ivory- and gold-rich ports of Ethiopia. At the same time, other Middle Eastern mariners forged a link between the Persian Gulf and the Red Sea to gain access to the same ports. Greek merchants from Egypt took a prominent part in this expansion and were to maintain a dominant role for the next thousand years, using Egyptian ports as entrepôts for the flourishing trade between the Mediterranean and the Indian Ocean.

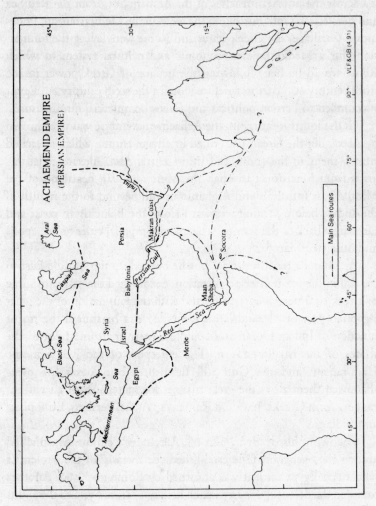

Map 4: Achaemenid Empire (Persian Empire)

The contact between east and west that developed under the Persian peace, proceeded by land—across the Iranian heartland, through Afghanistan and into the Indus and Ganges valleys, and by sea across the northern reaches of the Arabian Sea, from the Red Sea and the Persian Gulf. Further to the west, in the Mediterranean, Phoenician Carthage, the Greek states and Rome were laying the foundations for a Mediterranean economic and cultural system to which Rome would be heir, following the decline of Greek power in the third century BC. After its brief freedom in the sixth century BC, Egypt succumbed to Persian political and Greek commercial domination.

In the fourth century BC the Achaemenid empire was overthrown by Alexander the Great, who ruled briefly an empire which stretched from Athens to the Indus and into Central Asia. Alexander led his army from Macedonia through the Mesopotamian heartland of the Middle East into Iran and Afghanistan and beyond to the mouth of the Indus, before turning westward along the Baluchistan coast and ultimately back to the former Achaemenid imperial cities of Persepolis and Susa (see Map 5).

Alexander's reign was brief but he opened up the Middle East to the full influence of Greek civilization, encouraged the eastward surge of Greek commercial enterprise, and with the foundation of the great Egyptian port of Alexandria on the Nile delta he shifted the major junction of Indian Ocean and Middle Eastern maritime trade to the shores of the Mediterranean. The entrepôts of the Red Sea, the Hadhramaut and the Gulf still flourished, but Alexandria overshadowed them all as the great magnet for merchants of all nations ranging from Greeks, Jews and Romans to Arabs, Persians, Ethiopians and Indians.

Following his death in 323 BC, Alexander's empire was divided among rival generals. One established the dynasty of the Ptolemies who ruled Egypt until it was absorbed by Rome in 30 BC. Another founded the Seleucid dynasty which held sway from Syria to the Indus valley. The Seleucid empire collapsed in 63 BC, succumbing to the power of Rome and a revived Persia under the Parthians, who settled in Iran after migrating from Central Asia in the third century BC. The Parthians struggled with Rome for control of Syria and Mesopotamia, inaugurating a centuries-long rivalry which continued under their successors, the native Persian Sasanid dynasty, which came to power in AD 224.

In the Indo-Gangetic plain, during the centuries of Persian power and Greek influence to the west, urban life and long-distance trade flourished, as the centre of population and economic activity moved from the Indus valley to the Ganges valley, as jungles were cleared for intensive rice farming. Manufacturing and mercantile activity kept pace with the rapid increase in agricultural production. A complex network of overland and maritime trade routes linked previously isolated parts of South Asia into a greater subcontinental economy, in which the agricultural wealth of the Indo-Gangetic plain and the tropical south and Sri Lanka were linked via the mineral-rich Deccan. Trade links with the Persian empire and Central Asia were also consolidated during these centuries, as were maritime links with insular South East Asia.

This expansion of trade networks prompted the rise of urban centres such as Pataliputra, Kashi, Kanauj and Mathura in the Ganges valley, whose lifeblood was trade and not simply agriculture, and whose waxing and waning reflected the economic rhythms of South Asia. The growth of this new type of urban centre in turn encouraged the rise to prominence of new groups such as merchants and artisans. The services these groups provided in the marketplace were important to ruling groups, who were concerned to gain access to the profits of trade and to the market place as a means of converting agricultural produce, which they gathered as taxes, into luxury commodities and precious metals.

By about 600 BC the first South Asian states were in existence. The best articulated were located in the Ganges valley, but in succeeding centuries political units appeared in central and southern India and in northern Sri Lanka. By the fourth century BC coinage, brick-walled cities and writing had spread across the Ganges plain, and the dominant state in the area was Magadha, whose boundaries abutted the Indus province of the Achaemenid Persian empire.

Shortly after Alexander the Great defeated the Achaemenids and invaded the Indus, the throne of Magadha was seized by Chandragupta Maurya. He established the first South Asian imperial dynasty, which held power from c.322–185 BC. After Alexander died, Chandragupta

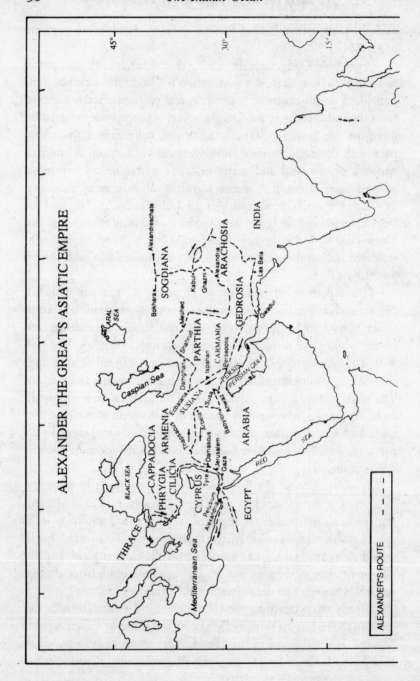

ALEXANDER THE GREAT'S ASIATIC EMPIRE

ALEXANDER'S ROUTE - - - - -

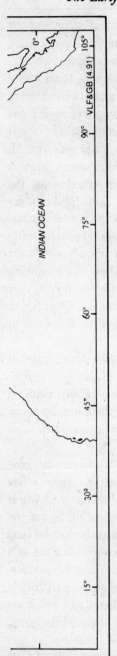

Map 5: Alexander the Great's Asiatic Empire

defeated the Seleucid emperor, Seleucus Nicator, and occupied both the Indus valley and parts of Afghanistan. The Mauryan empire reached its zenith under Chandragupta's grandson, Ashoka, who extended his authority over much of central and southern India.

Ashoka developed an elaborate administrative and tax-collecting system and built and maintained an extensive network of royal highways, reflecting and hastening the changing economic and social environment of South Asia. A new mercantile ethos was abroad, mirrored in the popularity of individualistic philosophies, such as Buddhism and Jainism, which provided a social sanction for the growing numbers of merchants and artisans. These philosophies evolved in an environment where merchants and artisans were increasingly important, but where the old tribal and village religion, an early form of Hinduism known as Brahmanism, was at odds with their urban lifestyle and aspirations. At a time when there was a growing hunger to the west for the exotic and the rare from South Asia, new élites—political, mercantile and religious—were emerging in South Asia, with strong appetites for the material and intellectual rewards of wealth and power.

In the realm of the material, for example, *The Periplus* records that the 'king' of Broach (Barugaza) imported 'expensive silver plate, musicians, pretty girls for the harem, first quality wine, unlined clothing of price [and] choice perfumes'.[11] In the realm of the mind, however, the rewards of wealth and power were the time and the freedom to speculate on the meaning of life.

Buddhism and Jainism evolved in a period of tremendous economic and intellectual ferment in South Asia. In the Ganges valley the spread of rice farming which returned better harvests than wheat farming in the Indus valley, the emergence of cities and the first states, challenges to old forms of religion and social organization by new élites and newly emerging social groups such as merchants, led to a questioning of traditional beliefs and social organization. Myriad answers were posed to new questions and to new problems, particularly among more cosmopolitan groups such as merchants and urban artisans. In response to the perceived shortcomings of early Hinduism,

[11] G. Huntingford, 1980, chapter 49.

new philosophies proposed new ideas and means for sustaining intellectual, spiritual and social life, particularly in urban areas. Within
Hinduism there were movements to develop traditional beliefs and
practices which in time would give shape to modern Hinduism, but
for many the answer was to seek new forms of salvation and of these
forms the most successful was undoubtedly Buddhism.

With its emphasis on individual initiative and the possibility of
salvation, with its rejection of old forms of social organization and
control, Buddhism won widespread support among urban dwellers
and then later among many rulers, who found in its message a means
for sustaining society in a rapidly changing world. The Mauryan emperor Ashoka was the greatest South Asian ruler to adopt Buddhism,
and his conversion mirrored similar processes among merchants and
traders in particular throughout South Asia. Adherents of Hinduism
in time adopted many aspects of Buddhism as they remoulded Hinduism to recapture ground lost to Buddhism in South Asia.

South Asian merchants and seafarers responded to the rise in
domestic and foreign interest in maritime trade by establishing communities in the Middle East and South East Asia. Apart from the
expatriate South Asian mercantile community on the island of Suqutra, South Asian merchants also lived in the great port of Alexandria,
and by the beginning of the present era similar communities were
established in South East Asia.

In this way, South Asian merchants created a domestic trade
network incorporating maritime links with the outside world. By the
beginning of the present era trade goods from both west and east were
also common in many South Asian ports—Roman and Middle Eastern ceramics, glass, wine, seals and cameos; Mediterranean coral;
copper, lead and tin from Britain and the Iberian peninsula; ivory
from East Africa, bronzeware and gold and silver coinage from the
west in general, along with tin from Malaya, silk from China and
cloves from the Moluccas. Such goods—augmented by the produce
of South Asia such as textiles, precious and semi-precious stones, ivory,
spices, pepper, pearls, tortoiseshell, wheat, rice, sesame oil and ghee[12]
—passed through ports such as Broach (Barugaza) on the Gulf of

[12] Ibid.

Cambay, Sopara (Souppara) to the north of Bombay, Cranganore (Mouziris) on the Malabar coast, Mantai on the north-west coast of Sri Lanka, Arikamedu (Podouke) on the southern reaches of the Coromandel coast and Masulipatnam (Masalia) on the Krishna delta, indicating a thriving maritime trade of considerable interest to many South Asian states.

Maritime trade was a significant factor in political life in central and southern India and Sri Lanka. While agriculture was the major prop which underpinned all states in South Asia, in parts of the subcontinent and Sri Lanka maritime trade generated revenue through levies and dues on markets and harbours, and provided a means of converting local farm produce, often gathered as taxes and tribute by ruling groups, into luxury commodities and precious metals. New coastal urban centres such as Broach (Barugaza), Cranganore (Mouziris) and Arikamedu (Podouke) developed during the last centuries of the first millennium BC, whose fortunes depended upon maritime trade, not upon agricultural and craft activities.

In this way access to the sea and the creation of coastal markets and harbours was one of the determining factors in the formation of many coastal states in South Asia, most particularly, along the Malabar, Coromandel and Orissa coasts and in Sri Lanka, where the prosperity of the great state of Anuradhapura was dependent upon trade through its port at Mantai and control of irrigation systems across northern Sri Lanka by the beginning of the present era. In the Deccan too, following the decline of the Mauryan empire in the second century BC, there were powerful states, the most notable of which was ruled by the Satavahana dynasty (*c.*50 BC–*c.*AD 225), whose rulers took a keen interest in maritime trade with the Arabian Sea and the Bay of Bengal through ports on the west coast of India such as Sopara (Souppara), Bankot (Mandagora) and Malvan (Ernnaoboas) and on the east coast such as Masulipatnam (Masalia). These ports were listed in *The Periplus* and were visited by ships from Egypt and the Persian Gulf crewed by Greeks, Egyptians, Arabs and Persians.

By the beginning of the present era South Asia exported a range of luxury goods to the west, along with more humble cargoes of grain, timber and metals to markets in the Gulf, Arabia, the Red Sea and the Somali coast in return for luxury goods, and above all, gold, silver and copper coinage. Roman coinage was so common in southern India and Sri Lanka that many local rulers minted copies as the most popular medium of exchange.

From this early period one of the most unique characteristics of South Asian trade until the eighteenth century AD is evident. Put most simply, South Asia exported a greater value of goods than it imported, with the result that huge quantities of gold and silver flowed into the subcontinent. At the beginning of the present era much of this gold came from Central Asia and Siberia, but in later centuries it also came from the Mediterranean, East and West Africa and South East Asia. Indeed, it was the lure of gold which first drew South Asian merchants into South East Asia some 2000 years ago.

The establishment of large states and imperial regimes in the Middle East and South Asia had a marked impact upon neighbouring peoples. Trade brought many into closer contact with the ideas and technology of the Middle East and South Asia. The increase in trade between areas with complex technologies and agricultural systems, and less developed areas, reinforced the growth of urban civilizations beyond the areas in which it first flourished. At certain points on the periphery of Middle Eastern and South Asian civilization, for example in south-western Arabia and in parts of South East Asia, dominant indigenous groups began to tax peasant farmers, organizing local markets to sell farm and jungle produce for imported goods and precious metals. The profits of this state-controlled trade supported religious and bureaucratic structures, modelled upon those of their more sophisticated trading partners, around which urban civilization took root on the peripheries of the Middle Eastern and South Asian civilizations.

Other Markets

The rise of Persia was mirrored in minor detail by the flowering of urban civilizations, both in Yemen in south-western Arabia, and across the Red Sea in the Ethiopian highlands where the state of Aksum took shape. With their monopoly of the incense trade, their access to valuable cargoes of African ivory, and their strategic position at the junction of the Red Sea and the Arabian Sea, ruling groups in the states of south-west Arabia, and later in Aksum, were able to exploit fully their geographical position as entrepôts between the Mediterranean and the Indian Ocean worlds. However, at its height Alexandria dominated these states and their ports as the leading western entrepôt for the trade of the Mediterranean and the Middle East with the Indian Ocean.

Less is known of the situation in the Persian Gulf, but it too acted as a general entrepôt area for maritime trade, linking in directly, through ports such as Charax and Hormuz, with the Persian imperial heartland and ports on the Mediterranean coast such as Tyre, Tripoli and Beirut via caravan cities such as Petra and Palmyra. What was increasingly evident was that the rhythms of mercantile life in the Red Sea were closely attuned to the economies of north-east Africa and the Mediterranean, while those in the Persian Gulf were attuned to the economies of Mesopotamia, Persia and Central Asia. Ports on the Arabian shore of the Gulf were also linked by desert routes to inland markets and ports in the Levant, providing an alternative to the Red Sea route for trade between the Mediterranean and the Indian Ocean.

In East Africa and South East Asia, the impact of political and economic developments in the Middle East and South Asia during the last millennium BC was more muted than in the highlands of Ethiopia and south-western Arabia. Maritime trade in East Africa, south of the Horn, remained desultory in terms of its links with the outside world, while South East Asians slowly integrated their maritime trading network with that of South Asia and China.

While many of the goods traded between the Middle East and South Asia were the sophisticated products of urban civilizations, the trading goods of East Africa, below the Horn, were primarily luxury raw materials such as ivory and rhinoceros horn, collected from the immediate hinterlands of coastal settlements. There is no evidence of trade networks linking the coast with the interior as was to be the case centuries later. Although *The Periplus* refers to African settlements south of the Horn stretching down the Somali and Kenyan coasts, which were involved directly in overseas trade at the beginning of the present era, such trade was an occasional event, based on annual expeditions comprising a few adventurous mariners and merchants from the Ethiopian coast, Yemen and the Hadhramaut, who exchanged goods such as ceramics and iron at *ad hoc* markets on the east coast of Africa.

By the beginning of the present era there was a rapid expansion of maritime trade linking South, South East and East Asia which had begun some centuries earlier. But South East Asia was not simply a transit area; the maritime traditions and technologies of its peoples were highly developed before they came into intimate contact with South and East Asia.

At least 2500 years ago, South East Asians had established a network of long-distant voyages which bound mainland and insular South East Asia and southern China into a remarkably complex trading world—as evidenced by the diffusion of rice cultivation, the presence of Moluccan cloves in China by the third century BC, and the distribution of the bronzeware of the Dong Son culture of Vietnam.

Also, by the beginning of the present era, people from South East Asia were settling Madagascar, and the cloves of the Moluccas in eastern Indonesia were a highly prized luxury in the markets of the Middle East and the Mediterranean where, by the first century AD the Roman statesman Pliny was complaining of the drain of gold currency to pay for spices and other luxury imports from the Indian Ocean. South East Asian trading vessels—carrying gold, spices, camphor, Chinese silk yarn and tin—were travelling west as far as the ports of Gujarat at the same time that South Asians were travelling east. South East Asians were not a geographically restricted people passively waiting for South Asians to integrate them into a larger economic and cultural world.

Many historians have viewed South East Asia as an area of relatively primitive economic and cultural life before the intrusion of South Asian culture and technology some two thousand years ago, and after that date as a mere halfway house linking the Indian Ocean with the South China Sea. Nothing could be further from the truth. Long before the arrival of South Asians and the Chinese, the area had developed its own complex cultural and economic systems based upon interactions between hunter gatherers, shifting cultivators and rice farmers. In parts of South East Asia as we have seen, rice farming was producing disposable surpluses which were used to support artisans and warriors, as well as for trade, and ceramics and metallurgical skills were highly developed long before intimate contact was developed with South Asia. In addition, an indigenous maritime trading network was in operation well before this time, even if it had not yet produced distinctive merchant groups and monumental civilizations such as existed in South and East Asia.

In the early centuries of the present era, South East Asian traders most probably came from itinerant maritime peoples, represented later by such groups as the Orang Laut of the Strait of Melaka and the Bugis of south-west Sulawesi. These people dealt mainly with local ruling groups for whom they collected and distributed trading goods both within South East Asia and with South Asia and China. Such groups probably pioneered South East Asia's first contacts with South Asia and, later, with China. When foreign merchants—mostly from South Asia, as the Greeks and the Romans do not appear to have ventured across the Bay of Bengal, while the Chinese were yet to sail the waters of South East Asia—appeared in South East Asia they were generally restricted to minor entrepôts on the periphery of the area in the Malay peninsula and on the Mekong delta. From such ports they secured cargoes from local intermediaries which they then redistributed to other parts of the Indian Ocean and East Asia.

Parochial influences prompted the evolution of the first complex societies in South East Asia, but the development of long-distance maritime trade linking insular South East Asia to the markets of the Mediterranean and China undoubtedly prompted the evolution of coastal trading states: for example, the production and trade in cloves, grown only on a group of five small islands in the Moluccas, transformed Moluccan society from 'scattered kin based communities of hunter-gatherers and shifting cultivators to stratified coastal trading states'.[13] Indeed, given that the island world of South East Asia is dominated both by sea and numerous river systems which link interior hinterlands to the ocean, control of river mouths conferred great political advantage. A river-mouth ruler had direct access to maritime trade, and by controlling riverine links to the interior could forge 'various alliances with upriver groups'.[14] Control of deltas and estuaries

[13] I.C. Glover, 1990, 1.
[14] K.R. Hall, 1985, 3.

gave shape to one type of state in insular South East Asia on Sumatra, the north coast of Java, Borneo, Sulawesi and the Moluccas. In contrast, elsewhere in the islands—in the hinterland interior of Java in particular—state formation was based on control of rice-rich farmlands.

By the second millennium of the present era foreign merchants began to intrude directly into the interior of South East Asia by sea and river from the periphery, particularly as demand for Moluccan cloves increased in the Middle East and Europe. South Asian merchants were the first foreigners to trade regularly with the peoples of South East Asia, and it was not until the ninth century that they faced serious competition from Chinese merchants.

South Asian and Chinese participation in South East Asian trade was made possible by the active co-operation of indigenous maritime peoples and local rulers. Foreigner merchants rarely penetrated indigenous societies beyond the port marketplace, and they remained reliant upon local producers, middlemen and rulers. Not until the late eighteenth century, with the advent of a new type of economic penetration by Europeans, did foreigners begin tightening their control over indigenous economies and rulers. This was achieved by territorial and economic domination as well as by controlling communications, as was the case, for example, with the sugar and coffee industries of Java and the Mascarenes, established after Europeans had taken control of both islands and of the sea routes which linked them to the outside world.

The same pattern of penetration by foreign merchants was repeated along the East African coast, if we consider the penetration of Arabian and Persian merchants southward beyond modern Kenya to Mozambique, the Comoros and Madagascar. In both East Africa and South East Asia, Middle Eastern, South Asian and Chinese merchants infiltrated old indigenous maritime trading networks, continuing to do so up until the twentieth century.

By the beginning of the present era a range of cultures and economies on the shores of the Indian Ocean were slowly merging to form a distinctive 'world' defined by the sea routes and land routes, along which travelled peoples from many civilizations. Maritime trade in particular defined the limits of the Indian Ocean world, which was

cemented by an increasing number of economic and cultural commonalities encompassing the Middle East, and South and South East
Asia, with peripheral maritime linkages to East Africa and East Asia.

In the coming centuries the internal economic and cultural bonds
of this world would strengthen, as would the maritime trade in staple
goods as opposed to luxuries. It would expand to include East Africa
and East Asia, in terms of its inhabitants' economic and cultural
boundaries, and the Mediterranean and Central Asia as peripheral
economic areas which were partially incorporated into the worldview
of Indian Ocean peoples. Not until the nineteenth century, due to
the workings of capitalism, would this world become a region of a
much larger cultural, political and economic world. Until then the
Indian Ocean world possessed its own strong internal stimuli for
cultural and economic growth; some of this growth was due to the
mercantile and cultural expansion of the Mediterranean world and of
China, but for the most part it was generated by forces from within
the Indian Ocean world.

Certainly, in the Middle East and around the Mediterranean,
Persians, Greeks and Romans provided a remarkable period of relative
political and economic stability which lasted more than a thousand
years, to the seventh century AD, encouraging considerable cultural
interaction as well as generating a steady expansion in maritime trade.
But it is doubtful if the growth in power and wealth of empires in
this area was responsible for the rapid growth in trade across the Indian
Ocean during the same period. We do know that Roman emperors
were concerned by the loss of gold and silver in pursuit of Indian
pepper, Indonesian spices and Chinese silk, but neither pepper nor
silk were produced solely for Mediterranean markets. By the beginning
of the present era, cargoes moved across the Indian Ocean in response
to flourishing local markets, more frequently than they did to supply
markets in the Mediterranean.

Mediterranean trade with the Indian Ocean declined considerably
during the third century AD as a result of legal, agricultural, financial
and administrative crises within the Roman empire. The weakened
Roman monetary system adversely affected trade, and was in part,
responsible for a contraction of urban life in the western half of the
empire. In the eastern half of the Roman empire, which included

Egypt, Syria and parts of Mesopotamia, the impact was less dramatic, and from the third century AD these lands, whose cities had been culturally influenced by Greece since the time of Alexander the Great, were politically, culturally and economically oriented eastward from the Mediterranean. Their overland trade to the east was, however, blocked by the hostile Sasanians, forcing Roman merchants to patronize the Aksumite port of Adulis to gain access to Indian Ocean trade.

During this period of decline in the western Roman empire, and following its collapse in the fifth century, there was a drop in the supply of gold to the Middle East and South Asia from Central Asia, due to folk movements in the area. This disruption of gold supplies, combined with the continuing hostility of Sasanian Persia, precipitated attempts by the emperors of Byzantium (the eastern rump of the Roman empire which survived the collapse of the western Roman empire) to seek access to the profits of Indian Ocean trade, via Alexandria, the Red Sea and Arabian and Ethiopian ports. The emperor Justinian (in the sixth century AD), for example, established close diplomatic relations with the ruler of Aksum, whom he encouraged to invade the Sasanian client-states of south-west Arabia, under the pretext that they were ruled by converts to Judaism. The real reason was the ambition of the Byzantine emperors to outflank the Sasanian empire—which had occupied much of coastal Oman and the resin-rich Dhofar coast—by gaining ready access to the Red Sea and beyond to the Arabian Sea. The decline in gold supplies may also have been another factor which further weakened South Asian interest in trade towards the west and north for some time, and encouraged a greater interest in the gold of South East Asia.

These changes in Mediterranean trade with the Indian Ocean led to a change in the hierarchy of Egyptian, Red Sea and Arabian ports. Alexandria was still a brilliant, wealthy and cosmopolitan port, but it now served a much reduced Mediterranean and European hinterland and turned more firmly towards the Indian Ocean as a source of commercial profit. This refocussing made Alexandria more dependent upon the entrepôts of Ethiopia, the Red Sea and the Hadhramaut which linked Byzantium to the markets of East Africa, South Asia and beyond to South East Asia and China.

Changes within the Roman empire from the third century AD had little appreciable effect upon the overall patterns of Indian Ocean maritime trade. A few ports and trading towns in Arabia and parts of South Asia, which were excessively dependent upon Mediterranean and Central Asian markets, declined. But their decline was matched by the growth of ports on the Aksumite coast of the Red Sea, on the Hadhramaut and Dhofar coasts, in the Persian Gulf, in Sri Lanka and in insular South East Asia. From these ports cargoes of African ivory, Sri Lankan gemstones and elephants, South East Asian spices and aromatics, and Middle Eastern manufactures (particularly ceramics and glassware) and resins were despatched to a growing number of markets within the Indian Ocean world, and beyond to southern China, by the third and fourth centuries.

For these reasons the contraction of Mediterranean markets seems to have had only marginally adverse effects around the Indian Ocean. Nor were the goods that had been imported from the Mediterranean central to any economy in the Indian Ocean; even the gold of Rome could be matched by that of South East Asia. The contraction of Roman maritime trade was matched by an expansion of Persian maritime trade under the Sasanid dynasty. Persia, which since the second century AD had controlled the western end of the Silk Road across Central Asia, found its overland trade with China interrupted by chaos in Central Asia and turned increasingly to the development of a maritime silk route. Sasanian ships, merchants and sailors—among whom were many Nestorian Christians—dominated the triangular trade of the western Indian Ocean between South Asia, the Middle East and East Africa, from the third or fourth century.[15]

Further compensation was provided by the maturing of maritime links with China by the first centuries of the present era. In the second century BC China incorporated the rice-rich tropical lands of the Yangtse and beyond, including the lands of the seagoing Yuëh tribes who provided a sophisticated body of maritime skills, thereby gaining easier maritime access to South East Asia and the Indian Ocean. In the reign of the emperor Han Wu-ti (ruled 141–87 BC) imperial envoys were dispatched, with the assistance of Yuëh sailors, to search the southern seas for rare and precious items. Over the next few

[15] André Wink, 1990, 48.

centuries Chinese maritime skills slowly developed, and by the third and fourth centuries Chinese ships were visiting porterage points on the Malay peninsula, from where cargoes of silk and ceramics were transhipped westward across the Indian Ocean in South and South East Asian ships. It was not until the sixth century, however, under the Sui dynasty (AD 581–618) that the Chinese began to explore the South China Sea systematically, and not until three centuries later that they became a major maritime mercantile force in the area.[16]

It is tempting to see the economic power of Rome as a major influence on the expansion of South Asian long-distance maritime trade, and to link the advent of Buddhism and Jainism with their emphasis on individual initiative, to the expansion of South Asian trade with South East Asia. It can be argued that Roman-South Asian economic linkages grew out of the economic expansion of South Asia, as much as out of the economic expansion of the Mediterranean world. Similarly, Buddhism and Jainism can be seen as reflecting, rather than creating, social attitudes, insofar as they grew out of an environment where individual initiative was beginning to rival corporate activity. In both cases the causes must be sought in a broader historical context. Certainly the collapse of empires often reflected a decline in agricultural production and hence of trade. Nevertheless, there was life aplenty beyond the boundaries of imperial Rome, Persia, India and China, generating its own powerful economic and cultural forces which impacted upon the expanding maritime trade network of the Indian Ocean.

Across the Indian Ocean the expansion of maritime trade was the result of the growth of various economic systems in East Africa, the Middle East, and South and South East Asia. The blending of various maritime traditions facilitated the movement of trade goods, but the growth of seaborne trade was slow and erratic, mirroring the different rates of economic development in the lands surrounding the Indian Ocean.

As maritime trade developed and trade itself became a distinct occupation separated from other activities such as the crafts, agriculture and fishing, new occupational groups evolved which were vitally

[16] O.W. Wolters, 1967.

dependent upon the sea—either as sailors or merchants—for survival. Such groups would play central roles in creating an oceanic trading network which linked a great variety of cultures, creating a distinctive human identity for the Indian Ocean world.

Fishermen, Sailors and Merchants

Undoubtedly, the first mariners were drawn from coastal fishing communities. But fisherfolk, like their peasant counterparts, are the lost people of history: its silent actors. Although they provided a vital pool of labour and maritime skills, fisherfolk were dominated, politically and economically, by more articulate groups such as merchants and ruling élites.

Initially there was no occupational divide between fishermen, maritime merchants and seamen. Around the Indian Ocean, fishermen performed all these functions as the first tentative steps were taken towards maritime trade, but as trade became more complex there was increasing occupational specialization. When men had to travel long-distances to get commodities, the exchange of goods could no longer be a supplementary activity alongside the work of crafts and farming, and a new division of labour took place giving rise to trade as an occupation.[17]

At least 5000 years ago, in Mesopotamia and the Indus valley, merchants, sailors and fishermen formed separate and distinct groups with the emergence of sophisticated city-dominated economies and societies. In contrast, in East Africa and South East Asia, clear occupational divisions did not emerge until well into the present era. Not until the eleventh or twelfth centuries AD is there evidence of powerful groups of merchants active along the coast of East Africa, where they ruled city states such as the ports of Mogadishu, Zanzibar and Kilwa. In much of South East Asia, where most large states drew their wealth from control of farming lands, rulers and nobles were often the chief merchants whose agents dealt with foreign traders, and there is little evidence of local merchant communities emerging until the fourteenth and fifteenth centuries AD, when independent trading cities developed across insular South East Asia.

[17] Ernest Mandel, 1968, 56.

The development of occupational divisions marginalized fisherfolk in many parts of the Indian Ocean. Dominant economic and political roles were assumed by those who controlled agriculture. Markets and ports became more central to economic activity than fishing settlements, which often literally, and always metaphorically, survived on the margins of urban civilization.

In their subordinate role, some fishing communities provided recruits to man deep-sea sailing craft; some were involved in petty trade or as ferrymen and lightermen to supplement their income from fishing; some were involved in shipbuilding and agriculture when the monsoon kept them from fishing; while others found alternative means to harvest the sea and became involved in the extraction of marine 'cash crops' such as pearls, cowries, shell and coral.[18] Yet others took to piracy, harvesting passing ships in narrow straits and shallow seas from the Red Sea to the Strait of Melaka.

Most fisherfolk, however, remained tied to their coastal settlements under the control of urban-based mercantile and political élites for whom they formed a community which provided both tax revenue and marketable commodities.[19] In their political, social and economic subordination to others, fisherfolk and seamen shared the same fate.

For most of human history sailors were recruited from fishing communities. But as long-distance maritime trade developed, sailors were also recruited from the unskilled inhabitants of ports and their immediate hinterlands. In time, many of the more substantial ports came to include communities of hereditary seafarers, and particular coastal peoples came to have a reputation as sailors. Arabs and Persians from ports on the Arabian peninsula and in the Persian Gulf were noted sailors 2000 years ago as were, centuries later, particular communities of coastal people in Gujarat and along the Malabar and Coromandel coasts of South Asia.

By the middle of the first millennium BC, merchant activity had increased around the Indian Ocean. The growth of large empires in the Fertile Crescent and the renewal of urban life in South Asia

[18] W.G. White, 1922.
[19] P. Reeves, 1992.

encouraged the development of long-distance voyaging to obtain goods, and the emergence of well-established merchant communities at major ports on the Asian shore of the Arabian Sea. From this period the increasing complexity of trade and the growth of long-distance sea routes confirmed the development of trade as a distinct and full-time occupation, separate from fishing and seafaring. In addition, in areas such as the Middle East and South Asia, there was an intimate association between the development of urban life, market networks, trade and the evolution of writing. The need to record and transmit information was vital to complex economic life and, in the Fertile Crescent, Egypt, Arabia and the Indus valley, the earliest scripts and alphabets provide strong evidence of the impact trade had upon their development.

Little evidence remains for us to write in detail of the precise nature of the groups involved in trade, but what is clearly evident is the existence of merchant and artisan quarters in all urban centres across Eurasia by the first millennium BC, and of the first primitive banking networks. In addition, merchants in both the Middle East and South Asia had begun to evolve corporate activity through the formation of guilds which protected the group's commercial, political and welfare interests and which often acted as sponsors of various types of civic and religious activity, ranging from the feeding of the poor to the establishment of shrines, temples and monasteries. In South Asia, merchant and artisan groups were particularly active in these types of activities from the early days of Buddhism and, in addition, had evolved into hereditary castes unlike their counterparts in the Middle East. In both East Africa and South East Asia there are no signs of the formation of similar merchant and artisan groups. Artisanal activity undoubtedly flourished but its social position remains obscure, while mercantile activity was controlled by ruling élites who utilised the services of agents whose limited freedom of action in no way compared with the relatively unrestricted self-interest of merchants in South Asia and the Middle East.

By the beginning of the present era it is clear from *The Periplus* that there were flourishing and well-established ports from the Red Sea to the Bay of Bengal. However, given the generally restricted nature of long-distance maritime trade and its focus upon luxury cargoes, such mercantile activities involved relatively few people. But in some specific areas the production of export goods sustained large coastal societies. For example, the frankincense and myrrh trade of south-western Arabia and the Dhofar coast of Oman was one of the mainstays of local prosperity, as was the production of pepper for export on the Malabar coast and perhaps textile industries in Gujarat and the Tamil country.

Although long-distance maritime trade at the beginning of the present era was still posited upon luxury products, and the number of merchants involved was relatively small, the trade was sufficiently complex and rewarding to encourage the formation of the earliest migrant merchants communities. Merchants from South Asia formed distinct expatriate communities in ports from the Red Sea to the Strait of Melaka. Arabs, Persians and Jews also filtered eastward to form diasporas on the Malabar and Coromandel coasts as mercantile intermediaries between southern India, the Gulf and the Red Sea. On the other hand, in East Africa, south of the Horn, foreign merchants were irregular visitors before the advent of Islam in the seventh century AD, and there is little evidence of the existence of African mercantile communities at the beginning of the present era, apart from tantalizing brief references in *The Periplus* to ports such as Rhapta on the Tanzanian coast, which were inhabited by indigenous peoples.

Such migrations of merchants in the western half of the Indian Ocean had little impact upon their host societies until the rise of Islamic commercial power, from the eighth century AD, when Arabs and Persians played a key role in the diffusion of Islam and Middle Eastern culture. On land, however, the picture was more complex.

Undoubtedly, the earliest processes of cultural adaptation and diffusion were the result of the migration of peoples. The various waves of settlement which led to the populating of Australia, beginning perhaps 100,000 years ago, are marked by the adaptation of new ideas and technologies across the continent by older groups of inhabitants. The Middle East did, and still does, reflect layer upon layer of peoples and cultures representing the migrations of many peoples over the millennia. In south-east India it has long been believed that there is an association between the migration of unknown peoples and the spread of megalithic technology and cultural forms, which are found across much of Europe and Asia, although this is now disputed.[20] In South East Asia, the migrations of Austronesian-speaking peoples, beginning perhaps some 10,000 years ago, led to a diffusion of agricultural and maritime technologies which were to ultimately affect many societies from East Africa to Polynesia, where Austronesian-speakers settled.

Central Asia was one of the great reservoirs for the populating of lands stretching from Europe through the Middle East and South Asia to East Asia. During the third millennium BC, Indo-European speaking steppe peoples domesticated the horse, developed the bow and improved their agricultural and metallurgical technologies. The first two developments gave them a military advantage over neighbours, including the more sophisticated civilizations of Mesopotamia, the Indus valley and the Yellow River valley of China. Akkadians, Guttians, Elamites, Amorites, Hittites and Kassites swooped down from the encircling mountains to fasten upon the fertile plains of the Tigris and Euphrates; related peoples settled the Iranian highlands, while others filtered into the Indus valley. Peoples sharing technologies similar to those of Mesopotamia and Central Asia—perhaps transmitted along trade routes across Central Asia—came to dominate the Yellow River heartland of Chinese civilization during the second millennium BC.

In the Middle East the invaders from Central Asia were periodically joined by other pastoral people moving north from the arid grazing lands of the Arabian peninsula. These Semitic-speaking people, like the invaders from Central Asia, were in time absorbed into the mainstream of Middle Eastern civilization. Both streams of invaders grafted tribal concepts of authority and tribal military technology on to older civilizations, reinvigorating them and providing the ideological and technological impetus for the first empires in the area. Many of these invaders were to gain temporary control of Mesopotamia, beginning with Sargon of Akkad who, in 2350 BC, established the first major territorial state in the Middle East outside the Nile valley. In time, many of these nomads merged into the mainstream of Middle Eastern civilization, establishing a host of petty states

[20] K.A.R. Kennedy, 1975.

and distinctive sub-cultures of which the Jew and Arab were to be heir.

While invaders from Central Asia in this early period achieved initial spectacular success, the states they established were ephemeral and they soon lost their group and linguistic identity. The dynasties established by the Semitic invaders proved equally ephemeral, but the infiltration of these people continued steadily over thousands of years until Semitic languages replaced the older languages of the area. The Semitic settlers also left the Middle East with the clear legacy of two distinct yet intertwined cultural traditions: that of the settled farmer and that of the pastoral nomad.

During the first millennium BC the rise of Assyria and the creation of a Mediterranean-wide Phoenician trading empire spurred the extension of Middle Eastern cultural and technological forms. Previously, Egyptian art had influenced the peoples of the Levant and the Greek islands, but, during the first millennium BC, Mesopotamian and Phoenician technologies and art forms, most particularly written scripts and mathematics, were adopted and adapted by emerging societies in Greece and Italy.

By the fifth century BC Greek civilization was, in turn, influencing many Mediterranean peoples from Italy to the Levant and, ironically, was setting new fashions and styles in the Middle East. This was particularly evident after the Persian Achaemenid dynasty destroyed Assyria and established an empire which incorporated Greece, opening up the heartlands of the Middle East to Greek merchants, mercenaries, artisans and scholars. Colonies of Greek merchants took over the foreign trade of Persian-occupied Egypt and moved eastward, carrying their ideas and culture into the Persian homeland and as far as the Indo-Gangetic plain.

The success of the Greeks in carrying their ideas and culture to the Middle East was undoubtedly associated with the expansion of long-distance trade which occurred from the Mediterranean to South Asia during the first millennium BC. Trade was the product of economic prosperity and such prosperity encouraged the growth of new centres of wealth and power. Greek culture provided a model for newly emerging urban groups and provided fashionable and sophisticated forms which were freely adopted and adapted by élites across the

Middle East. Older cultural forms survived among both the masses and the élites, but in towns and cities from the Levant to the Indus valley sophisticates aped the ways of Greece.

In eastern Africa, during the first millennium BC, at least two major processes of cultural interaction were taking place. One was certainly associated with the development of overland trade, and to an extent also, with the development of short-haul trade across the Red Sea. The other was associated with major movements of peoples.

In the highlands of northern Ethiopia, a merging of peoples and cultures from Africa and southwest Arabia was taking place. As we have seen, about *c.*500 BC this gave rise to the complex agricultural-based civilization of Aksum. Greeks, Egyptians, Arabs and South Asians were regular visitors to the Aksumite port of Adulis through which Christian missionaries from Alexandria in Byzantine-controlled Egypt were to eventually convert the kingdom, beginning in the fifth century AD.

Parallelling the rise of Aksum, Bantu-speaking peoples were moving into the East African hinterland where they mingled with, and absorbed, local peoples and culture. This movement lasted over many centuries and resulted in the spread of Bantu languages almost to the tip of Africa, giving shape to all the indigenous cultures of southern and eastern Africa. Little is known of this great folk movement, but it did result in the fusion and transmission of cultures from the Atlantic to the Indian Ocean, linked by a series of complex transcontinental trade routes.

At least 4000 years ago, overland routes through the mountains of Baluchistan and across the Iranian highlands provided a tenuous link between the civilizations of Mesopotamia and the Indus valley. We know little about the goods traded along these routes but there are clues, marked by the eastward passage of ceramic styles, indicating a movement of peoples and cultures between the two areas. Similarly, there were overland routes which linked the Indus valley north into the Hindu Kush and Afghanistan to the edge of the great plains of Central Asia. In the coming centuries, both sets of routes were to be used by waves of Indo-European, Scythian and Hun settlers, who brought with them new languages, religious ideas and technologies which were to be absorbed into the mainstream of South Asian life.

The Indo-European invaders of South Asia were part of that great movement of Indo-European speaking peoples which moved out of Central Asia to settle Europe, Mesopotamia, Persia and the Indus valley. In Europe their language and culture overwhelmed older languages and culture; in the Middle East, as we have seen, they left a much more limited legacy; while in Persia and the Indus valley they left a cultural and linguistic imprint which helped shape the civilizations of modern Iran and the states of South Asia. In both Europe and Persia the Indo-Europeans found peoples with similar levels of technological and agricultural skills. But in the Indus valley they came upon a sophisticated but decaying civilization. Much of the old civilization vanished, but the process was far from even and the Indo-Europeans absorbed some of the technology and culture of the Indus valley peoples. The great cities of the Indus valley—Mohenjo-daro and Harappa—were abandoned and forgotten, but popular religious practices, agricultural techniques, cotton weaving and various crafts survived the collapse of urban life and were absorbed by the invaders.

The history of these first invaders, and later invaders such as the Scythians and Huns, are still largely unknown except in broadest outline, and they have left little material evidence of their presence in South Asia. But during the centuries of Persian and Greek influence over the Middle East, from the sixth century BC, Greeks—merchants, artisans and mercenaries—filtered eastward. They founded trading cities such as Taxila in north-west Pakistan, Qandahar in Afghanistan, and the many cities in Bactria on the edge of the steppes, which linked both South Asia and the Middle East heartland into the great overland trade routes stretching across Central Asia to China. These Indo-Greek settlements and petty states were islands of Hellenized urban life, complete with temples and built according to classical Greek rules concerning urban planning. Although abandoned in the early centuries of the present era, these cities and their inhabitants left a deep imprint upon the sculptural and architectural forms of Buddhist art in South Asia, which were in part derived from Indo-Greek art.

The Hellenized inhabitants of these trading cities were early converts to Buddhism, and they served as a catalyst for a selective process of cultural adaptation whose influence can still be traced in Buddhist iconography from South Asia to Japan. So powerful was their legacy

that even though their cities were devastated by invaders from Central
Asia, such as the Kushans (who established a short-lived empire which
included Bactria, Afghanistan, the Indus valley and much of northern
India in the first centuries AD), their conquerors became patrons of
the arts and crafts of the Hellenized peoples of the area and incorporated them firmly into the cultural mainstream of South Asia.

Although Greek civilization left a legacy in the Middle East and
on the western borderlands of South Asia, there is only minimal
evidence of any legacy of South Asian civilization westward from the
subcontinent in the same period. South Asian merchants and travellers
moved as far afield as the Mediterranean, but apart from some influence upon Greek fables and philosophical writings their cultural
impact was minimal.[21] South Asian luxury goods spread throughout
the Mediterranean and the Middle East, but neither the goods themselves nor the South Asian merchants who brought them to Egypt
and Persia influenced local cultural practices to any great degree.

Eastward from the Indian subcontinent the situation was markedly
different. Here the forms and ideas of South Asian civilization penetrated more deeply than had Greek forms and ideas along the western
boundary of South Asia. By the beginning of the present era Hindu
and Buddhist merchants were becoming increasingly familiar figures,
from the Irrawaddy valley in Burma and the Strait of Melaka to the
shores of Vietnam. They were entering an area where there were no
great established empires, but where the spread of settled farming was
beginning to produce significant agricultural surpluses in specific
locations, giving rise to more complex social, religious and economic
systems. Throughout South East Asia, rapidly changing societies,
moving towards the formation of the first urban centres and states,
were continuously exposed to merchants drawn from the sophisticated
civilization of South Asia. Such merchants were not the vanguard of
a great South Asian migration into South East Asia, but were the
precursors of a movement of literate and skilled South Asians to ports
and royal cities in South East Asia, in search of profit and employment.[22]

[21] J.W. Sedlar, 1980.
[22] I.C. Glover, 1990, 6–7.

Hindu Brahmin priests, Buddhist monks, architects, scribes, artisans and perhaps even some warriors from South Asia found outlets for their skills across South East Asia from Burma to southern Vietnam. They introduced new ideas and practices which were readily adopted and adapted by local rulers, eager to consolidate their power and wealth. Various South Asian written scripts were adapted for use in royal courts; Hindu and Buddhist religious symbolism was used to surround local rulers with more ritual and sanctity; and South Asian architectural, technological and artistic traditions influenced the development of monumental architecture, agriculture and the decorative arts, from Burma to southern Vietnam.[23]

As elsewhere on the shores of the Indian Ocean, the first processes of cultural diffusion and interaction in South East Asia were the result of migrations of peoples. The Austronesians were the dominant group until the beginning of the present era, but in succeeding centuries they were followed by other peoples—Mon, Pyu, Khmer, Burmans, Lao, Shan, Thai and Karin to name a few—creating overlays of linguistic and cultural traditions which mingled at various levels to form the varied and rich cultural mosaic of mainland South East Asia. In the Malay peninsula and insular South East Asia, where the Austronesian-speakers remained the dominant group, there is a greater degree of linguistic and cultural homogeneity, but, as in the rest of South East Asia, different environmental conditions and patterns of population dispersion led to considerable cultural variation. Throughout South East Asia, however, the uniformity of environmental conditions in areas of densest human settlement led to the evolution of widely dispersed cultural and technological commonalities, based upon the use of maritime resources and the sea as the common highway; the production of rice, palm sugar and wine, and betel nut; and the exploitation of tropical and equatorial forests.

During the first millennium BC, Greeks, Arabs, Persians and South Asians were the pioneers who, by land and sea, began to integrate the trading economies of the Middle East and South and South East Asia. But the cultural results of these emerging linkages varied enormously. The Greeks in South Asia formed isolated outposts of Hellenic

[23] J.C. Heesterman, 1989.

civilization in close proximity to the sophisticated urban civilization
of South Asia. The complex civilization of South Asia needed little
from Greek civilization, except in very specific areas such as Buddhist
iconography, where Greek artistic forms helped shape Buddhist sculptural traditions from the second century BC. In South East Asia on
the other hand, there is no evidence of South Asian settlement, but
rather of South Asians coming into contact with vigorous peoples
undergoing rapid economic and social change.

South Asian mariners and merchants were central to the processes
of cultural borrowing and adaptation which occurred between South
and South East Asia. Westward from South Asia, however, they simply
provided an economic link between great sophisticated civilizations,
whereas eastward from South Asia they provided a linkage for both
economic and cultural interaction between an established civilization
and a range of societies undergoing rapid economic and social change.

Chinese maritime contact with South East Asia, as distinct from
Chinese maritime exploration,[24] was relatively limited until the tenth
century AD, and the first substantial external contacts the people of
South East Asia had were with South Asia. In the early stages of this
contact, South Asians were attracted to South East Asia as a source of
rare commodities and not as a halfway house to China. In this period
the seas of South East Asia were very much an extension of the growing
maritime world of the Indian Ocean. However, once trade along the
Silk Road became more dangerous and expensive in the fifth and sixth
centuries AD, and Chinese control of the lands to the south of the
Yangtze became more effective in the same period, then the sea route
to China via South East Asia became an attraction in itself and the
seas of South East Asia assumed the role of linkage point between the
Indian and Pacific Oceans.

Throughout South East Asia the influence of Hinduism was almost entirely restricted to ruling élites who cast themselves as avatars
or god-kings, remote from their subjects, with the result that the
success and failure of Hinduism in South East Asia was, for the most
part, related to the success and failure of particular dynasties and states.
The fate of Buddhism was more complex. It too was utilised by rulers

[24] Paul Wheatley, 1980.

in various parts of South East Asia as a means of bolstering status and legitimacy, but it had more widespread appeal as a result of considerable missionary activity and its more egalitarian appeal to groups who were not part of any élite. Buddhism in South East Asia was much more successful than Hinduism in striking deep root among the masses and consequently was less subject to the vagaries of political fortune than Hinduism. Hinduism on mainland South East Asia was intimately associated with the ritual and cosmology of large agrarian-based dynasties such as the great Cambodian Khmer empire: when the Khmer dynasty went into decline so did Hinduism, whereas Buddhism retained its place as a focal point of popular religion albeit intertwined with more ancient indigenous beliefs and practices. While Buddhism was to surpass Hinduism as the more popular faith throughout South East Asia, until it was rivalled by Islam from the thirteenth century AD, Hindu influences lingered on in various forms. Brahmans survived in many royal courts until the present century as priests in various royal rituals, and at the popular level, Hindu deities and beliefs mixed with Buddhist beliefs and even more ancient animistic beliefs to form complex, and distinctively South East Asian, religious systems.

By the beginning of the present era, maritime trade was beginning to provide linkages for the transmission of both tangible and intangible cargoes. Along some routes the movement comprised only physical commodities, but along others there was a passage of foreign ideas and forms which spread beyond marketplaces to influence the shape of emerging civilizations. In coming centuries this process was to gather pace around the Indian Ocean, giving rise to a cosmopolitan Indian Ocean world bound by a range of common religious, cultural and mercantile practices.

2

Commercial Imperialism

Overview

For a thousand or more years from the beginning of the present era there was a spectacular flowering of civilization and long-distance trade across the Indian Ocean. From the age when the Romans dominated the Mediterranean and much of the Middle East to the collapse of the great Arab empire in the thirteenth century AD, maritime trade evolved from the passage of small quantities of luxury goods to annual movements of thousands of small vessels carrying everything from luxuries to more common daily necessities. In the process, previously isolated peoples were brought into closer contact, leading to intensive cultural interaction between African and Asian civilizations.

During these centuries South Asia was at the centre of maritime trade network linking the Arabian Sea and the Bay of Bengal. South Asian mariners and merchants integrated the local trade networks of South East Asia into a larger Indian Ocean economic world, and in the process facilitated the selective adoption of South Asian religions, cultural forms and technology by the peoples of South East Asia.

The processes of South Asian commercial penetration of South East Asia continued over the centuries, as the Roman, Byzantine and Persian empires flourished in the Mediterranean and the Middle East, and as successive Chinese dynasties evolved the civilization and boundaries of China. The most visible results of South Asian enterprise in South East Asia were the wider diffusion of South East Asian commodities such as spices, rare timbers and gemstones, as well as the rise of 'Indianized' kingdoms scattered from the Burma to Java and southern Vietnam.

In the seventh and eighth centuries AD, with the advent of Islam and the spectacular economic growth of China, beginning with the T'ang dynasty, Muslim Middle Eastern merchants and Chinese merchants became increasingly active, challenging the predominance of

South Asian merchants. Muslim merchants controlled the trade of the Arabian Sea, infiltrating the indigenous coastal trade networks of East Africa and reaching as far east as southern China. At the same time, Chinese merchants and mariners became more regular visitors to South East Asia, occasionally sailing as far west as Sri Lanka and southern India. South Asia remained central to Indian Ocean maritime trade, with South Asian merchant communities scattered from East Africa to the Malay peninsula. But there were other merchant communities comprising Arabs and Persians who, in South Asia and East Africa, began the Islamization of coastal peoples, from the eighth century.

By the beginning of the present era, maritime trade was not only stimulating the growth of numerous cosmopolitan ports around the Arabian Sea and the Bay of Bengal, but was also becoming an instrument of state policy in many parts of Asia, where it was perceived to be a vital source of profit to royal treasuries. In South and South East Asia in particular, dynasties took a close interest in the promotion and protection of maritime trade to the extent that, by the eleventh century, international relations around the Bay of Bengal in particular were marked by periods of intense rivalry over the freedom and profits of maritime trade.

Throughout these centuries, maritime trade provided the means for the transmission of religions and cultures around the shores of the Indian Ocean. South Asia exported Hinduism and Buddhism from the time of the Mauryas. From the seventh century, Islam and its cultural values were carried out of the Middle East to the peoples of coastal East Africa and to South Asia, and from the thirteenth century to insular South East Asia. The impact of China was less marked. After the ninth century Chinese maritime enterprise in South East Asia was certainly of great importance to South East Asian economies, but it remained marginal to China itself. There was also a certain inconsistency in Chinese mercantile activity which was tied to the rhythms of the rise and fall of ruling dynasties. Chinese merchants sallied briefly beyond South East Asia into the Indian Ocean between the twelfth and fifteenth centuries, but only in pursuit of luxury cargoes. Their intervention barely caused a ripple in the workings of Indian Ocean trade, beyond an intensification of the trade in pepper, ceramics and silk from the twelfth century, without any diffusion of Chinese culture.

By the fifteenth century, Muslims—from the Middle East and South Asia—were the dominant force in maritime trade across the Indian Ocean. They were involved in both the long and short-haul trade, and they carried Islam to ports around the Ocean, from the Mozambique coast to the Moluccas on the edge of the Pacific.

Luxuries, Staples and the Nature of Maritime Trade

Many historians have regarded the maritime trade of the Indian Ocean until the fifteenth century, in the words of Edward Gibbon's writing in the eighteenth century, as 'splendid but trifling'. It has been described as a pedlar's trade involving only luxuries based upon irregular and erratic commercial contacts.[1] Such characterizations are generalizations which obscure the complexities of Indian Ocean trade, and which do nothing to explain the development of great cosmopolitan ports and complex processes of cultural interaction which were under way by the early centuries of the present era.

From very early times the trade of the Indian Ocean comprised both luxuries and necessities, and was much more regular and better organized than was previously believed.

For economists the terms 'luxuries' and 'necessities' have precise meanings, and it is worthwhile bearing these in mind if we are to lay the ghost of Gibbon's generalization. A necessity is a good whose consumption does not increase in proportion with income; a luxury is one whose consumption increases more than proportionately. It is true that pre-capitalist societies were more economically self-sufficient than their modern counterparts and that their trade in necessities was limited, but this self-sufficiency has been exaggerated. The majority of the products of pre-capitalist societies were consumed directly by those who produced them. The proportion of goods available for trade was relatively small, and the demand for imported goods was generally restricted within any society to the groups who controlled most local resources. Such people were only interested in what we would describe

[1] J.C. van Leur, 1955; K.N. Chaudhuri, 1985, 39; Ravi Arvind Palat, 1988, 269.

as luxuries; nevertheless, there were some necessities which were traded over great distances in large quantities. The trade in grain, salt, ceramics, timber and cheap cotton cloth across the Indian Ocean, for example, constituted a great trade which grew rapidly over the centuries, although ignored by historians until recently. Pre-capitalist maritime trade across the Indian Ocean was in fact a mixture of luxuries and necessities, the ephemeral and the staple.

The histories of Indian Ocean trade to the seventeenth century, are replete with details of exotic cargoes made up of splendid goods. 'As that great authority, McPherson [*sic*]', in the 'History of Commerce with India' tells us:

> To that city (Malacca) were carried the cloves, nutmegs and mace of the Moluco and Banda Islands, the sandalwood of Timor, the camphor of Borneo, the gold and silver of Luconia, the pepper, drugs and dye stuffs, the perfumery, rich silks and porcelain, and all the vast variety of merchandise produced and manufactured in China, Java, Siam and the neighbouring countries or islands. There the merchants from all the more Eastern countries met with those of Hindoostan and the Western Coasts of the Indian Ocean; and every one procured what was in request in exchange for what was redundant in his own country. The cities of Calicut, and Cambay on the west side of Hindoostan, Ormus in the Persian Gulf, and Aden on the South Coast of Arabia, were particularly enriched by the trade of Malacca; and they also trade to Pegu for rubies and lacker, to Bengal for cloths, (now called piece goods), to Calicare (or Kilcare) for pearls, to Narsinga for diamonds, to Ceylon for cinnamon and rubies, and to the coast of Malabar for pepper, ginger, and many other kinds of spices.[2]

The focus is firmly on the luxurious. But it is a distorted focus, a half-truth, revealing imaginations captured by the legend of Sindbad, by the fantasies of medieval commentators and by the vision of epic voyages from Arabia to China and back. It excludes the more regular and mundane maritime trade in cargoes of necessities which underpinned the passage of luxuries destined for select clients.

There were undoubtedly real-life Sindbads whose vessels plied the

[2] W.H. Coates, 1911, 16–17.

seas between the Middle East and the fabled marts of China, but the realities of maritime trade across the Indian Ocean were found in the less glamorous short-haul voyages. It was along these shorter routes, often coastal, that the basic rhythms of maritime trade were established—an enduring traffic less vulnerable to those sudden changes in taste, wealth and power which caused wild fluctuations in the luxury trade. This mundane trade was the mainspring of the movement of peoples across the Indian Ocean, which made possible spectacular processes of cultural interaction.

These realities have been further obscured by the vagueness of the term 'luxury trade' as used by many historians. A luxury in one society is not necessarily a luxury in another. Even within the same society, what is a luxury to one class is not necessarily a luxury for another.

Ivory, pepper, cowries and Chinese ceramics at their point of origin were not luxuries, but were relatively cheap export commodities which, after they were transported over great distances to markets where they were a rarity, became much more expensive and were regarded as a luxury. But even at this point one must be careful in using the term luxury: a ruler, for example, may have regarded an expensive import as a necessity, whereas to a peasant farmer such an import was an entirely useless luxury representing in value a lifetime's income. To further complicate the argument, but hopefully to underline the impossibility of treating pre-modern trade as unsophisticated, consider the generally accepted belief that gold and silver are nothing but luxuries. This may be true if one thinks of jewellery, but in other circumstances gold and silver are necessities: in all ages they have underpinned the stability of financial systems. Without the trade in gold and silver it would have been impossible to sustain the minting of gold and silver coins which, from the early centuries of the present era underpinned commerce in many parts of the Indian Ocean.

There is no universal formula to resolve what was, or what was not, a luxury item. All that we can do is to note that merchants sought a maximum return for a minimum outlay. If cargoes were to travel great distances and be exposed to great risks and handling and transportation costs, the margin of profit had to be equally great. Before the advent of steam vessels and modern communication technology, long-distance maritime trade was an extremely risky business. Storms, inadequately charted waters, relatively small and frail craft, pirates, and the great distances that had to be travelled, posed constant threats: the challenge was successfully taken by many people over the ages, but compensation was sought by a high profit margin on cargoes. On the other hand, short-haul traffic was less risky, and consequently costs were lower and profits less spectacular than those of the successful long-distance voyagers. In addition, short-haul traffic could concentrate upon bulkier and more mundane necessities such as grain and cheap cloth, and direct itself to markets which included buyers other than locally dominant groups.

The differentiation between 'luxuries' and 'necessities' in precapitalist cargoes across the Indian Ocean became less clear over time. As maritime trade matured, long-haul voyages were replaced by a series of segmented voyages determined by the rhythms of the monsoon winds. Such cargoes typically comprised both staples carried for one voyage only, and luxury items possibly intended for offloading to another vessel bound for more distant ports. No vessel could safely sail with a small cargo of luxury items without some form of ballast, preferably with commercial value: rice, ceramics, sugar, timber, iron ingots, and building materials. As cargo exchange became more frequent with time, few items of ballast were carried which did not have some market value.

Increasingly, over time, bulk cargoes of farm produce and raw materials were carried on long-haul voyages as the main source of profit. Famine, and the development of ports without an agricultural hinterland were incentives for the movement of such cargoes over long distances. Rice, for example, was a widespread cargo, not only because it could be kept for several years (unlike wheat, which soon deteriorated), and was central to the diet of many peoples in Asia and Africa, but also because it comprised a great number of varieties, rare and common, which appealed to a range of market tastes. Thus Bengal supplied particular varieties of rice to Sri Lanka, the Maldives and Gujarat; rice from Madagascar and the Comoros was traded with East Africa; and the varied rice types of Java, Sulawesi, southern Thailand, central Burma and the Mekong delta were found in markets scattered across South East Asia. South Asia also supplied shipbuilding timber for the great trading ports of Arabia and the Gulf, while East Africa

supplied the Gulf with mangrove timber for house construction and
ingots of iron for metal industries in the Middle East.

Human cargo presents even more complex problems of categoriza-
tion. Systems of slavery existed across the ancient world from the
Mediterranean to China. Africa and South East Asia were major
sources of slaves within the Indian Ocean, although the latter system
appears to have been geographically restricted to South East Asia itself.
By the fourth century AD, Africa, from Ethiopia to Madagascar, was
a source of slaves for markets as distant as Europe and China.[3] Unlike
the great exodus of slaves which began from Africa in the ninth
century, the numbers involved in this earlier trade were relatively small.
Few slaves appear to have been used as a source of cheap labour, and
were considered luxuries and assets, not simply beasts of burden to be
mindlessly exploited.

While the luxury trade returned great profit, it was based upon a
refined market demand: the ability of the rich to maintain high levels
of consumption. On the other hand trade in necessities was grounded
in broadly based market demand, and was less subject therefore to
radical changes in the fortunes of élites. Trade in luxuries was more
vulnerable to the random event—the death of a Caesar, the collapse
of a dynasty, the sack of a city, the debasement of a currency—than
the trade in necessities.

The more humble trade in necessities, while also subject to market
forces, was broadly based in terms of demand. It too could be disrupted
by random human and natural catastrophes, but the more universal
the demand, the fewer the possibilities for any sustained disruption
of trade. Depending upon the development stage of the societies
concerned, basic commodities such as foodstuffs, cheap cloth and raw
materials like timber for house construction and shipbuilding, were
in greater and more constant demand than the glamorous trifles which
provided the splendid facade for the maritime trade of the Indian
Ocean.

The Rise of South Asia

The spread of urban civilization across South Asia by the beginning

[3] André Wink, 1990, 14.

of the present era was central to the development of long-distance maritime trade across the Indian Ocean. The growth of cities and marketplaces in South Asia reflected the emergence of a conglomeration of increasingly prosperous societies with growing wealth. The subcontinent was the major supplier of export cargoes in the Indian Ocean. Furthermore, as the junction between the western and eastern halves of the ocean, many of its coastal markets were entrepôts for goods passing along an east-west axis. But South Asia was also the major importer of foreign commodities in the Indian Ocean. Its ports provided a link between the sea and the South Asian hinterland, also serving as the Ocean's main gateways to the overland trade routes of Central Asia, which swept in a huge arc from Persia to China.

The complex factors governing the ebb and flow of long-distance maritime trade across the Indian Ocean cannot be linked to the fortunes of one economic area. By virtue of their sheer size and complexity, South Asian economies exerted a profound and lasting influence on the history of Indian Ocean trade. Just as foreign merchants, mariners and travellers thronged the ports of South Asia, South Asian merchants, mariners and travellers reached every corner of the Indian Ocean littoral from East Africa to the Indonesian archipelago, selling and collecting a variety of goods from a growing number of markets.

During the early centuries of the present era, there was a spectacular growth in seaborne trade eastward from the Coromandel coast and Sri Lanka. *The Periplus* mentions that Indonesian outriggers visited the eastern coast of India, and this probably stimulated South Asian interest in the gold, tin (vital for the growing bronze industry of southern India and Sri Lanka, based upon the mixing of copper and tin), spices, Chinese silk and ceramics, and exotic jungle products available in lands across the Bay of Bengal. This South East Asian trade impacted profoundly upon the Tamil country of southern India, which by the second and third centuries AD were in regular contact with South East Asia through ports such as Arikamedu (Podouke), Kayal and Kamara.

Tamil civilization entered its classic *sangam* phase which was marked by spectacular cultural activity, the spread of Brahmanical Hinduism, and the area's first major period of urban growth. Various dynasties lavishly endowed shrines and priests out of piety and for the more pragmatic reason of reinforcing their legitimacy. Hinduism in particular benefited from this process, as rulers patronized the priestly Brahmin castes with lavish land grants and temple foundations as a means of opening up new agricultural land, encouraging the growth of local markets which were traditionally associated with temple feast days, and securing popular support through the agency of priests wedded to royal patronage. It was in the south in particular that Hinduism transformed itself, by developing a broadly-based popular content, which enabled it to weaken and then destroy the hold of Buddhism which appears to have lost much of its early egalitarianism and to have become institutionalized and remote from the masses in South Asia. Rulers viewed temples not only as symbols of royal legitimacy but also as centres of commerce, for most were associated with fairs and marketplaces, and as such were a central part of the economic integration of southern India with both land and sea trade routes.

On both the Malabar and Coromandel coasts major states had evolved by the beginning of the present era. On the Coromandel coast, Tamil states developed under the Chola, Pandya and Pallava dynasties, and under the Cheras on the Malabar coast. As early as 20 BC there was a mission to the Roman ruler Augustus from the Pandya ruler of Madurai, and from the second and third centuries AD all these states were locked in convoluted naval and military struggles with one another, the Sinhalese kingdom of Anuradhapura, various kingdoms in Burma and the Sumatran-based empire of Srivijaya, to dominate the maritime trade of the Bay of Bengal. All these dynasties were great patrons of the arts and religion, leaving magnificent literary and monumental legacies, and until the twelfth and thirteenth centuries AD they and their successors maintained an intimate interest in the maritime trade of the Bay of Bengal.

In contrast to this rapid expansion of South Asia's overseas contacts, maritime links between China and the outside world did not become regular until the tropical south beyond the Yangtze was fully incorporated into the Chinese state in the third century AD, under the Han (202 BC–AD 220) dynasty. Only then was Chinese official interest in maritime enterprise roused by the prospect of readily accessible luxuries from the south, at a time when Persian extortions on the caravan traffic at the western end of the Silk Road through Central Asia, increased the price of imported luxury goods in China. Sea trade to the south offered a new source of revenue and cheaper luxuries, as well as providing an alternative route to unstable Central Asia for Chinese pilgrims to reach Buddhist centres of learning in northern India and Sri Lanka.

A further explanation of why Chinese trade to South East Asia was so slow to mature may be that South Asians had acclimatized earlier to tropical disease conditions than the Chinese. Widespread parasitic diseases in South Asia prepared South Asian travellers for the intense microparasitism of South East Asia. In contrast, the Chinese had little resistance to tropical diseases until several centuries after they had absorbed the tropical lands to the south of the Yangtze.[4]

By the first century AD South Asian merchants had penetrated as far east as the Mekong delta. Entrepôts developed along the route from Mantai on the west coast of Sri Lanka and Arikamedu (Podouke) on the Coromandel coast (both rich sources of Roman and Persian artefacts), across the Kra Isthmus to Oc-eo on the western side of the Mekong delta, where South Asian, Roman and Persian artefacts have been found. South Asian merchants also traded with the Irrawaddy valley in Burma for Chinese silk and jade which came overland from Yunnan.

In this eastward expansion, South Asian merchants took advantage of the extensive maritime trade network that already existed within South East Asian waters. Their rise to pre-eminence in the long-distance trade of the area was facilitated by the absence both of a South East Asian merchant class and a significant Chinese mercantile presence. Indigenous long-distance trade was controlled by local élites who dealt through agents with foreign merchants, inhibiting the growth of local merchant communities.

South Asian mercantile penetration was also encouraged by the growth of agricultural-based riverine and coastal states in Burma and Thailand, on the Mekong delta, and on the coastal plains of Vietnam, during the early centuries of the present era. Rulers of states such as

[4] William McNeil, 1976.

Dvaravati, Funnan and Champa eagerly exchanged local commodities such as gemstones, tin and exotic jungle products for the sophisticated manufactures of South Asia.

In South Asia, local rulers also actively encouraged foreign merchant communities as a means of promoting maritime trade and increasing their tax revenue. Along the Malabar coast in particular, foreign merchants such as Jews, Nestorian Christians, Arabs and Persians had their own distinct quarters in all major ports by the fifth and sixth centuries AD. Local rulers frequently granted such groups agricultural land to support their religious establishments and permitted them what were in effect extra-territorial privileges. However, unlike South East Asia, there is remarkably little evidence of significant cultural interaction between the foreign settlers and their host community. Most probably this was due to the fact that neither side had much to offer the other. With a few exceptions, civilization in the Middle East and South Asia was on a technological par. Neither side was in a period where there was rapid social or economic change which may have encouraged the search for new answers or ideas, with the result that neither side was particularly receptive to foreign cultural influences.

The major exception to this generalization concerns Christians. By the sixth century Christianity had spread beyond the confines of scattered mercantile ghettoes to include indigenous converts drawn from artisan and agricultural groups. However, until the coming of Europeans in the sixteenth century significant Christian communities existed only along the Malabar coast. To an even more limited extent Judaism also made converts, largely through intermarriage, on the Malabar coast and then later in Maharashtra on the Konkan coast. On the other hand, until the coming of Islam, communities of Arabs and Persians in South Asia remained exotic enclaves outside the mainstream of South Asian civilization.

But trade links with the Middle East and South East Asia, whatever their cultural consequences, did set the seal upon the maritime orientation of certain parts of South Asia 2000 years ago.

On the western flank of the subcontinent Gujarat, with its great port at Broach and with its ready access to the great food- and textile-producing areas of northern India and the trade routes of

Central Asia via the Punjab and Afghanistan, became a focal point of South Asian trade with the Middle East and East Africa, and a cosmopolitan area where people of many lands lived side by side. The Konkan ports to the south of Gujarat such as Bankot (Mandagora) and Malvan (Erannoboas?), with their mineral-rich hinterland in the Deccan, exported metals and gemstones westward in return for a range of goods. Malabar sent teak, coir and pepper to Middle Eastern markets on the Arabian and Persian coasts from ports such as Cranganore (Mouziris); while the Maldives, astride the monsoon winds, provided an alternative entrepôt to the ports of South Asia for the passage of goods between the Middle East and South East and East Asia, and were an ideal revictualling base as well as a supplier of cowries, coir rope, salted fish and beach-gathered ambergris.

On the south-eastern flank of the subcontinent, the Sri Lankan port of Mantai was similarly situated at the junction between the eastern and western Ocean. It was also a major producer of gemstones, ivory, pearls, elephants, cinnamon and arecanut, which were widely sought after across Asia. Like Gujarat, the Coromandel coast with its ports at Arikamedu (Podouke), Kayal, Kamara and Masulipatnam (Masalia) was an outlet for a major cotton textile-producing and rice-surplus area, as well as the key to the Deccan, serving as a major entrepôt area for trade with South East and East Asia. The Orissa coast likewise provided access to the mineral-rich Deccan, while Bengal's hinterland—the eastern extension of the great Indo-Gangetic plain—was rich in cotton cloth, rice, indigo and other dye stuffs. The evolution of ports in these latter two areas appears to have occurred later than elsewhere in South Asia. In part, this probably reflects the relatively underdeveloped nature of the Orissa hinterland and the deltaic nature of the Bengal coast with its constantly shifting channels and inlets which provided ready access to great inland waterways, but which also made the establishment of permanent port sites next to impossible.

In the hinterlands of all these areas, foodstuffs, manufactured goods and raw materials were produced for both domestic and foreign consumption. Ceramics, textiles, metal goods, sugar, rice, pepper, ghee, wheat, salted and dried fish, salt, coconuts, vegetables, spices and fruit were moved by river and sea within the area, and at times,

further afield to markets in East Africa, the Middle East and South
East Asia.

The monsoons set the rhythms for coastal traffic, as they did for
long-distance maritime traffic and agriculture. The movement of coastal traffic corresponded closely to agricultural cycles and was most
active towards the close of the harvest seasons across the Indo-Gangetic
plain, when northern fleets sailed south with cargoes of grain and cloth
for southern ports. Their arrival on the Malabar and Coromandel
coasts coincided with the arrival of fleets carrying cargoes of spices,
manufactures and raw materials from East Africa, the Middle East,
South East and East Asia. Return coastal traffic carried cargoes from
the south, Sri Lanka, and from other parts of the Indian Ocean, the
Mediterranean and East Asia.

From the period of Roman domination of the Mediterranean to
the rise of Islam in the seventh century AD, South Asian maritime
enterprise had a profound effect upon economic activity from the Red
Sea to the South China Sea. However, the main thrust of South Asian
maritime enterprise was to the east, from about the third century AD,
as trade to the west declined, and in following centuries Persians,
Aksumites and Arabs came to dominate the carrying trade of the
Arabian Sea. Conversely, along the eastern seaboard of India and from
Sri Lanka, local merchants and mariners dominated the sea routes to
the east, and maintained and extended various ancient indigenous
maritime traditions and technologies which appear to have been
strongly influenced by South East Asian technology.[5]

As previously noted, during the first few centuries of the present
era, maritime trade was sufficiently important to involve various South
Asian states in political intervention to secure its profits. But it was
in the south and in Sri Lanka that maritime trade and politics inter-
sected to greatest effect. On the Coromandel and Malabar coasts
during the first millennium AD, various dynasties and kingdoms, while
drawing most of their power from control of the agricultural surplus,
paid close attention to the fortunes of maritime trade, to the extent
of forging state policy towards the furtherance of that trade by warfare
and diplomacy. Revenue derived from trade no doubt greatly appealed

[5] P.Y. Manguin, 1985, 13–15.

to rulers who usually derived the bulk of their resources through local landholding intermediaries. Such intermediaries were not always willing to disgorge their surpluses without concessions from the central authorities. In addition, an increasing amount of land revenue was alienated by grants to temples and Brahmins, and although such acts may have had indirect benefits, they further reduced royal revenue. The profits of trade, therefore, offered rulers a chance to decrease their dependency upon too powerful subordinates and to compensate them for their generous piety.

On the Coromandel coast, dynasties such as the Pandyas, Pallavas and Cholas fought the rulers of Sri Lanka over a period of a 1000 years or more, for control of the pearl and shell rich Palk Strait and the Gulf of Manaar, at the junction of trade routes between the western and eastern Indian Oceans. South Indian and Sri Lankan dynasties also embarked on ambitious overseas naval campaigns,[6] as for example, in the eleventh century, when they were involved in disputes with kingdoms in Bengal, Burma and Sumatra, over maritime trade. They were also involved in warfare with one another across the northern plains of Sri Lanka, which resulted in the abandonment of the Sinhalese capital of Anuradhapura and its port at Mantai in the eleventh century, in favour of Polonnaruwa further to the south. Ruling groups on the Malabar coast, most notably the Chera dynasty, extended their control over the Lakshadweep islands, gaining access to their coir and coconut production, and control of an oceanic staging post on the route between the Persian Gulf and southern India.

While none of these contending dynasties and states had standing navies, control of trade routes and ports was a vital part of political life, and the overseas campaigns of various south Indian and Sri Lankan rulers were directed towards the protection and extension of their trading interests. The same can be said of the activities of the various Muslim city states along the coast of East Africa during the fourteenth and fifteenth centuries, and the great political manoeuvring which took place between Srivijaya and various other South East Asian states for control over the Kra Isthmus, during the era of Srivijayan domination of Sumatra and the Strait of Melaka, from the seventh to the

[6] See O.W. Wolters, 1970; Paul Wheatley, 1980, Chp. XIII; Janet L. Abu-Lughod, 1989, 269–70; André Wink, 1990, 309–27.

fourteenth century. Violence intruded into all these political situa-
tions, and it was a violence aimed at dominating maritime trade.

From the time of the Mauryan dynasty to the establishment of
the Islamic Arab empire in the seventh and eight centuries AD, South
Asia passed through a period of remarkable economic and political
stability. Its history is admittedly full of a multitude of contending
kingdoms and would-be empires, but compared with the history of
the Middle East, northern Africa, China and Europe, it was a period
generally free from wide-ranging wars and devastating invasions. Invaders, such as the Scythians and Kushans from Central Asia and
Greeks from Bactria and Iran, who did breach the wall of protecting
mountains were soon absorbed into the mainstream of local life and
civilization. Greeks and Scythians established a number of states in
western and central India, the Kushans established a short-lived empire
which stretched from the Caspian Sea to the Indus valley, then in the
fourth century a dynasty based in the ancient kingdom of Magadha
established the Gupta empire (*c.* 320–499 AD) which at its height
stretched from the Indus valley to Bengal. Following the decline of
the Gupta dynasty north India was divided among a variety of con-
tenders for imperial authority with none achieving paramountcy. In
the Deccan the same pattern of political fragmentation was repeated
with the Satavahanas, Vakatakas, Kadambas, Chalukyas and Hoysalas
succeeding one another in the quest for domination of the area.

During these centuries of relative isolation and widespread peace,
technological and economic evolution changed the human and geographic face of South Asia. Vast tracts of land came under the plough,
urban life flourished, there was a rapid development of the arts, and
expanding trade networks integrated markets from the Maldives to
the Punjab into a subcontinental wide economic system. In addition,
it was a period in which Hinduism, particularly under the Guptas,
was transformed from an elitist tribal based religion into a vast and
amorphous socio-religious system, which incorporated the most sophisticated philosophical speculation alongside a pantheon of local deities
and religious practices. Its eclecticism undermined Buddhism in South
Asia where it retained its hold only in Sri Lanka.

The relative political isolation of South Asia was not however
matched by maritime isolation. The ancient ports of Maurya India

flourished under the Kushans and other north Indian dynasties, while the Deccan states maintained a lively interest in foreign commerce matched by the vigorous kingdoms of the Malabar and Coromandel coasts and Sri Lanka. During these centuries, Arabs, Persians, Jews, Christians and Ethiopians continued to visit the ports of western India and Sri Lanka, while from the Malabar coast, Sri Lanka and the eastern seaboard of India, local merchants and mariners sailed the Bay of Bengal to the kingdoms of mainland and insular South East Asia.

The Impact of the Islamic and Chinese Empires

The creation of an Arab Islamic empire extending from the Atlantic to the Arabian Sea and into Central Asia in the seventh and eighth centuries, and the parallel growth of a reinvigorated Chinese empire stretching from Central Asia to the Pacific under the T'ang and Song dynasties (619–1279), were further stimuli for the expansion of Indian Ocean trade in the eighth and ninth centuries, and for the evolution of another great cultural system in the Middle East.

The impact of each empire upon maritime trade was different. Chinese maritime ventures into the Indian Ocean were largely confined to the South China Sea and the Bay of Bengal, as far west as the Malabar coast and Sri Lanka. However, traders from the Islamic empire established a commercial network which at its peak reached across Eurasia from the Atlantic to the Pacific. Not since the time of Alexander the Great, some 1000 years earlier, had the Mediterranean and the Indian Ocean been linked by a single state which encompassed the lands of the Middle East from Egypt to Iran (See Map 6).

When the Prophet Muhammad preached the message of Islam in the seventh century, the Middle East was divided between the empire of Byzantium, the surviving eastern half of the Roman empire, and Sasanid Persia, with a string of minor trading states in the Gulf and Arabia.

The Indian Ocean trade of the Middle East was maintained through ports on the Red Sea and the Persian Gulf, some of which were under Byzantine and Sasanid control, or through entrepôts in Yemen and on the Ethiopian and Hadhramaut coasts. Arabian ports, although nominally independent, lived under the shadows of Byzan-

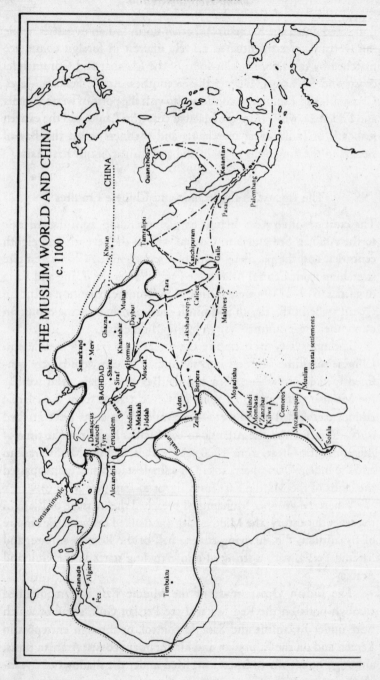

THE MUSLIM WORLD AND CHINA
c. 1100

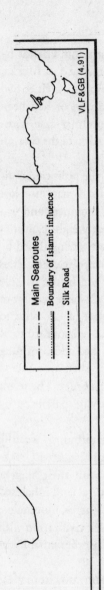

Map 6: The Muslim World and China, *c.* 1100

Legend:
- Main Searoutes
- Boundary of Islamic influence
- Silk Road

VLF&GB (4.91)

tium and Persia, and were linked to their economic hinterlands by overland trading routes through oasis trading cities, such as Mekka, Medinah and Petra. By the seventh century many of these cities had been incorporated into Byzantine or Persian territory, or had been ruined by the incessant wars between the two. In either case, most had declined in importance, with the probable exception of the caravan cities of the Hejaz: Mekka and Medinah.

The formation of the Islamic empire reshaped the political boundaries of the Middle East and the Mediterranean. Byzantium lost control of its Middle Eastern and North African provinces and was driven back to the mountains of Anatolia. For nearly eight centuries Byzantium was to struggle against Islam, until it was extinguished by Muslim Ottoman Turks in 1453. Sasanid Persia collapsed after a series of military defeats which left the Arabs in command of the Middle Eastern heartland, from the Mediterranean to the Caspian Sea. From North Africa Islamic armies moved across the Strait of Gibraltar to conquer the Iberian peninsula and a single dominant religious, cultural and political system held sway from the Tagus to the Indus, forming a huge *Dar al-Islam* or Abode of Islam, where the shari'a or Sacred Law of Islam was the theoretical foundation of social order. The result was an outpouring of cultural and economic activity, paralleled by similar developments in T'ang (618–907) China.

The Arabs inherited a culturally complex and enormously wealthy empire. In the Middle East they conquered the sophisticated Greek-speaking cities of Egypt, the Levant and Syria with their ancient cosmopolitan cultures; vast tracts of fertile agricultural land inhabited by Semitic-speaking peasants from Egypt to the Zagros mountains; and in Persia they humbled an ancient and complex civilization with its distinctive language and culture set apart from the other inhabitants of the Middle East.

At first the desert Arabs ruled their new empire uneasily from great citadels, little inclined to interfere in local life beyond the collection of taxes. But the realities of imperial rule and the attractions of urban life rapidly undermined Arab insularity. Islam gained an increasing number of adherents and the complex imperial bureaucracy needed local collaboration and participation. The new ruling élite evolved a culture which reflected their mixed inheritance. Local scholars and artisans who became part of the new order helped shape classical Arab civilization, and in doing so produced a dynamic urban culture which reflected much that was best in the legacy of Greece, Rome and Persia, at a time when in Western Europe urban life had all but vanished.

The term Arab soon came to be applied to most of the inhabitants of North Africa, Egypt, Syria, Palestine, the Levant and Mesopotamia, as conversion led to the incorporation of the masses into Islam. Mass conversions to Islam occurred in Persia too, but there Arabic failed to replace the old language as it did elsewhere in the Arab empire, with the result that the Persians retained a strong sense of national and cultural identity apart from their Arab co-religionists.

Long before the advent of Islam, Arab and Persian sailors and merchants were active in the great ports of the Arabian Sea, as were Nestorian Christians from the Sasanid empire who travelled as far east as South East Asia. A body of Middle Eastern literature, drawn from Persian, Greek, Roman and South Asian sources relating to the lands, routes and ports of the Indian Ocean, was available to the first Muslim merchants and sailors who sailed routes and dealt in cargoes long familiar to the mercantile communities of the Middle East.

The Islamic empire created an environment favouring a growth in urban centres as well as economic activity, by restoring peace to the agricultural lands of the Middle East, which had been long ravaged by wars between the Persian and Byzantine empires. The empire integrated an awesome range of manufacturing, farming and cultural systems from the Atlantic to the Arabian Sea. This was the biggest empire and largest collection of economies and cultures under one political system that the world had seen. A sophisticated and cosmopolitan Islamic culture and society grew out of this blending of old and new, incorporating ancient merchant communities and traditions which were to flourish under the peace which was established by the foundation of the Islamic empire.

The imperial élite were acutely aware of the advantages of trade which they consciously and vigorously encouraged. Non-Muslim and non-Arab merchants—Jews (such as the very successful *radhaniya* merchants financed by Jewish bankers in Baghdad during the ninth and tenth centuries), Nestorian and Coptic (Egyptian) Christians and Persians—prospered within the empire, where their ancient cultural and trade networks were integrated into a broader imperial system. The new rulers also took an active interest in the promotion and extension of agriculture, undertaking in Mesopotamia (later known as Iraq) in particular, a reclamation of waste land to produce a range of cash crops such as sugar and dates. These fed into the export trade of the Gulf.

Once the empire was established, the economic energies released and channelled had an astounding impact upon the Middle East, the Mediterranean world, Central Asia, and many parts of the Indian Ocean world. The outpouring of Middle Eastern energy from the seventh century onwards gave the Indian Ocean trading world the shape it retained for the next nine centuries, and added yet another layer to the complex of cultures which formed the Indian Ocean world.

In the Arab and Chinese empires economic prosperity and peace prompted a flowering of the arts and learning. In the Middle East the conquering Arabs incorporated the ancient urban Romano-Greek culture of Byzantium, and the even more ancient civilization of Persia, into the culture they brought out of the desert. Intellectual life flourished as the wealth of the empire increased.

During the eighth and ninth centuries the economic growth of the Middle East promoted a revival of internal and external trade networks. Trade along the Silk Road through Central Asia increased, as the Arabs and Chinese pacified the area, and there was an intensification of maritime trade with other parts of the Indian Ocean, most notably South Asia and East Africa. The great age of Middle Eastern merchants and sailors had begun. Arab, Persian, Christian and Jewish merchants from the Middle East now travelled to the farthest reaches of the Indian Ocean.

With the establishment of the Arab imperial capital at Baghdad, from where Khalifs who claimed descent from the Prophet ruled as the temporal and spiritual leaders of the Islamic empire, the Persian Gulf became the main artery for Middle Eastern trade with the Indian Ocean. Ports such as Basra in Mesopotamia, Bahrain on the Arabian shore, Siraf and Hormuz on the Persian coast, and Sohar and Muscat on the Gulf of Oman, forged stronger links with the East African coast south of the Horn and South Asia.

Middle Eastern bullion flowed into the ports of southern India such as Calicut, in return for pepper, pearls, textiles and gemstones as well as for goods transhipped from across the Bay of Bengal. North Indian ports from Daybul on the Indus delta to Thana near modern Bombay also benefited from this upsurge in trade, but political fragmentation in northern India circumscribed their growth in comparison with their southern rivals who, apart from their entrepôt functions, serviced fewer and larger states.

By the ninth century, Middle Eastern merchants and mariners had established communities from the Comoros to Quanzhou in southern China, creating a maritime Silk Road as well as a commercial and information network of unparalleled proportions. Traces of Middle Eastern trade goods, mainly ceramics and glass, have been found in considerable quantities at sites dating from this period, around the Indian Ocean, as have the remains of the first mosques constructed outside the boundaries of the *Dar al-Islam*.

The brilliance of the Arab Muslim empire was matched by the glories of T'ang and Song China (960–1279). China had been trading by sea with South East Asia and beyond from the third century, but that trade only assumed significant proportions during the period between the fall of the Han dynasty and the rise of the T'ang. During the fifth and sixth centuries, southern China was ruled by a series of dynasties denied access to the trade of the Silk Road by their northern counterparts. In recompense, southern China turned towards South East Asia as a source of luxury imports, particularly pepper and aromatics, and as an outlet for exports, most particularly silk and ceramics. The navigators of insular South East Asia in particular, provided maritime expertise which linked southern China to the markets of the Indian Ocean.

Under the T'ang and Song dynasties, central authority was restored, control over the Silk Road reasserted, and the profitable southern seaborne trade expanded. Some South East Asian commodities —such as the aromatics and medicinal drugs extracted from pine resin and benzoin—were imported as cheaper substitutes for goods previously carried from west Asia by Persian merchants who controlled the frankincense and myrrh trade from Oman. But, as we have seen, South East Asia also provided a growing number of unique luxury items which ensured it a permanent place in China's overseas trade.

As a result of this growth of Chinese maritime activity, Middle Eastern merchants who had reached as far east as Quanzhou by the eighth century were, from the ninth century, faced with increasing Chinese competition in the South China Sea and the Bay of Bengal. Foreign trading communities in Chinese ports declined as the Chinese imperial authorities, merchants and mariners, became aware of the potential gains of direct participation in the Indian Ocean trade, in tandem with the indigenous merchants of South East Asia.

However, the impact of Chinese maritime trade until the twelfth century should not be exaggerated, for it was subject to considerable ebbs and flows. Generally, within China, revenue derived from trade never rivalled the efficiently collected revenue raised from taxes on peasants and was consequently of little concern to most dynasties. Also, maritime trade was still very much based on the demand for luxuries by wealthy Chinese, and remained dependent upon China's political stability and economic prosperity. At times of dynastic weakness, or the collapse of central authority, Chinese maritime enterprise declined alongside the ability of rulers to collect taxes from the peasantry.

The Chinese bureaucracy was suspicious of money and power accumulating in merchant hands, and there were frequent attempts to curb the growth of a large Chinese merchant class which might challenge the authority of the landowning élite which traditionally provided recruits to the imperial civil service. At the same time, wealthy Chinese sought foreign luxury goods, so the imperial bureaucracy encouraged the settlement of South Asian and Middle Eastern merchants in southern Chinese ports, particularly under the Song dynasty, as the safest and easiest way of gaining access to foreign luxury goods.

Before the twelfth century, Chinese maritime trade centred mostly on the importation of small cargoes of exotic luxuries in exchange for cargoes of ceramics, silk, copper coins, luxury manufactures, and medicinal items. Such trade was far removed from the mundane seaborne traffic within South East Asia, and from the large-scale traffic in cotton cloth which paid for South Asia's imports from South East Asia.

During the twelfth century there were changes in the pattern of China's maritime trade: the volume and value of imports grew, and to pay for them the Chinese greatly increased their exports of mass-produced ceramics. With increasing prosperity and urbanization under the Song dynasty, Chinese luxury imports increased dramatically, but imports of bulk commodities such as cheap cloth, pepper, rice, sugar, timber and salt increased even more dramatically as domestic demand for them spread beyond the relatively small number of wealthy landowning families who were the traditional buyers of imported goods.

When the Song court was forced by the Jurchen invaders to move south in 1127, the government encouraged the export trade in mass-produced ceramics and silk to finance military activity against the usurpers. In the next century, the Mongol Yuan dynasty (1276–1368) pursued an even more vigorous overseas trade policy. By the fourteenth century, Chinese merchants were active throughout South East Asia, trading great quantities of ceramics (particularly the new blue and white porcelain). Such ceramics ranged in quality from the rare and expensive to the mass-produced export ware which could be found in marketplaces throughout Asia and East Africa well into the twentieth century.

The magnet of Chinese prosperity attracted merchants from other parts of the Indian Ocean, and by the twelfth century the southern ports once more hosted large communities of foreign Muslims and Hindus. But cultural interaction was limited. The Chinese absorbed little from the outside world, exhibiting a high degree of cultural self-sufficiency. Similarly the outside world—beyond a small number of countries such as Vietnam, Japan and Korea, on the borders of China—adopted little from China, apart from ceramic technologies and designs, and the secrets of the silk worm.

Between the eighth and thirteenth centuries, the Islamic and Chinese empires enjoyed an unprecedented degree of prosperity which spurred the development and extension of maritime trade. The two imperial systems altered the rhythms of maritime trade, but the nature of this influence can only be understood by examining maritime trade beyond the boundaries of empire within the Indian Ocean world.

Beyond the Empires

Beyond the political boundaries of the Arab and Chinese empires between the eighth and thirteenth centuries, there was a steady expansion of the Islamic faith and culture. East Africa, and South and South East Asia were intimately affected by the spread of Islam—both in terms of the expansion of maritime trade and the conversion of local peoples.

Until the seventh and eighth centuries, the coast of East Africa, south of the Horn, was largely *terra incognita* to outsiders. Ivory was the main attraction, but it could be obtained closer to markets in the Mediterranean, the Middle East, and South Asia through Aksum, and much of the East African coast remained peripheral to mariners and merchants from other parts of the Indian Ocean. By the seventh century, however, over-hunting had reduced the elephant herds of north-east Africa, and foreign merchants were seeking alternative supplies south of the Horn.

South East Asia's contacts with South and East Asia were much more regular and substantial as merchants were attracted by its plentiful supplies of very profitable trading commodities. The Malay peninsula also served as an entrepôt for the exchange of cargoes between the Indian Ocean and the South China Sea, and was divided among a number of states whose prosperity depended upon trade with South and East Asia. The history of these states remains obscure, but from the third century there are references to them in Chinese writings which would indicate that both the west and east coast of the Malay peninsula, and the east coast of Sumatra, were dotted with a large number of small, thriving port city states whose prosperity was based on their entrepôt functions.[7]

Until the sixth and seventh centuries AD, many of these tiny states appear to have maintained a tenuous independence. Between the fifth and sixth centuries they were probably dominated by the kingdom of Funnan, located in what is now southern Vietnam and Cambodia. Following the decline of Funnan in the sixth century, the peninsula states came under the influence of Funnan's successor, the Khmer empire centred upon Cambodia, and the great Sumatran-based trading empire of Srivijaya (c. 650–c. 1400), with their mixed Hindu, Buddhist and indigenous cultural and religious practices. Srivijaya, despite

[7] P. Wheatley, 1980.

Khmer attempts to gain access to the Indian Ocean shore via the Kra Isthmus, proved the more successful in dominating the maritime trade routes which linked the Indian Ocean and the South China Sea.

Srivijaya's success resulted from several factors. Among them was the ability of its rulers to secure the services of itinerant maritime groups such as the Orang Laut, who were recruited to man its ships which serviced the major ports on the periphery visited by foreign merchants and ships. Another was its diversion of trade between the Indian Ocean and the South China Sea from the previously popular porterage route across the Kra Isthmus to the route through the Strait of Melaka. Allied with these factors was the successful substitution of commodities from South East Asia for the expensive goods China had previously imported along the Silk Road.

During the late fifth century China reshaped its foreign policy in South East Asia. The imperial court cut diplomatic links with Funnan, concentrating its attention upon the rival Cham kingdom of coastal southern Vietnam which lay on the main sea route between China and Java Sea centres. The eastern coast of Sumatra, with its many riverine systems and proximity to the Strait of Melaka, was the main focus of Chinese attention. But the riverine systems of northern Java also attracted foreigners. These rivers formed the cores of tiny states which, in time, were linked to the rice-rich interior where great states were taking shape in the fifth and sixth centuries. In addition, these riverine states were entrepôts on the maritime trade routes snaking eastward from Java to the Moluccas.

Despite challenges from the Khmers and the Cholas of southern India, Srivijaya maintained its maritime supremacy for more than 700 years. Funnan and the Khmers at times attempted to extend their control across Thailand to the Malay porterage routes on the Kra Isthmus, but with little lasting success. The Cholas were equally unsuccessful with punitive naval raids on the heartland of Srivijaya, in protest against its monopoly over the flow of goods between the Indian Ocean and the South China Sea.

The core of the trading empire was the ports located on the many inlets along the Sumatran shore of the Strait of Melaka which serviced both local shipping and vessels passing between the Indian Ocean and the South China Sea. Ports such as Palembang were not only cos-

mopolitan meeting places for sailors and merchants from the Middle
East and South and South East Asia, but they were also great centres
of Buddhist faith and culture, matched in South East Asia only by
the great Buddhist centres at Pagan in Burma, Borobodur in central
Java and Angkor Wat in Cambodia. Only from the eleventh century,
when Chinese vessels appeared in insular South East Asia to collect
such commodities at their source, was the hegemony of Srivijaya
challenged and finally destroyed.[8] (See Map 7)

From the eighth century, Islam began its slow expansion along
the coast of East Africa and into the Comoros and northern Madagascar. By the eleventh century, from the Benadir coast of Somalia to
Zanzibar on the Swahili coast, Arab and Persian Muslim merchants,
as well as merchants from South Asia, were making more sustained
inroads into seaborne trade, spurred on by rising demand in the
Middle East and South Asia. The pre-existing indigenous African
seaborne trading network and ports integrated into a wider Indian
Ocean mercantile system, with the export of hinterland commodities
to far distant markets. Cowries, foreign and locally minted silver
coinage, most particularly the beautiful and pure gold coinage of the
Arab empire, were now used in many markets along the coast.

The coastal settlements such as Malindi, Mombasa, Kilwa and
Sofala—and offshore settlements such as Zanzibar—began exploiting
their hinterlands (in somewhat similar manner to the delta states of
South East Asia) as demand rose for the products of the interior.
Merchants from the Middle East ventured more frequently past the
Horn and down the Somali and Kenyan coast as far as Kilwa, where
the monsoon winds faded. South of Kilwa, foreign traders travelled
less frequently, and the coastal traffic carrying cargoes of local foodstuffs and export commodities, as well as cargoes of foreign goods such
as ceramics and textiles, was organized by African merchants and
mariners. These cargoes were redistributed via the northern entrepôts,
most particularly the great redistribution port of Mogadishu on the
Benadir coast, to the Middle East and South Asia along monsoon-
driven sea routes.

The Muslim mercantile penetration of coastal East Africa made a

[8] O.W. Wolters, 1967 and 1970.

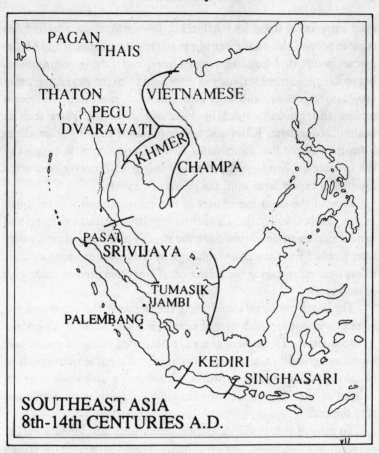

**SOUTHEAST ASIA
8th-14th CENTURIES A.D.**

Map 7: South East Asia 8th–14th Centuries AD

deep impression upon its inhabitants, from Eritrea on the Red Sea coast to Mogadishu on the Benadir coast, and the Comoros and Madagascar. South of Mogadishu, agricultural and fishing communities began to engage more seriously in trade, and from the eleventh century grew into large towns and cities with communities of Arab and Persian settlers and generally ruled by merchant dynasties. Ports such as Malindi, Mombasa, Kilwa and Sofala obtained export commodities from their immediate hinterlands as well as trading with peoples of the interior for ivory, gold and slaves. But gold, however, was not a significant export item until the thirteenth century.

Beyond the coast the impact of foreign merchants was minimal. In the Zambezi valley and Zimbabwe highlands, African pastoral and agricultural states developed from the twelfth century. Culturally they were isolated from the coast, although by the thirteenth century their rulers were encouraging the collection of ivory and gold to trade with coastal cities.

The main problem inhibiting trade between the coast and the interior was not so much rugged terrain, but the nature of economies in the interior. These were generally not based upon extensive and intensive agriculture, and rarely produced sufficient surplus goods to sustain complex trading networks. Urbanization and trade were restricted in the interior, and the demand for Asian trade goods was very limited.

To resolve this problem, coastal settlements developed a variety of mercantile functions. The inhabitants of these settlements imported sophisticated goods—ceramics, silk, glassware, metal goods and carpets—and foodstuffs from the Middle East, South Asia and China, mainly for their own consumption. But in addition they produced primary and manufactured goods—particular types of cotton cloth, shell beads, local cowries, iron, foodstuffs and salt—which were traded in the interior for goods sought by the outside world.

The only Asian commodities to gain wide acceptance in the interior were glass beads from the Middle East and South Asia, and Maldivian cowries, which achieved an amazing universality of value throughout Africa as a decorative material, symbol of fertility and wealth, and as a form of currency in trade transactions.[9] Their

[9] B.M. Fagan, 1970, 35.

abundance in the Maldives ensured those scattered atolls a central place in the maritime trading network, as Middle Eastern and South Asian merchants realized the full potential of the humble shell, distributing it westward into Africa and eastward to South East Asia and China.

Trade between the coast and the interior was desultory, with the exception of the gold trade between Zimbabwe and Sofala on the Mozambique coast, which flourished from the thirteenth century. Goods from the interior did not pass directly from producer to coastal market, but from market to market in the interior until they reached the coast. Coastal people did not penetrate the rugged and disease-ridden terrain of the interior but maintained contact with their suppliers through intermediaries.

On the Red Sea coast of Africa the Muslim impact was more substantial. From the late seventh century, Muslim merchants, settlers and warriors drove Christians from the coast. Aksum and its port of Adulis declined, and during the next 500 years the successor Christian states to Aksum retreated to the mountainous core of Ethiopia, cut off from the rest of Christianity by the Islamic lands of the Sudan, Eritrea and the Horn of Africa. Trade and navigation in the Red Sea was now the exclusive domain of Muslims.

The great Arab empire fell with sack of Baghdad by the Mongols in 1258. In reality, for several centuries it had been little more than a collection of squabbling principalities paying lip service to the Baghdad Khilafat, with important provinces such as Egypt, Persia and Spain all but independent. In the central lands of the empire, political instability had been accompanied by declines in population and agricultural production since the tenth century, with a consequent decline in trade which gravitated towards the more prosperous Nile valley and the Red Sea maritime trade route. The once-prosperous cities of Mesopotamia began their long decline into obscurity as the centres of Middle Eastern political and economic activity moved to the periphery of the area: to places such as Egypt, the Levant, Anatolia and Persia.

The sack of Baghdad, the ravaging of Mesopotamia, and the Mongol occupation of Persia, led to a further catastrophic decline in the population and farming in much of the Persian Gulf hinterland. There was a sharp fall in its maritime trade, whose centre of activity moved from Baghdad's outlet of Basra at the head of the Gulf, to the island port of Hormuz at the entrance to the Gulf. Hormuz served the great Persian cultural centre of Shiraz which had escaped the Mongol devastation, and Tabriz, the capital of the Mongol Il-Khan dynasty, which replaced Baghdad as the main junction of trans-Persian routes linking the Mediterranean, Central Asia and the Indian Ocean.

In contrast, the seaborne trade of the Red Sea flourished, and the waterway became the link between a reviving Mediterranean trade network and the Indian Ocean. From the seventh century, when the Arabs occupied the great entrepôt of Alexandria, the port had been in decline. Basra, the Persian Gulf and the ports of the Levant had attracted trade away from Alexandria, but from the twelfth century it began to recover some of its lost glory as one of the great clearing houses for trade between the Mediterranean and the Indian Ocean. From Suez, Cairo and Alexandria, Muslim and Jewish merchants embarked on ships at Suez which carried them to the ports of East Africa and South Asia whose goods once more appeared in the warehouses of Alexandria.

The fall of Baghdad had political and cultural consequences beyond the heartland of the Middle East. The Mongols cut the umbilical cord between the old political and cultural élites of the Middle East and the vigorous Turkish Muslim frontiersmen who had carved out semi-independent states in Egypt, Anatolia, Afghanistan and northern India between the ninth and thirteenth centuries. In the wake of the Mongol invasion, such states formed the scattered centres of a series of Islamic revivals which preserved the glories of classical Muslim civilization. Although the Mongols invaded many other parts of Asia, ranging from raids into northern India in the 1240s and an abortive sea invasion of Java in 1293, they fell most heavily upon the central lands of the Middle East from where Muslim intellectuals, craftsmen and soldiers were dispersed to the Turkish states on the periphery of the *Dar al-Islam* and beyond.

Between the eighth and twelfth centuries, Muslim political power did not extend into South Asia beyond Sind. During these centuries the subcontinent was divided among a host of Hindu states. Gujarat and Bengal were ruled as separate states, while the central Ganges valley and the Indus were divided among a variety of feuding dynasties.

Occasionally, northern India was disrupted by invaders, but they were absorbed into the fabric of Hindu life. Political fragmentation was also, as we have seen, the norm in central and southern India.

In the early centuries of the present era the most active South Asian ports were located in southern India and Sri Lanka: a host of small ports along the Malabar and Coromandel coasts as well as the great Sri Lankan port of Mantai which flourished until it was abandoned in the eleventh century after devastating wars between Sri Lanka and south Indian invaders. But with the establishment of the Arab empire, and the economic decline of Western Christendom, trade between the Middle East and northern India expanded rapidly. Ports in Gujarat such as Cambay and Surat, and on the Ganges delta such as Satgaon, responded to the growing wealth of the northern kingdoms, and they overshadowed south Indian and Sri Lankan ports with respect to both the Middle Eastern and South East Asian trade, until the rise of Chinese maritime enterprise under the Song dynasty.

The growth of Chinese maritime trade restored the maritime fortunes of the south as the pivot of trade between the Arabian Sea and the Bay of Bengal. Foreign merchants, eager to participate in the expanding trade with China and South East Asia, flocked to ports such as Mangalore, Cannanore, Calicut, Cochin, Quilon, Rameshwaram and Kanci as well as to Galle in Sri Lanka. By the eleventh century, southern India was experiencing its second period of rapid urban growth and vigorous political activity associated with an upsurge in maritime trade. In this same period Islam spread on the Malabar and Coromandel coasts. Hindu rulers on both coasts encouraged the settlement of foreign Muslim merchants and mariners who, through intermarriage, established substantial communities of Muslim merchants, mariners and artisans in most southern ports. These communities did not form discrete enclaves of foreigners but rather comprised people who in language and dress were barely distinguishable from their Hindu compatriots. (See Map 8).

As southern ports grew in importance once more, new invaders threatened northern India. Vigorous Turkish Muslim tribesmen from the mountains of Afghanistan launched devastating raids across the Indus. By the early thirteenth century these tribesmen had established themselves as permanent overlords of the Punjab, and shortly there-

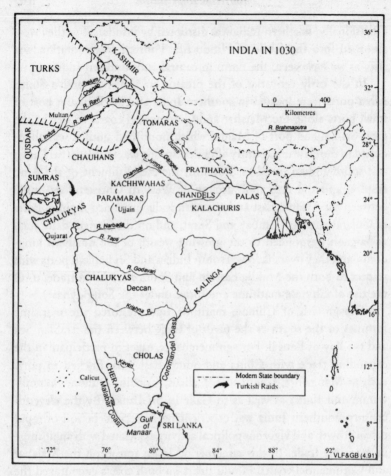

INDIA IN 1030

TURKS

KASHMIR

Jhelum
Chenab
R. Ravi　Lahore
Multan　*R. Sutlej*
R. Indus

QUSDAR

TOMARAS

R. Brahmaputra

CHAUHANS

Gaini
R. Jumna
R. Ganges

SUMRAS

Chambal
KACHHWAHAS
PARAMARAS
Ujjain

PRATIHARAS

CHANDELS　　PALAS
KALACHURIS

CHALUKYAS

Gujarat

R. Narbada
R. Tapi

CHALUKYAS

Deccan

R. Godavari

Krishna R.

KALINGA

Coromandel Coast

CHOLAS

Calicut
CHERAS
Malabar Coast

Kaveri

SRI LANKA
Gulf
of
Manaar

0 ———— 400
Kilometres

— · —	Modern State boundary
→	Turkish Raids

VLF&GB (4.91)

72°　76°　80°　84°　88°　92°
8°　12°　16°　20°　24°　28°　32°　36°

Map 8: India in 1030

after of the entire northern plains, from the Indus to the Ganges delta. In addition, the wealthy ports of Gujarat and Bengal had passed under their control.

A large Muslim state, the Delhi Sultanate, replaced a host of feuding Hindu states, from the Indus to the Bay of Bengal and into the Deccan. Once settled, the Turkish Muslim frontiersmen took a sophisticated and sustained interest in the operations of their domain. They used the skills and services of Muslim refugees from Mesopotamia and Persia to keep an eye on both the peasant farm and the marketplace: the former as a source of revenue, the latter as the agency for the conversion of goods received as payment of taxes.

From the thirteenth century, port marketplaces in northern India took on a new lease of life, and along the coast of Gujarat in particular there was a flowering of maritime activity. Muslim overlords did not bring anything new to the practices of administration, apart from the application of the shari'a to public life, rather, they simply took a more profound interest in public administration. In addition, there was an increase in South Asian demand for imported goods, notably spices from insular South East Asia. This was due to increasing domestic prosperity, the emergence of larger more efficient revenue collecting states, and to rising demand in Christian Europe from the thirteenth century. Middle Eastern Muslims and Jews were the intermediaries in this trade and moved eastward in increasing numbers to South Asia and beyond to collect cargoes.

The Turkish Muslim invasion led to the conversion of large numbers of merchants and artisans, particularly in the ports of Gujarat and Bengal. Even in southern India, on the Malabar and Coromandel coasts beyond the pale of north Indian Muslim political influence, apart from a brief period in the late thirteenth and early fourteenth centuries, there was an increase in the Muslim population as Arab and Persian trading communities grew. The result was a rise in the number of Muslims engaged in maritime trade, most notably eastward from India into insular South East Asia, and the establishment of petty Muslim trading states along the south east coast of India. Some of these Muslim merchants and rulers were from the Middle East, but the greater number were from maritime mercantile areas of South Asia, and were drawn from convert communities whose ancestors, as

Hindus or Buddhists, had long been engaged in commerce between the Middle East and South and South East Asia.

After Middle Eastern merchants lost their pre-eminent position in the long-distance maritime trade of South East and East Asia, to South Asian and Chinese merchants in the late ninth century, the easternmost outposts of Muslim mercantile activity in the Indian Ocean world were located in southern India, Sri Lanka and Bengal. Here, for the next four centuries, foreign and local Muslims slowly cornered a greater share of maritime trade and began to venture eastward once more.

The spread of Islam across the Indian subcontinent from the twelfth century paralleled the emergence of larger states on the ruins of a host of petty states. The majority of these new states were ruled by Muslims who, in the process of conquest and conversion, broke down the insularity which had bound Hindu South Asia for many centuries. In one form or another the Delhi Sultanate loomed large during these centuries, but at times of weakness ambitious Muslims in Gujarat, Bengal and the Deccan sought their independence.

The rulers of such states were frequently vitally concerned with the profits of trade and sponsored its increase as a means of filling state coffers. In addition, such rulers were eager to prove their legitimacy and their authority as leaders of Islam, and to do so they gathered around them at their courts Muslim mercenaries, scholars and artisans from the great centres of Muslim civilization in the Middle East and Central Asia.

So it was that people and ideas were gathered in from the Middle East and Central Asia, passing along land and sea routes to the great ports of South Asia, where they stimulated intellectual and economic growth. Much of the Indian subcontinent was now part of the *Dar al-Islam*, and many of its inhabitants were believers in a religious and cultural system whose boundaries stretched beyond the Indian Ocean. The creation of larger states across the subcontinent, and the evolution of more efficient revenue gathering regimes, boosted internal commerce and international trade, particularly with the Muslim lands to the west, where the demand for South Asian products was rising.

The Flowering of South East Asian and East African Trade

In South East Asia there was a steady growth of long-distance maritime trade between the seventh and thirteenth centuries. At the beginning of the period, foreign trade focused on the axis between Burma, the Kra Isthmus and Funnan on the lower Mekong, leading to southern China via coastal Vietnam. In the following centuries, under the influence of Srivijaya, the axis of trade moved south, centring upon the Strait of Melaka and the islands of the Indonesian archipelago.

Mainland South East Asia did not drop from the picture. Indeed, these centuries saw the rise of two important empires—that of the Khmers in Cambodia and Thailand, and of the Burmans of Pagan—but most foreign merchants tended to focus their attention upon the ports of insular South East Asia, where the goods of the entire area were gathered by local mariners for export. This focus on the islands was strengthened by their monopoly on spice production and their wealth of other exotic and valuable products.

The Strait of Melaka was the key to insular South East Asia. For 600 years, from the seventh century, it was controlled by Srivijaya, whose fortunes were founded upon small but rich rice lands, the entrepôt functions of its ports, and its ability to limit piracy in the Strait of Melaka. But while Srivijaya waxed powerful as the result of its stranglehold over the Strait, it did not lack envious rivals. The ambitious Chola dynasty of the Coromandel coast launched seaborne raids on Srivijaya to break its trade monopoly through the Strait. There was enmity between Srivijaya, Sri Lanka and various states stretching from Burma to Cambodia for much the same reason, while from the seventh and eighth centuries various Javanese kingdoms, with their abundant rice lands and proximity to the spice-rich Moluccas, proved more enduring rivals for political and commercial power among the islands of South East Asia.

By the eleventh century the power of Srivijaya was waning, challenged by an increase in Chinese and South Asian shipping in the South China Sea and within the Indonesian archipelago by the rise of states such as Singhasari in southern Sumatra and Majapahit in Java. This heightened activity was associated with rising demand for South East Asian commodities from the Mediterranean to China, and with a decline in traffic on the Silk Road, the only land-based trade route across Eurasia. By the fourteenth century, under onslaughts from Mongol armies and epidemic diseases in Central Asia, the Silk Route was fast approaching the end of its days as the major overland route between West and East. The depredations of the Mongol Tamerlane, in the fourteenth century, hastened this decline, and the Silk Route was finally abandoned by the Chinese when the Ming dynasty (1368–1644) strictly limited trade contacts with the outside world in the late fifteenth century.

From the late thirteenth century an increasing amount of China's foreign trade was carried by sea through South East Asia and into the Indian Ocean. Not only were southern Chinese merchants and mariners active in the ports of Srivijaya, but they were also found as far west as Galle in Sri Lanka and Calicut in southern India. China's officially sanctioned private participation in Indian Ocean trade, first formally organized by the Song in the tenth century when they declared maritime trade a state monopoly, lasted until the Ming dynasty outlawed Chinese civilian involvement in maritime commerce in 1368.

Official involvement ceased after the epic state-sponsored trading voyages of the Muslim admiral Zheng He ('Cheng Ho') across the Indian Ocean, between 1404 and 1433, when contact with the outside world was limited to a small number of ports open to foreign merchants and ships. Xenophobia, the expulsion of the Chinese army of occupation from Vietnam in 1427, Beijing's suspicions of the loyalty of southern Chinese merchants, and the poor returns on maritime trade for the central treasury, were factors which influenced the imperial authorities to curb maritime commerce.

Muslim merchants, particularly those from South Asia, were the major foreign beneficiaries of the growth of insular South East Asia's long-distance trade. From the thirteenth century Muslim merchants and seafarers appeared more regularly and in greater numbers throughout South East Asia, particularly once the Song and Yuan dynasties actively encouraged foreign Muslim involvement in the trade of southern Chinese ports. Srivijaya crumbled and was replaced by Melaka (c. 1403–1511), the great entrepôt on the Malay coast of the Strait, whose ruler converted to Islam in 1436; by Hindu Majapahit on Java (*c.* 1350–1527), and by a chain of smaller ports stretching away to the east through the Indonesian archipelago. With the disintegration of Srivijaya, a formidable barrier to intensive foreign penetration of the archipelago was removed. Foreign merchants moved deeper into the Indonesian archipelago, and greater numbers of local merchants were involved in more direct and prosperous trade with the world beyond South East Asia. This increased their exposure to cultural and political systems other than those imposed by the great Hindu-Buddhist states of Sumatra and Java.

Prior to the rise of Melaka it is doubtful if there were similar great ports in South East Asia. Most ports would have been at river mouths or on the thousands of creeks which linked sea and land throughout insular South East Asia and on the Malay peninsula. Apart from the monuments at Angkor, Pagan and Borobodur, most buildings in South East Asia were constructed of readily degradable material such as bamboo and atap and as such have left few remains from which we can construct a picture of port life. Unlike South Asia, few ancient ports in South East Asia appear to have survived as working ports until the present, and most likely such ports were relatively small urban centres whose existence was ephemeral, depending upon the shifting political and economic fortunes of the hinterlands they serviced.

In addition, until the thirteenth and fourteenth centuries there is little evidence of independent merchant groups in South East Asia compared with the great merchant communities of East Asia, the Indian subcontinent, the Middle East and East Africa. Such groups shaped and dominated port life in these areas, whereas in South East Asia indigenous trade was controlled by agricultural-based ruling groups through the agency of factors and servants who did not form a definable social or economic group. There were undoubtable ancient communities of seafarers—such as the Bugis and the Orang Laut—but they existed in a symbiotic relationship with the trade representatives of ruling groups and do not appear to have formed significant merchant groups such as existed in many other parts of the Indian Ocean.

The Strait of Melaka remained the funnel through which the maritime trade of South East Asia passed. Following the collapse of Srivijaya, various independent ports on either side of the Strait rose to prominence at Aceh, Pasai, Kedah and Melaka. The most notable of these was Melaka, which by the middle of the fifteenth century, was the greatest entrepôt in South East Asia, with a cosmopolitan merchant population drawn from many parts of South and South East Asia. Melaka set the pattern for developments elsewhere in insular South East Asia, in its commercial practices and by its conversion to Islam.

Melaka set a new pattern for port life in South East Asia in that its rulers consciously and assiduously cultivated the settlement of foreign merchants as well as facilitating the development of indigenous trading groups drawn from communities throughout South East Asia. The rulers of the port welcomed Hindu and Muslim merchants from Gujarat and the Malabar and Coromandel coasts and granted them a degree of self-government as well as a voice in the management of port activities. Chinese merchants also established a permanent presence in the port alongside traders from Sumatra, Java, Sulawesi and the Moluccas, who emerged from obscurity at this time to take shape as distinctive communities of independent merchants who were no longer simply the agents of local rulers, although the goodwill and cooperation of local rulers was vital for the successful prosecution of maritime commerce throughout South East Asia.

Beyond Melaka, local merchants in ports stretching from Java to the Moluccas, prospered during the fifteenth century, as a result of the upsurge in maritime trade and followed Melaka into the fold of Islam. The Islamic Malay culture of Melaka became the model for port culture in insular South East Asia where a large number of new port city states developed from the thirteenth and fourteenth centuries. The ethos of such cities was in direct opposition to the hierarchical Hindu-Buddhist mixture of the great agricultural states such as Majapahit on Java, which came into increasing conflict with the power, wealth and pretensions of their port-based merchant communities. Trade and Islam sundered the fabric of ancient cultural and political forms in insular South East Asia, replacing it with a new élite culture, religion and mercantile ethos based on that of Malay Melaka.

Along the coast of East Africa during these centuries there were some remarkable parallels in economic and cultural evolution. Until the thirteenth century, Mogadishu on the Benadir coast was the major entrepôt for foreign merchants. But during that century, Muslim immigrants from the Middle East spread further south, extending Islam into eastern Africa at the same time co-religionists were extending it into South and South East Asia. Expanding Muslim settlement led to the emergence of more complex Afro-Islamic communities in ports along the Kenyan and Tanzanian coasts, where Islam had already taken root among indigenous merchant communities in larger African coastal settlements. The focus of political power and foreign trade moved south, centring upon Mombasa and Kilwa, which dominated the invaluable gold trade of Sofala on the coast of southern Mozambique (See Map 9).

From the thirteenth century these ports grew into substantial urban settlements with great stone mosques and palaces inhabited by the merchant élites who governed the cities. The wealthier inhabitants of these ports adapted Middle Eastern and South Asian Islamic culture to highlight their role as leaders of society. Some of these leaders were undoubtedly of Middle Eastern and South Asian descent, but the majority were either of mixed Afro-Asian origin or were purely African. Indeed, these urban settlements remained predominantly African in population and contained a spectrum of African groups. These ranged from non-Islamic Africans who formed a living bridge between the Islamic élite and the peoples of the interior, to groups who, in linguistic and cultural terms, laid claim to being part of the greater Islamic world.

This expansion of Islam into coastal East Africa was associated with a strengthening of trade across the Arabian Sea between the port of Cambay in Gujarat and ports such as Suakin and Aydhab on the Red Sea. This trade was underpinned by a growing westward flow of spices and pepper in particular, for the expanding markets of the Mediterranean and Europe.

During the thirteenth and fourteenth centuries the Mameluke rulers of Egypt took a keener interest in the Red Sea trade, extending their power as far south as the Sudanese port of Suakin, and encouraging a general expansion of maritime trade in the triangle bounded by Aden, Cambay and Kilwa. In exchange for South Asian and Chinese manufactures the major ports of East Africa supplied increasing amounts of gold, ivory, timber, ambergris and iron. It is impossible to quantify this trade, except to note that as early as the twelfth century

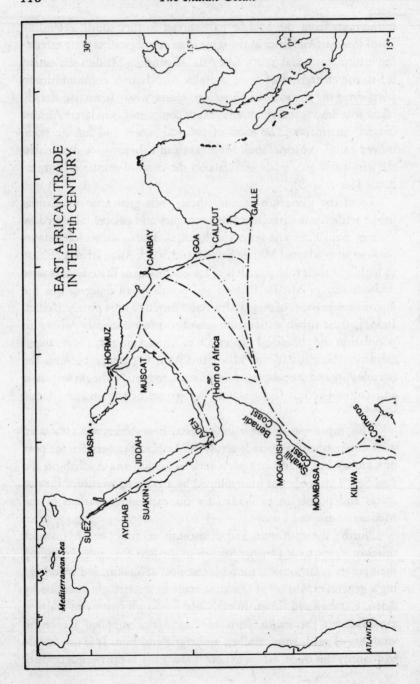

EAST AFRICAN TRADE
IN THE 14th CENTURY

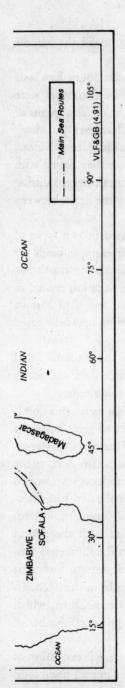

Map 9: East African Trade in the 14th Century

coastal East Africa was the leading producer of iron for the Middle East.

The similarities between East Africa and insular South East Asia during this period are striking. In both areas, communities were defined by a physical insularity which favoured the sea as a means of communication; in both areas, indigenous peoples developed maritime trade networks before the arrival of foreign traders; in both areas, foreign traders congregated in specific ports where they liaised with local traders; and in both areas, rival port city states emerged during the fourteenth and fifteenth centuries, confirming the nexus between maritime trade and politics.

The littoral markets of East Africa participated in two types of trade: they bartered goods with the interior—for example beads for ivory—and utilized foreign and locally-minted coins to conduct trade with the Middle East and South Asia. The same situation existed in South East Asia where the entrepôts of Srivijaya, and then Melaka and other great ports, were at the junction of trading networks based on barter and the use of coins.

From the eighth to the fifteenth centuries the economic and cultural relationships of East Africa with the Middle East, and South and East Asia with South East Asia were remarkably similar.

In both East Africa and South East Asia, foreign merchants dominated external maritime trade through a number of great entrepôts linked in with local maritime networks. Over the centuries, foreigners penetrated further into both East Africa and South East Asia, as the demand for East African and South East Asian products increased in the Middle East, South Asia, East Asia and then finally in the Mediterranean and northern Europe. The 'golden age' of commerce in both East Africa and South East Asia areas coincided with the rise in international trade across the Indian Ocean from the thirteenth century. This was associated with growing demand for imports from East Africa and South East Asia in markets stretching from the Mediterranean, through the Middle East and South Asia to China, which prompted the rise to power and influence of a growing number of ports and their mercantile élites.

In both East Africa and insular South East Asia, the expansion of maritime trade up to the fifteenth century, and its impact upon local economic and political relationships, was responsible for the adaptation of foreign cultural forms, ranging from religion to architecture, by the indigenous inhabitants of ports. Such processes of adaptation— relating to Hinduism, Buddhism and Islam in insular South East Asia, and to Islam in East Africa—were to lead to major local cultural and religious changes among the élite of both areas, resulting in the selective Islamization of both coastal East Africa and insular South East Asia by the fifteenth century.

In East Africa the process of Islamization resulted, in part, from the settlement of foreign Muslims who established port colonies whose culture mirrored that of their Arabian or Persian homeland. But more frequently Islamization occurred along the coast where maritime trade prompted the evolution of more complex African settlements. In these settlements, trade was responsible for the growth of civic life with all its complexities, and in this environment Islamic culture and religion provided the ordering for new lifestyles, particularly among those Africans who mingled most closely with foreign traders. The language of these ports remained essentially African, but it borrowed terms relating to trade and technology from Arabic, Persian and the languages of South Asia, and in architecture and dress, local élites adopted and adapted Middle Eastern models. Intermarriage encouraged such processes of cultural adaptation, but the prime causes relate to the impact that sustained foreign trade had upon the economic and social organization of African life on the coast.

In insular South East Asia by the thirteenth century Islam was beginning to make inroads and, within three hundred years had become the major religion in the ports of the area. As with the earlier 'Indianization' of South East Asia, the spread of Islam can only be explained by a conjunction of circumstances. From the thirteenth century maritime trade increased throughout insular South East Asia, leading to greater prosperity in port cities. At the same time an increasing number of South Asian Muslims were penetrating beyond the decaying empire of Srivijaya. Many settled in ports stretching as far east as Sulawesi and Brunei and are often claimed as the founders of Islam in the area, just as legend claims the same for Arabs and Persians in East Africa.

This may indeed be part of the truth, but a more prosaic reality is that Islam first took root only in ports and then spread slowly into agricultural hinterlands. The key is obviously the port, the area where the economic impact of increased maritime trade was greatest and where traditional social relationships and power structures were most radically affected by the new prosperity. Islam, with its egalitarian doctrines and concept of universality was undoubtedly attractive to emerging mercantile groups, in contrast to the conservative hierarchical rule of the traditional agricultural ruling groups. Islam offered a new ordering of life as well as tangible benefits in the form of linkages into the great Islamic trade network, and to this extent had a vital role to play in the formation of new states in insular South East Asia.[10]

In cultural terms many of the Islamic practices which reached insular South East Asia had been filtered through the lens of South Asia, where Sufis (Muslim mystical adepts) were an important factor in the peaceful spread of Islam. With their focus on personal devotion, *pir* (saint) worship and relative pragmatism about doctrinal formalities, Sufis provided 'a natural bridge between Muslim worship and the beliefs of non-Muslim groups in many different regions of Asia and Africa'.[11] In southern India Sufis subtly modified local traditions and practices to accommodate them within the wider Islamic community. By the time Islam reached insular South East Asia the practice of accommodation with local traditions was well established, and much of the Hindu-Buddhist heritage of Sumatra and Java passed into popular Islam.

In mainland South East Asia, however, the necessary preconditions for the spread of Islam were absent. While maritime trade was important it never challenged agriculture as a source of wealth and power to the extent that it did to the south. The external trade of the states and dynasties of mainland South East Asia was handled by royal agents who liaised with foreign merchants and shipowners. There was no increase in this trade from the thirteenth century, comparable with the growth in maritime trade throughout insular South East Asia, nor was there a growth of powerful port-based merchant communities to challenge the traditional social ordering and open a gap in the social fabric for Islam to take root and flourish.

[10] Taufik Abdullah, 1989.
[11] Susan Bayly, 1989, 74–75; Muzaffar Alam, 1989.

Although the seaborne trade of mainland South East Asia was not as voluminous or valuable as that of the islands, it was nevertheless impressive. From Burma to Vietnam, gemstones, pearls, ceramics, timber, rice, bamboo, lacquer goods and rare jungle produce were traded with Arabs, Indians, Persians, Chinese and the Malays of the islands for the produce of their homelands.

While political and economic events in the Middle East, South Asia and China undoubtedly exerted a growing influence upon the rhythms of Indian Ocean maritime trade by the twelfth and thirteenth centuries, the importance of South East Asia and East Africa to this trade should not be underestimated. Both areas supplied invaluable export cargoes to the great civilizations of Eurasia; however, their importance as importers of foreign goods was tempered by their relatively small populations whose size was restricted by endemic tropical diseases.

By the fifteenth century the maritime trading network of the Indian Ocean linked ports which stretched from Quanzhou in southern China to Sofala on the southern coast of Mozambique. Great entrepôts—such as Melaka, Calicut, Cambay, Hormuz, Aden and Kilwa—loomed large in it, but none could lay claim to domination, apart from their physical situation at the junction of major sea and land routes. The rhythms of maritime trade were set by a host of factors relating to climate, topography and the pace of a large number of economies. Certainly the powerful economies of South Asia exerted great influence upon the operation of this network, but this influence cannot be excised from the total spectrum of economic activity around the Indian Ocean, which was moulded by a mix of local and international market forces.

Overall, there were certainly some modifications in the volume and direction of Indian Ocean maritime trade during the fourteenth and fifteenth centuries. In the Persian Gulf and the Red Sea, political events combined with the demographic disaster of the Black Death to reduce mercantile activity; in Sri Lanka, the abandonment of the great irrigation systems of the Dry Zone, due to centuries of warfare with south Indian dynasties, left the traditional rice lands of the islands a malaria-infested jungle wilderness, with much the same happening in Cambodia, following the collapse of the great Khmer kingdom under pressure from the Thais.[12] In both Sri Lanka and Cambodia these developments had an adverse impact upon external trade linkages, but at the same time elsewhere in South and South East Asia other states were taking a more prominent role in long-distance maritime trade.

Despite these localized modifications, the commercial world of the Indian Ocean by the fourteenth and fifteenth centuries was more dynamic than ever, and it was worked by merchants and mariners from all the ports which stretched from the Mozambique coast to the Moluccas on the edge of the Pacific.

Indian Ocean Worlds

The peak of indigenous maritime activity was, in what Ashin Das Gupta has described as the 'high medieval period', between the fourteenth and sixteenth centuries.[13] It was a period when Middle Eastern merchants and sailors, along with smaller numbers of South Asian Muslims and Hindus, controlled the traffic of the western Indian Ocean. Across the Bay of Bengal, South Asians dominated sea-lanes linking in with flourishing South East Asian and Chinese mercantile systems. These workers of the sea were served by a large number of cosmopolitan ports which integrated local economies into a wider Indian Ocean trading network.

To understand the nature of the interlocked world of the Indian Ocean, we need to understand the people who bound it together. The workers of the sea and littoral societies gave the Ocean its human face, and were the agents for the dissemination of cultures and technologies across the Ocean.

A coastal or littoral society has been described as a human coastal frontier which is porous, flexible and unspecific.[14] Some coastal people are obviously members of a littoral society in that their livelihood comes from the sea. Fisherfolk; many inhabitants of port cities such as merchants, artisans, dockside labourers and innkeepers; and farmers whose crops are exported, are cases in point. But there are also farmers,

[12] K.N. Chaudhuri, 1990, 37.
[13] Ashin Das Gupta, 1967, 7.
[14] M.N. Pearson, 1985, 1–9.

artisans and many other occupational groups living on the coast, unaffected by the sea. A similar vagueness surrounds the inland boundaries of coastal societies. Most societies in insular South East Asia, given the intimate nexus between sea and land, were littoral societies; so too were the coastal East African Muslim enclaves, the Maldives and the Lakshadweep islands. Similarly, inland traders, carriers and producers whose livelihood depends upon the movement of exports and imports by sea are bound in with the fate, if not the daily life, of littoral societies. Such societies have several obvious characteristics: they tend to be more cosmopolitan and pluralistic than inland societies; their economic and social life is more dominated by the rhythms of the monsoons, and more clearly geared to overseas and other coastal markets than inland societies. In the pre-modern world, human boundaries were radically different from those many of us accept today. It is likely that most people of the Indian Ocean region identified with a religion, language or civilization in describing the world they inhabited.

People working the Indian Ocean before the coming of Europeans also defined different boundaries for the Indian Ocean world. They perceived different combinations of markets and cultures as part of their particular worldview. Merchants, seamen, fishermen and pilgrims operated within various, and often different, information and cultural networks which set the horizons of their worlds. This world of merchants was defined by various economic, informational and cultural boundaries; for seamen and fishermen by tangible geographic constraints, and for pilgrims by religious boundaries. But for all of them it was a world dominated by the rhythms of the monsoons.

Before the understanding of the monsoon winds there was no Indian Ocean world. People on the shores of the Ocean used the sea sparingly, and had limited horizons operating in discrete enclaves such as the Red Sea and the Persian Gulf, or among the islands of South East Asia. But with the discovery of the monsoons the boundaries of these enclaves expanded, so that the Arabian Sea and the Bay of Bengal became the arenas for growing mercantile activity. By the beginning of the present era, two interlocking mercantile information networks formed an Indian Ocean merchant's world which, although still primitive and segmented, linked the Mediterranean and southern China.

The first network—the Indian Ocean world of *The Periplus*—was worked by Egyptian Romano-Greek, Arab and Persian merchants and sailors through the Red Sea and Persian Gulf, and by merchants and sailors from the Aksumite coast and South Asia. Such people had access to shipping manuals and geographies outlining a world bounded by the Arabian peninsula, the Benadir coast, western India and Sri Lanka. Beyond these lands, fantasy and rumour marked the limits of accurate knowledge and physical penetration by merchants from the west.

The second network was demarcated by the Bay of Bengal and linked into insular South East Asia and the South China Sea. For peoples to the west of India it was the mysterious world of silk, spices and gold; of strange peoples and fabulous creatures. It was a maritime trading world worked by the Austronesian-speaking peoples of insular South East Asia and southern China and, increasingly, by merchants and sailors from South Asia seeking the legendary 'Golden Land', *Suvarnabhumi*. In the succeeding centuries these two mercantile networks integrated and became more complex, expanding to include parts of East Africa as well as land linkages through Central Asia.

The advent of Islam set the final form on the mercantile boundaries of the Indian Ocean world. As a universal religious and cultural system, Islam provided its followers with a worldview which stretched from the Atlantic to the Pacific and deep into mainland Asia by the fifteenth century. Within this cultural and religious system, Muslims—merchants, seamen, divines, intellectuals, mercenaries, craftsmen and pilgrims—moved with relative familiarity, and drew upon a huge body of information as well as the support and comfort of co-religionists scattered across the Ocean. To a lesser extent, the same worldview existed for the Jewish, and later Armenian, mercantile communities of the Middle East and South Asia, whose communal links stretched into the Mediterranean world.

The great annual Muslim pilgrimage, the *hajj*, focussed upon the Holy Cities of Mekka and Medinah in the Hejaz, remains a living symbol of the universality of Islam. From the earliest centuries of Islam tens of thousands of Muslim pilgrims, from Morocco to insular South East Asia, have taken part each year in the hajj. The Holy Cities were at the centre of a great Islamic cultural and information network which, by the fifteenth century, linked Muslim communities from West Africa to southern China and the Philippines, across Central Asia and the Indian Ocean.

But other, older, Indian Ocean boundaries existed, based on more ancient religious affiliation. From the third century BC, when the first Buddhist missionaries left South Asia, a Buddhist Indian Ocean world was created, defined by the Silk Route which linked South, Central and East Asia, and by sea routes through South East Asia into East Asia. Until the end of the first millennium AD, northern India, birthplace of Buddhism and centre of Buddhist intellectual activity, drew Buddhist pilgrims and merchants from across Asia. Muslim invasions, and the revival of Hinduism, extinguished Buddhism on the subcontinent by the thirteenth century. However, it survived in Sri Lanka, which, as a centre of orthodoxy until the sixteenth century, attracted Buddhist clerical and lay pilgrims from China and the Buddhist kingdoms of South East Asia.

The boundaries of this world were not impermeable. Buddhists moved westward to the Middle East and the Mediterranean. But their numbers and visits were few compared with the concourse of Buddhists travelling the Bay of Bengal and the South China Sea.

Paralleling the evolution of a Buddhist world was an even more ancient Hindu world. In strictly religious terms this was much more geographically defined than Buddhism. The Hindu belief system was physically defined by the geographic limits of South Asia, within which were contained all its sacred sites and mythology. It was not a universal religious system with a proselytising mission like Buddhism, Christianity and Islam. Along with Buddhism, Hinduism spread eastward following trade, as first Hindu merchants and sailors, and then Hindu priests and laity, settled in South East Asia at important ports and marketplaces.

Hinduism, unlike Buddhism, did not strike deep roots in South East Asia. It remained the adopted religion of local élites in areas such as Cambodia and Java and, unlike Buddhism, failed to win mass support. In part this was due to the very selective adaptation of Hindu doctrine and practice, and in part to the absence of a missionary drive—so prominent a feature of Buddhism—in South Asian Hinduism.

The boundaries of these various worldviews were not constant and they frequently overlapped. Physically, most indigenous merchants and seafarers operated in a world defined by the waters of the Ocean and the South China Sea, but intellectually, and in terms of imagination and information there were constantly changing boundaries defined by the spread of particular religious and cultural systems.

This was most obviously the case with Muslim merchants and seafarers who were, for the most part, physically restricted to the waters of the Indian Ocean and the South China Sea, but whose religious, cultural and mercantile worldviews were formed by a background knowledge of a physically much larger Muslim world, the *Dar al-Islam* or 'Abode of Islam'. The political boundaries of the *Dar al-Islam* were in a state of flux as Muslim states rose and fell. On the other hand, the cultural and religious world of Islam constantly expanded between the seventh and sixteenth centuries, to reach from the Atlantic to the Pacific.

From the seventh century AD, the *Dar al-Islam* was a centre of tremendous intellectual and cultural activity. Islamic civilization in the Middle East absorbed, preserved and extended the cultural legacy of classical Greece and Rome which entered the mainstream of Muslim civilization, spreading with Islam across Asia and into Africa. But in addition, it was this eclectic Islamic civilization which enabled Europe to recover much of its ancient cultural inheritance from the tenth century on. Muslim and Jewish intellectuals in the great Islamic cities of Spain reintroduced their Christian neighbours to the glories of Greek philosophy and mathematics, and this process continued during the next couple of centuries when the Latin Crusaders briefly established kingdoms in Palestine and along the Levant coast. This brief but intimate contact with Islamic civilization introduced many Europeans—scholars, soldiers and merchants—to the intellectual and physical wealth of medieval Islam, helping to revive European intellectual and mercantile activity in the Christian lands of the Mediterranean, as well as in the first universities which began to emerge at this time in France, England and the German lands. Thus, the cultural legacy of Islam is not to be found only in 'the East' but was a major force in the reshaping and revival of European learning and civilization.

One effect of the expansion of the *Dar al-Islam* was to add new groups of people to the cosmopolitan trading world of the Indian Ocean. In Middle Eastern ports, Arabs, Persians, Turks, Egyptians, Moroccans, Mongols, Tunisians, Algerians, Spanish Muslims, Asian Christians of a multitude of sects, Jews and the occasional European traveller such as Marco Polo, thronged marketplaces and harbours, boarding ships which carried them to all the major ports of the Indian Ocean.

For non-Muslims in the Indian Ocean, world boundaries contracted during the same period. The Buddhist world, after the decline of Buddhism during the latter half of the first millennium AD in Central Asia and the Indian subcontinent, functioned on a Sri Lanka–South East Asia axis. The same held true of the Hindu world which at its height extended from the Indus to the Mekong. By the twelfth century, following the Turkish Muslim conquest of northern India and the decline of the great Cambodian Hindu Khmer empire, Hinduism had contracted to its ancient heartland, with external contacts restricted entirely to the short-term ventures of merchants and sailors overseas.

To state the obvious, the major focus of human interest in the Indian Ocean in the pre-modern period was inextricably linked for the most part with the ebb and flow of maritime trade. Trade was the sole reason for the existence of ports, the economic force which sustained most long-distance travel and the primary means for cultural interaction. The major exceptions to this general statement were pilgrims and fisherfolk. For pilgrims the Ocean was simply a highway; for fisherfolk the working of the sea was primarily directed at the extraction of marine products, rather than upon using the sea as a highway between markets or religious shrines.

As we have seen, maritime trade was sufficiently complex and rewarding from the early centuries of the present era to encourage the migration many peoples. Merchants from South Asia formed distinct expatriate communities at ports in the Middle East, while others were beginning the South Asian commercial penetration of South East Asia—from Burma to Vietnam—where they formed communities on the Kra Isthmus at porterage points on the route to the South China Sea. Arabs, Persians, Nestorian Christians and Jews also filtered east to settle on the Malabar and Coromandel coasts as mercantile intermediaries between southern India, the Persian Gulf and the Red Sea. On the other hand, in East Africa, south of the Horn, foreign merchants were irregular visitors before the advent of Islam in the seventh century.

The spread of Hinduism and Buddhism into South East Asia and then into China added to the numbers of people travelling by sea. Missionaries, priests, monks and craftsmen sailed from South Asia to provide expertise and religious orthodoxy for the 'Indianized' courts of South East Asia which evolved during this period. In addition, there were movements of Chinese and South East Asian Buddhist monks and laity visiting Buddhist sacred sites and universities in northern India and Sri Lanka. It is impossible to quantify this early passenger traffic, but glimpses are provided by the Chinese Buddhist monk, Fa-hsien, who, in 413–14, travelled from Sri Lanka to southern China in ships which carried 200 passengers and crew. A similar report comes from another Chinese monk, I-Ching, who visited northern India, the Malay peninsula and Sumatra in the period between 671 and 695.

Pilgrim, priest, monk or artisan, most people travelled with a cache of goods to sell or exchange along the way as a means of paying their passage. Trade goods were a universal currency for all travellers in the pre-modern world, leading to a greater and more diffuse movement of goods than indicated by any study of formal commercial systems.

While Middle Eastern and South Asian merchants were pre-eminent in this human traffic, as we have seen they had no real South East Asian equivalents. Maritime trade remained a royal prerogative in mainland South East Asia until the last few centuries, and it was not until the thirteenth and fourteenth centuries that distinctive local mercantile groups began to emerge in insular South East Asia.

State envoys and diplomats also travelled the Indian Ocean from the first few centuries of the present era, invariably accompanied by trade goods as tribute and presents. Various South Asian rulers sent embassies to Roman and Sasanian courts, while from the fifth century there were regular seaborne diplomatic exchanges between the states of South East Asia and the Chinese imperial authorities.[15]

On the eve of the establishment of Islam in the seventh century

[15] P. Wheatley, 1980.

the range and type of people travelling by sea was increasing. The most prominent were Middle Eastern and South Asian merchants of various religious backgrounds. But they jostled for space on the small ships which crossed the Ocean with merchants from other lands, diplomats, artisans, pilgrims and slaves.

With the establishment of the Arab Islamic empire, maritime merchants, as individuals and as distinct economic groups, begin to emerge more clearly. The great expansion of maritime trade which occurred with the foundation of the Arab Islamic empire pushed the merchant to the forefront of the history of the Indian Ocean world.

In the Middle East, South Asia and East Asia, most merchants of substance were landbound. However, petty itinerant merchants and devout Muslims embarking on the hajj with their small bundles of goods, crowded aboard ships along with agents guarding large cargoes consigned by the merchant magnates, and sailors with their small bundles and chests filled with trade goods.

The majority of travelling merchants moved with small quantities of goods, but there were merchant princes who owned considerable numbers of vessels and dealt in large quantities of goods. There were also conglomerations of merchants who combined their fortunes to mount annual trading fleets down the Red Sea and Persian Gulf to the ports of East Africa and South Asia. The great *Karimi* Muslim and Jewish merchants of Cairo, who flourished during the eleventh and twelfth centuries, are examples of the latter type of merchant whose complex trading world stretched from the Mediterranean to the African and Asian shores of the Arabian Sea. They flourished by combining their capital to promote joint annual voyages and by utilising the services of co-religionists scattered in ports from southern Europe to Sri Lanka.

Few, if any, of these merchants were launching themselves into an unknown world. They were embarking for well-known markets where they were reasonably sure of selling their goods and obtaining return cargoes. The risks they faced were not the risks of the unknown, but the risks of the known which they had to calculate: the rhythms of the monsoons, of poorly charted waters, of storms at sea, of ship-wreck, of market gluts, of piracy and war—all events which could upset the best laid commercial plans and which were beyond the control of anyone. Naturally, precautions had to be taken, but in the pre-modern era they were few, given technological restrictions relating to ships and the rapid dissemination of information.

The most efficient way to provide a tolerable degree of control over a difficult world was to establish a sympathetic commercial network through collective mercantile activity, based upon interaction between people bonded by a common culture, religion and language. To do this, members of the same mercantile community settled in foreign marketplaces. This dispersal was encouraged by the monsoonal rhythms imposed on maritime and mercantile activity. Men and cargoes could not sail the year round, and it was frequently necessary for merchants and mariners to stay over a season in foreign ports if they missed the monsoons. It was also necessary for some merchants to set up home in foreign ports as agents for their compatriots.

These merchant settlements also acted as intermediaries between different cultures.[16] The links they maintained with their homelands helped sustain their communal identity, and provided cultural and technological conduits between cultures. Such settlements had a distinct and visible identity in ports around the Indian Ocean. Each community had its own quarter, centred upon a focal point such as a marketplace, mosque, temple or church which marked the distinctive identity of the group. The group provided hospitality for travelling compatriots, administered group law and charity, engaged in mercantile activity, supported religious leaders, and its spokesmen represented the group in its relations with the local ruler. Each community was a window into a foreign culture; not all its members were literate, but its leading members—the most successful merchants, and the keepers of mosque, temple and church—were. Through them it was possible to glimpse other worlds, and, when the occasion was right, they were to be vital players in the processes of cultural interaction and diffusion.

Not all merchants and seafarers moved on an axis bounded by welcoming communities of compatriots. Only the most important marketplaces would have contained expatriate communities, and there were many markets and harbours where the foreigner was an exotic

---

[16] See André Wink, 1987, for a critical discussion of the concept of mercantile diasporas.

visitor. But the visiting merchant was a valued participant in any market, and as such was protected by local law where rulers wished to encourage overseas trade.

Muslims had the widest network of communities in foreign ports. Initially, Persians were at the forefront of Muslim maritime expansion and pioneered the great sea route from the Gulf to southern China. By the ninth century Persians had been supplanted by Arabs, and Muslim mercantile diasporas had moved beyond the political boundaries of Islam, effectively laying the foundations for a greater *Dar al-Islam* which would reach its greatest extent in the sixteenth century. A universal brotherhood and information system was unfolding which would incorporate Muslims from all the major cultures on the shores of the Indian Ocean.

The first expatriate Muslim communities were located on the north-east coast of Africa, in Ethiopia and Somalia, and along the coasts of southern India and Sri Lanka. In time these expatriate communities became an integral part of local life; no longer exotic they frequently established their own expatriate communities, thereby pushing the boundaries of Islam further to the south and east. Mogadishu and Kilwa were major agents in the Islamisation of ports and peoples to the south; the Muslim settlements along the Malabar and Coromandel coasts were vital to the Islamization of insular South East Asia.

By the fourteenth century Chinese communities appeared in South East Asia. Their late evolution was due to the preference of the Chinese authorities for foreign merchants to visit China instead of Chinese merchants dispersing overseas. As a result, Chinese merchants did not build up strong links with South and South East Asia until the eleventh and twelfth centuries, and it was not until the fourteenth century that there is any confirmed evidence of an overseas Chinese commercial community in South East Asia.[17]

But merchants were not the only people travelling the high seas. By the fifteenth century thousands of Muslims from around the Indian Ocean were involved in the hajj each year.[18] Also, the Mongol holo-

[17] Paul Wheatley, 1980, 84–85.
[18] M.N. Pearson, 1985.

caust and the collapse of the Baghdad Khilafat in the thirteenth century caused an exodus of Muslim refugees from Central Asia, Mesopotamia and Persia which spread over several generations. Many refugees were attracted to Muslim states in East Africa and South and South East Asia, which expanded the boundaries of the *Dar al-Islam*, providing new opportunities for skilled and adventurous Muslims from across the old Muslim world.

Dispossessed Muslim divines, craftsmen and soldiers joined missionaries and Muslim intellectuals in a great migration south and east by land and sea, seeking service in the frontier Muslim states in East Africa, northern India, the Deccan, the Maldives and South East Asia, from the thirteenth century. As representatives of sophisticated Muslim civilization they were welcomed by newly-established Muslim rulers, providing an atmosphere of sophistication and the tangible skills needed to create the ideal religious and cultural *Dar al-Islam*.

In South Asia Muslim refugees were vital to the processes of Islamization. They brought with them skills and traditions of the great urban civilization of the Middle East and Central Asia, leaving tangible imprints upon the monumental architecture of Muslim cities across South Asia, as well as preserving classical Islamic learning and creating a new body of South Asian Islamic literature and learning, derived both from foreign and internal sources. Persian became the language of high society, both Muslim and Hindu, in Muslim ruled areas, setting the mould for South Asian Islamic courtly culture which existed until the nineteenth century.

In all the cities which stretched across the northern plains of India, foreign Muslims found a welcome. In the great city of Delhi sultans surrounded themselves with Moroccan, Persian and Central Asian mercenaries, divines, intellectuals and artisans who frequently moved from one city to another, seeking royal or noble patronage and binding this new frontier of Islam more closely to the Middle Eastern heartland of Islamic civilization. In lesser Muslim courts and administrative centres in the Deccan, and even in the Maldives, such travelling Muslims found an equally warm welcome from local Muslim élites as they attempted to mould an idealized Islamic lifestyle.[19]

[19] R.E. Dunn, 1989.

But not all of South Asian Islamic civilization derived from foreign sources. Much of the Persian and Central Asian Islamic tradition was eclectic, and in South Asia quickly adapted local forms and idioms, both as a means of affecting conversions among the rural masses in areas such as Bengal,[20] and because of the necessity of incorporating non-Muslims in the administration and the performing and plastic arts. Apart from areas such as the Indus valley and Bengal, mass conversion was the exception rather than the rule, and Islam remained an essentially urban religion and culture, deriving its wealth and power from the labour of a predominantly Hindu peasantry, and alliances with many small Hindu states which accepted the overlordship of Muslim rulers.

From the fourteenth century Muslims from the Middle East and South Asia migrated further east in greater numbers, as Islam made inroads into the states of insular South East Asia. Apart from scholars, artisans and religious leaders, Muslim mercenaries, particularly cavalrymen, found a welcome in South and South East Asia at Muslim and non-Muslim courts. Few courts of any note were without their contingent of Muslim cavalrymen, just as most rulers of any note employed some foreign Muslims as their commercial and political agents in dealings with other foreigners.

Diasporas of merchants, artisans, religious leaders and mercenaries were central to processes of cultural diffusion around the Indian Ocean. The presence of foreign communities within a society did not automatically mean that cultural diffusion and interaction were under way, but without such intimate contact such processes were not possible.

The two most obvious instances of foreign communities acting as catalysts for cultural interaction and diffusion relate to Middle Eastern diasporas in East Africa, and South Asian diasporas in South East Asia.

As we have seen, in East Africa from the eighth century, growing international trade ushered in new processes of social and economic change among indigenous peoples on the coast. The development of regular long-distance trade linkages encouraged the growth of urban centres, and the differentiation of indigenous society to accommodate

[20] Asim Roy, 1984.

new occupational groups such as merchants and artisans. Communities of Arabs and Persians along the coast provided local peoples with access to new economic, cultural and religious models to suit their changing circumstances. Islam, the religion and civilization, provided the model for new local urban élites who converted, at the same time adopting many of its cultural forms and values. Undoubtedly, too, there was also intermarriage between local élites and members of the foreign Islamic merchant communities.

The end result was the creation of an Afro-Asian Islamic civilization, the Swahili civilization, which stretched from Kenya to the northern coast of Madagascar. It was a society dominated by merchants who ruled port city states scattered along the coast of East Africa. Superficially, such port cities were enclaves of Islamic settlement and civilization on the coast, with little but trade to tie them to the African hinterland. In reality, however, such settlements were part of the spectrum of African responses to external stimuli: in this instance to the stimuli of foreign trade and the presence of foreign Muslims. In religion, architecture, government and trade, the Middle East and South Asia influenced forms and practice in these port cities. But linguistically, racially and in terms of popular culture (ranging from food to folklore), the basic forms remained those of Africa, linking the inhabitants of such settlements to the people of the African hinterland.

Similar processes occurred in South East Asia where communities of South Asians—Hindu, Buddhist and later Muslim—acted as link groups, enabling local élites to borrow and adapt from the civilization of South Asia. As in East Africa, the reasons for the adoption and adaptation of foreign religious, cultural and technological forms relate to changes within local societies which made aspects of foreign civilization attractive and useful to local élites.

The spread of Hinduism and Buddhism throughout South East Asia was associated with increases in rice cultivation which led to greater productivity and wealth. Rulers emerged to control these increasingly complex and wealthy societies, and the first South East Asian states took shape. As in East Africa, the presence of foreign communities gave access to a more sophisticated civilization, aspects of which were attractive and of use to rulers emerging in a rapidly changing social and economic environment. The result was the very conscious borrowing of Hindu ideas of kingship, of the ritual and priests to legitimize kingship, and the architectural and art forms associated with the expression of kingship and the state.

The spread of Buddhism into South East Asia was more complex, including the involvement of both rulers and rules. Buddhist merchants from South Asia were central to this process, but so too were Buddhist missionaries who, in contrast to their Hindu counterparts, spread the values of Buddhism among the masses. Although Hinduism has left many spectacular monuments throughout South East Asia, it has left only vestigial practices at royal courts and on the Indonesian island of Bali. Buddhism on the other hand, was less dependent upon royal patronage and provided a popular alternative to the élitist practice of Hinduism in South East Asia. The end result was the triumph of Buddhism on mainland South East Asia and the virtual eclipse of Hinduism.

In insular South East Asia the story was not quite the same. Until the fifteenth and sixteenth centuries, Hinduism and Buddhism intertwined to form a complex cultural mélange unique to the islands. In addition, the wealth of states in the area was primarily derived from either agriculture or trade: for example, Srivijaya's fortunes depended upon trade, whereas the wealth of the kingdoms of Java was derived from control of agricultural lands. During the thirteenth and fourteenth centuries, however, increasing maritime trade with South Asia and China had begun to put pressure on traditional social and economic structures throughout insular South East Asia. Merchants groups, foreign and local, became more important, as did trade and port cities. The power of many rulers, traditionally based upon agriculture, began to weaken as maritime trade created new wealth and aspirations among coastal groups involved with trade. As in previous centuries, South Asian merchant communities, now made up mostly of converts to Islam, provided alternative systems for such people to live by and Islam began its slow penetration of insular South East Asia.

In insular South East Asia, however, Islam came into contact with an ancient civilization steeped in Hindu and Buddhist influences. Unlike East Africa, insular South East Asia was an area of complex urban-based civilizations underpinned by an enormously productive wet-rice farming peasantry. As it progressed through the islands, Islam constantly had to accommodate itself to ancient beliefs and practices among complex societies. In East Africa, on the other hand, Islam was an urban-based religious and cultural system which helped shape the life of relatively isolated groups of people undergoing rapid social and cultural change as maritime trade became central to their livelihood.

In both East Africa and South East Asia, communities of foreign merchants were vital to the early stages of cultural diffusion and adaptation. It was not their presence alone that precipitated such processes. The precipitating causes were more closely associated with the social and economic changes that foreign trade either began or hastened among local peoples. Once the processes of cultural adaptation were under way, foreign communities had a minor role to play, and the fate of such processes were associated with developments within local societies. It is important to note also that the five centuries or more which separated the spread of Islam into East Africa and insular South East Asia were crucial to the role Islam played in these areas. In East Africa Islam helped construct a civilization, in insular South East Asia 'Islam did not construct a civilization, it appropriated one' that was already ancient by the fourteenth century.[21]

[21] C. Geertz, 1971, 11.

3

The Age of Commerce 1450–1700

Overview

By the fifteenth century the peoples of the Indian Ocean lands, from East Africa to South East Asia, were linked by a flourishing maritime system which indirectly served markets as far afield as Europe and Japan. This complex network of maritime trade was worked by numerous mercantile groups, many of whom converted to Islam as it spread eastward from South Asia into insular South East Asia. These groups were vital parts of a dynamic economic, social and political indigenous world in which ideas as well as tangible commodities passed between peoples.

The rhythms of this mercantile system were set by the monsoon winds and human political and economic activity on land. The monsoon winds enabled rapid long-distance passage by sea, but human activity on land determined the volume and direction of trade. The rise and fall of states, the expansion and contraction of economies, famine and plenty, were all factors which finely tuned the flow of goods and ideas around the Indian Ocean.

Despite the influence of forces beyond the control of merchants, the economic system they evolved was far from primitive and was more substantial than any casual peddling trade, and was sustained by great communities of merchants in a large number of port cities over many centuries.

The arrival of Europeans in the last decade of the fifteenth century did not destroy the indigenous world of the Indian Ocean. The Portuguese and the later European arrivals disrupted ancient economic linkages and mercantile fortunes, but in essence their mercantile activities during the sixteenth and seventeenth centuries were founded upon intimate collaboration with indigenous merchants and seafarers.

Europeans active across the Indian Ocean during these centuries did not face declining or decayed indigenous economic and political systems. The expansion of European mercantile activity was paralleled by the rise of vigorous, powerful and culturally vibrant indigenous states in the Middle East, South Asia, and South East and East Asia, which were more than a match for the interlopers on land.

Nevertheless, the Europeans began the process of linking indigenous maritime trading networks with new maritime trading networks in the Atlantic and the Pacific during these centuries. This laid the groundwork for their domination of Indian Ocean trade during the eighteenth century, when changing circumstances in Europe and Asia gave Europeans advantages which led them to world-wide economic and political hegemony.

An Age of Stereotypes

In *South East Asia in the Age of Commerce 1450–1650*, Anthony Reid cautioned his readers to shun stereotypes of an unchanging and declining east between the fifteenth and seventeenth centuries, just as Edward Said in his essay, *Orientalism*, warned the historian against defining parts of the world negatively by their difference from Europe.[1] Their messages have a validity for historians of the indigenous peoples of the Indian Ocean. Too often, the arrival of the Portuguese in the Indian Ocean in 1498 had been taken to mark the beginning of a new age, stereotyped as one of indigenous decline and the triumph of European enterprise. It is still seen by some historians as the great watershed between the 'modern' and 'pre-modern' world, following which the modern West overwhelmed and subjugated the anachronistic and unchanging East.[2] Undoubtedly, from the late seventeenth century the economic relationship between western Europe and the Afro-Asian lands of the Indian Ocean underwent fundamental changes, culminating in the political and economic triumph of Europe, but the victory of Europe cannot be pushed back to 1498.

While the arrival of the Portuguese marks the beginning of a well documented period concerning European mercantile activity in the Indian Ocean, it does not mark the beginning of a new epoch in the commercial and political history of the area. By the early fifteenth

[1] Anthony Reid, 1988, xv; Edward Said, 1985.
[2] I. Wallerstein, 1974; Janet L. Abu–Lughod, 1989.

century the maritime trade of South East Asia was rapidly expanding. At the centre of this growth was Melaka, with its burgeoning links into insular South East Asia, and its connections into vibrant systems of Chinese private trade and the vigorous networks of Gujarat, the Malabar and Coromandel coasts, Bengal and Burma. Similarly, across the Arabian Sea by the mid-fifteenth century, there was a marked growth of maritime commerce between the Malabar coast, Gujarat, the Persian Gulf, southern Arabia, the Red Sea, the Maldives and the coast of East Africa as far south as Sofala. Paralleling the rise of Melaka, ports such as Calicut, Cambay, Hormuz and Kilwa reached their greatest levels of prosperity, attracting merchants from all parts of the Indian Ocean, along with envoys from all the major courts of the area.

During the fifteenth century the Indian Ocean achieved a new unity based upon the spread of Islam. In insular South East Asia, Melaka, inheriting the mantle of Pasai on the north-east coast of Sumatra, which was the first port in the area to convert to Islam, was the focal point for the spread of Islam eastward. In East Africa the same was true of Mombasa and Kilwa. They had overhauled Mogadishu as focal points of commercial and political power on the coast, and were now centres for the spread of Islam south along the coasts of Tanzania and Mozambique. By 1450 a vast new Islamic commercial and cultural network had been created which was rapidly expanding to link East Africa, the Middle East and South and South East Asia into a Muslim-dominated mercantile system; this would survive into the seventeenth century.

Against this background of renewed vigorous indigenous commercial activity, the sixteenth and seventeenth centuries have been described as an 'Age of Contained Conflict' between indigenous peoples and Europeans, rather than as a clear-cut prelude to the establishment of formal political and economic European empires.[3] It was a period of considerable indigenous political, cultural and economic life, and a continual jostling between locals and intruders for a share of traditional commerce: not an age marked by the death throes of indigenous enterprise.

During the sixteenth and seventeenth centuries the superiority of

[3] Sanjay Subrahmanyam, 1990(a), Chp. 5.

Europe and the certainty of its triumph over indigenous political and commercial systems in the Indian Ocean was by no means clear. During these centuries, indigenous commerce flourished and expanded in both conflict and co-operation with European enterprise. In addition, politically and economically buoyant indigenous states emerged in the Middle East and South and South East Asia, containing Europeans on land and taking an active and aggressive interest in mercantile trade.

Apart from being characterized as 'An Age of Contained Conflict', these centuries have also been labelled as an 'Age of Partnership' during which indigenous groups facilitated European penetration of the Indian Ocean world.[4] It was an age both of conflict and apprenticeship with indigenous commercial groups for the Portuguese and other Europeans who followed them. No intruder was able to shape the commercial world of the Indian Ocean to European demand. Without exception they compromised and scuffled among themselves, and with indigenous groups, for a share of trade within the Ocean. The result was the placement of conflicting European commercial groups within the traditional trading world of the Indian Ocean rather than European domination.

In cultural terms this was not an age in which Europe came to dominate indigenous peoples. To an extent, Portuguese became a lingua franca of trade, but equally, European merchants and administrators had to learn local languages. Malay, for example, was widely used throughout insular South East Asia as the language of commerce by both European and indigenous merchants. Similarly, in South Asia, Persian remained the official language of communication for Europeans with many local rulers until well into the nineteenth century. Certainly, in many of their enclaves, Europeans attempted to reproduce their native lifestyles, but frequently they succumbed to common sense, and in food, clothing and social habits many discreetly—and some indiscreetly—adopted local custom, often to the disgust and concern of their newly-arrived compatriots. Climate and disease wreaked havoc among Europeans. Most European communities were

[4] Blair B. King and M.N. Pearson, 1979.

transient and driven by the dream of wealth, with only a small proportion of Europeans possessing either the time or the inclination to interact with local societies to any significant degree. The major exceptions to this generalization were the Portuguese and various orders of Roman Catholic missionaries, who, at least until the late eighteenth century, were the only Europeans who attempted to establish permanent settler colonies, proselytize indigenous peoples and investigate indigenous cultures.

Portuguese enterprise during this age has often been as crudely stereotyped as indigenous enterprise. It has been explained as an anti-Muslim crusade, fuelled by a ravenous desire for gold. The official Portuguese commercial organization in the Indian Ocean, known as the *Estado da India*, has been characterized as the first European colonial empire in the Indian Ocean, and as anachronistic, lawless, monolithic and moribund, compared with the supposedly more dynamic, better organized and essentially 'modern' Dutch, English and Danish joint stock mercantile companies, which appeared in the Indian Ocean in the seventeenth century. But the *Estado da India* was neither monolithic nor static. It was not the first of the territorial colonial empires, but was a trading network concerned with the distribution of goods rather than their production, and with relations between people, not with control over land: as such, its relations with indigenous peoples, and its commercial and political activities, changed with time, as various factions in Lisbon and the *Estado* struggled for influence, and conditions changed in the Indian Ocean.

Undoubtedly, some Portuguese were motivated simply by the desire for gold and souls, and some were devious and deceitful, but during the sixteenth century the policies of the *Estado da India* evolved and changed, as did relations between the Portuguese and indigenous peoples. Factions rose and fell within the organization, as Lisbon and the men on the spot reacted to changing stimuli from Europe and the Indian Ocean. From the early seventeenth century the Portuguese came under new pressures worldwide from the Dutch and the English. This provided new challenges which sorely tested the *Estado da India* as it fought desperately to survive in the Indian Ocean.

Tensions existed in Lisbon and the Indian Ocean between Portuguese policymakers and administrators regarding the goals of the

Estado da India, particularly with respect to the use of force.[5] The Portuguese did use force and terror; however, they were not the essence of Portuguese policies. Such policies were multifaceted and constantly changing, and, throughout the sixteenth century, consistently encompassed collaboration and alliances with peoples of all religious persuasions, ranging from Muslims to Buddhists. Undoubtedly, religious prejudice, dreams of territorial empire and greed motivated factions within the *Estado da India,* but during the sixteenth century Portuguese enterprise was essentially conceived and directed at promoting peaceful trade, although warfare was not avoided if it furthered commercial objectives.

In attempting to assess the impact of Portuguese enterprise upon the cultural, political and commercial world of the Indian Ocean, one cannot isolate the activities of the *Estado da India* from the indigenous world in which it operated, nor ignore the vigorous and long-lasting activity of Portuguese private traders, or of indigenous merchants who linked Portuguese enterprise into traditional mercantile networks. Official and private Portuguese enterprise constantly evolved in response to changing local conditions and was remarkably successful in blending into indigenous commercial networks.[6] If one judges Portuguese success on the basis of diverting trade to Europe, then they and other Europeans during this period must be judged only partially successful. But if one judges Portuguese success on the basis of their ability to find a niche within the traditional commercial world of the Indian Ocean, then they must be judged successful.

Certainly, the Dutch, English and the Danes during the seventeenth century patterned their commercial activities closely on those of the Portuguese, and introduced no new revolutionary ideas to direct more trade towards Europe.[7]

During this period no European group managed to break the relative cultural and economic insularity of the Indian Ocean world, which was to remain remarkably unchanged until the late seventeenth century. There were to be major internal realignments of trade due

[5] T.F. Earle & John Villiers, 1990.

[6] R. Ptak, 1987; R. Ptak & Dietmar Rothermund, 1991; Jorge Manuel Flores, 1990 and 1991.

[7] Leonard Blussé, 1988, 195–214.

to European activity, but this was not an age of partnership or conflict in which Europeans overwhelmed indigenous commerce, states or cultures, and subjugated the flow of goods to the demands of the European marketplace, as was to be the case from the eighteenth century.

The various European trading institutions during this period were very similar in their activities and fortunes, insofar as they all became part of the indigenous commercial system. Only from the late seventeenth century did changing patterns of economic activity in Europe, and the activities of private European traders, usher in profound changes in, first, the economic relationship, and later the political and cultural relationship, between Europe and the Indian Ocean. Changing European economies and private initiative linked the age of commerce to the age of capitalism, rather than the pioneer Portuguese, Dutch and English trading enterprises.

The Golden Age of Indigenous Trade

By the late fifteenth century the major civilizations on the shores of the Indian Ocean were linked together by an expanding and changing network of maritime trade routes and ports. These ports ranged from the self-governing city-states of East Africa, the Persian Gulf and insular South East Asia, through ports such as Cambay, Goa and many others on the Malabar and Coromandel coasts which owed allegiance to large states. Some, such as Kilwa, Hormuz and Melaka did not service an immediate hinterland but were great redistributive centres for more distant ports and markets.

All these ports were active centres of Muslim communal life and part of that Muslim intellectual and cultural world which stretched from the Atlantic to the Pacific. Even in areas beyond Muslim political control, such as southern India and Sri Lanka, Muslims had a disproportionate presence as merchants and mariners. Tamil-speaking Muslim merchant communities, such as the Marakkayars, flourished in ports along the Tamil littoral; Malayalam-speaking Mappila Muslims ruled some ports on the Malabar coast; while in Sri Lanka, foreign trade was almost entirely in the hands of Middle Eastern and south Indian Muslim merchant communities.

Across the centuries there was a steady evolution of maritime
technology, skills, trade and ports, from the days of the earliest fishing
communities to the full-blown bustle of great cosmopolitan ports.
The history of this process was complex and far from being 'simply a
monotonous repetition of the same events'.[8]

While trade between various areas of the Indian Ocean increased
over the centuries, differential rates of growth and a variety of political
events in the lands bordering the Ocean led to frequent changes in
the nature and workings of that trade. The fate and fortunes of ports
were dictated by similar factors, to which must be added the vagaries
of nature.

The variety and quantity of goods produced around the Indian
Ocean varied greatly. The Middle East and South Asia had, for
thousands of years, produced an enormous variety of sophisticated
manufactures and raw materials which fed into maritime trade. In
comparison, East Africa and South East Asia began to impact upon
that trade much later, while Australia had only the slimmest of links
as late as the early nineteenth century.

It needs to be noted, however, that within the Middle East and
South Asia there were as many different economies as there were
topographical variations. Both areas had fluctuating agrarian frontiers,
and while there were substantial enclaves of sophisticated mercantile
activity there were also large areas where subsistence agriculture and
barter dominated, and markets were few.

Fluctuating agrarian frontiers could impact directly upon the fortunes of ports servicing agrarian hinterlands. During the fifteenth
century, for example, there was an opening up of new agricultural
lands in southern India, as Telugu migrants moved from the central
Deccan into jungle tracts further south, in what is now Tamilnad.
This extension of farming obviously had a positive impact upon local
economies and the activity of local ports. Ancient ports such as
Masulipatnam on the Coromandel coast were joined by scores of new
harbours: many were simply beach roadsteads, others were located on
river-mouths and deltas, some—Nagapattinam and Nagore—were

[8] Fernand Braudel, v. 3, 1986, 485.

large urban centres, others were little more than villages with an occasional market for visiting mariners.

In the Middle East on the other hand, there was by the fifteenth century, a contraction of agricultural activity in both Mesopotamia and Persia which suffered from political instability, following the Mongol invasions and in the wake of the Black Death. Both these calamities led to depopulation, a failure in competent administration and a decline in farming, which was reflected in a drop in trade and a withering of such formerly great ports as Basra. The fate of Basra, which became a provincial backwater until the twentieth century, was less unkind than that of many other ports in the Gulf over the millennia: ancient Dilmun vanished from records some 3000 years ago when trade in the Gulf was affected by chaos in Mesopotamia; Failaka was deserted when Rome and Sasanian Persia developed alternative ports to access the Gulf trade some 2000 years ago; Siraf, once the gateway to Persia in the ninth and tenth centuries AD, was destroyed by earthquake and civil disturbance; while Sohar on the Oman coast, long the rival of Siraf, was sacked by an expeditionary force from Mesopotamia in the tenth century which was determined to destroy its maritime pre-eminence in the Gulf. On the Dhofar and Hadrahmaut coasts, in south-west Arabia and in the Red Sea, the same pattern of growth and contraction can be observed in the life of ports. With the collapse of the Yemenite state system in the sixth and seventh centuries the frankincense and myrrh trade dwindled, as did the fortunes of a string of ports from Yemen to the Dhofar coast; similarly, with the Arab occupation of Egypt, that country's maritime trade through the Red Sea declined for several centuries, and ancient ports such as Bernike and Muos Hormos were ruined. In time, other ports developed to take their place, but few ports in the area today can claim the ancient heritage of Aden which has survived for more than 2000 years.

The focus of demographic growth and economic and cultural activity in the Middle East had, in fact, switched back to Egypt in the eleventh and twelfth centuries before the catastrophes of the Mongol invasions and the Black Death, and the Red Sea replaced the Persian Gulf as the major sea route to the east. But even the operation of this route showed signs of change by the fifteenth century. Egypt too had been ravaged by the Black Death, and, as its agricultural infrastructure crumbled under the dual impact of inefficient Mameluke rule and massive population losses from plague, demand for imports declined. The great Muslim and Jewish merchant families of Cairo sank into poverty and obscurity, and formerly great ports such as Alexandria and Suez became primarily exchange centres for the spice and pepper trade between the Mediterranean and the Indian Ocean, where Europeans, such as the merchants of Venice and Genoa, copied and then improved upon indigenous mercantile techniques.

Despite the internal decay of Egypt the pilgrim markets of Mekka and Medinah continued to expand as centres for the redistribution of South Asian textiles and other commodities from the east, benefiting from the continuation and growth of the annual pilgrimage of the Muslim faithful, the hajj, to the Holy Cities of Islam.[9] By the fifteenth century large groups of pilgrims sailed annually from the ports of East Africa, Gujarat, the Malabar and Coromandel coasts, Sri Lanka and Melaka, carrying goods which they traded along the way and also in the great markets held to celebrate the arrival of pilgrims in Mekka and Medinah.

From Egypt to Persia the long-distance commerce of the Middle East was, by the fifteenth century, increasingly based upon the transit trade between the Mediterranean and the Indian Ocean rather than upon servicing local markets. Such trade was still enormously profitable and received the attention of rulers in Egypt, Persia and South Asia who maintained regular diplomatic contact to ensure its smooth working. New empires were emerging in the Middle East which would restore some of the faded glory of Islamic civilization, but agriculture and commerce were generally never to fully recover, despite attempts by Ottoman and Safavid rulers in the seventeenth and eighteenth centuries to encourage their revival. The reasons for this are complex, but in part relate to the slow death of the transit trade between the Indian Ocean and the Mediterranean from the sixteenth century.

In the Indian subcontinent on the other hand, by the fifteenth century, agriculture expanded and there was a consolidation of larger

[9] Suraiya Faroqhi, 1990; M.N. Pearson, 1986.

states—such as the Delhi Sultanate, the Deccan sultanates and Vijaya-nagara—which consciously associated the fortunes of agriculture with the interest of the state. Unlike the situation in the Middle East, there had been no overall catastrophic demographic or economic decline, although there were considerable local variations in fortune. In general the history of ports appears to have been less fickle in South Asia than in the Middle East. Occasionally ancient ports such as Broach (Baru-gaza) and many others, most particularly in Bengal, faced slow death as rivers shifted course and waterways silted up, but most ports mentioned in *The Periplus* were still active in the fifteenth century.

The major exception to these generalizations about South Asia was Sri Lanka. By the fifteenth century the abandonment of the irrigated Dry Zone, and the shift in population to the central highlands and the tropical coastal lands of the south-west, had led to a decline in the rice export trade. This was replaced by an increasing reliance upon the export of luxury commodities such as cinnamon, gemstones, ivory and elephants. In addition, the port of Galle on the south-west coast replaced ancient Mantai, facing India, as the country's major entrepôt for cargoes from the maritime networks of the western and eastern Indian Ocean.

Thus, different rates of economic activity and different political histories in both South Asia and the Middle East, over the centuries, imposed yet more rhythms upon the flow of maritime cargoes and the fate of ports.

Such cycles were also reflected in different patterns of cultural activity. By the twelfth and thirteenth centuries the most vibrant centres of Muslim cultural life in the Middle East had gravitated westward to prosperous Egypt, as Mesopotamia sank into political and economic chaos. Imperial Baghdad declined into provincial obscurity as Cairo became the Middle Eastern centre of Islamic intellectual and cultural life. But by the fifteenth century the pendulum swung eastward once more: Egypt was in decline and Persia re-emerged as a major centre of Muslim cultural activity, as its Mongol overlords converted to Islam and became patrons of Islamic culture.

In South Asia during the fifteenth century the Muslim states of the Deccan in central India emerged as major centres of Muslim culture, for a time rivalling the great Muslim cities of the Indo-Gangetic plains as economic activity in the Deccan expanded. From 1347–1526 the Deccan had been ruled by the Muslim Bahmani dynasty which had encouraged Muslim urban culture in cities such as Gulbarga and Bidar, and which also jealously guarded and encouraged maritime trade through its major port at Goa. The Muslim rulers of the Deccan maintained large cavalry forces and were reliant upon the trade in horses between the Middle East and Goa. In the late fifteenth century the Bahmani state began to disintegrate as provincial governors established their independence to form the sultanates of Ahmadnagar, Golconda, Bijapur, Berar and Bidar. The rulers of these states sponsored Muslim culture at their courts, and those with outlets to the sea took a keen interest in maritime trade: Ahmadnagar and Bijapur, through Chaul and Goa on the west coast of India, and Golconda through Masulipatnam on the Coromandel coast. In time the two landlocked sultanates, Berar and Bidar, were absorbed by Ahmadnagar and Bijapur, each of which were able to maintain substantial cavalry forces which were regularly replenished from Persia and Arabia through Chaul and Goa.

Further to the south, the Hindu empire of Vijayangara was responsible for a major revival of south Indian Hindu cultural life associated with the expansion of agriculture, trade and seaborne commerce through ports on the Coromandel and Malabar coasts. In contrast, in Sri Lanka the decline of the ancient agricultural system and the population shift to the more tropical south was accompanied by a decline in courtly culture and a degeneration of Buddhism, which was not halted until the nineteenth century.

Across the Bay of Bengal, in insular South East Asia, the great expansion of maritime trade, evident by the early fifteenth century, was central to the formation of new states, to the processes of Islamization and the spread of Malay Muslim élite culture, in an area stretching from Melaka to the Moluccas. The rise of indigenous and foreign commercial activity led to an appropriation of the mixed Hindu-Buddhist culture of the area by Islam,[10] and a reformation of political life to take greater account of the importance of maritime trade. During

[10] C. Geertz, 1971, 11.

the previous 1000 years South East Asian states had developed diplomatic links with the various dynasties which ruled China, partly as a means of securing trade and partly to legitimize their power locally with the blessing of the great empire. In the fifteenth century the Ming court was assiduously courted by newly emerging Muslim states in South East Asia for the same age-old reasons, just as they assiduously courted important Muslim mercantile groups from South Asia and the Middle East.

By the fifteenth century bustling ports on the Strait of Melaka (Aceh, Pasai, Kedah and Melaka) and on the northern coast of Java (Bantam, Jakarta, Demak and Gresik) were enjoying unprecedented prosperity. Tensions developed between these ports and agricultural states, such as the Thai kingdom of Ayuthia (1350–1767) in mainland South East Asia and Majapahit (*c.*1300–*c.*1527) on Java. In the instance of Ayuthia, tension was the result of that kingdoms' quest for access to greater maritime trading links with the outside world at the expense of ports such as Melaka on the Malay peninsula. In Java, on the other hand, maritime trade prompted the rise of new élites and new forms of wealth which threatened traditional ruling groups whose power and wealth came from agricultural taxes.

In this struggle new port-city states such as Melaka, whose fortunes were tied to international trade, frequently looked to foreign commercial and political powers to legitimize their rule and to offer protection against powerful and aggressive neighbours. Melaka, for example, secured the protection of China and extended special privileges to Hindu and Muslim South Asian merchants whose activities were central to long-distance trade in South East Asia.

Across South East Asia, in the fifteenth century, cultural activity flourished. In insular South East Asia wealthy Islamic courts in which local and foreign idioms were blended became centres of yet another distinctive South East Asian culture. On the mainland, Burmese, Mon and Thai rulers actively sponsored the development of distinctive local forms of Buddhist art and architecture, to the extent of carrying off artisans and artists from conquered rivals as a legitimate part of the booty of war.

Throughout history the flow of maritime trade and its cultural impact has been inextricably linked with patterns of political events.

In some instances they moulded patterns of maritime trade and cultural interaction, in other instances the imperatives of trade helped mould political and cultural activity.

In the Middle East, for example, the many wars between Byzantium and Sasanid Persia and their respective Christian allies in Aksum and Jewish allies in south-western Arabia, in the fifth and sixth centuries, contributed to the collapse of the states of Yemen and the diversion of overseas trade to other ports in the area. The relocation of the Arab imperial capital from Damascus to Baghdad in the late eighth century intensified the Persian Gulf trade, while the decline of Baghdad's political authority in Mesopotamia and Persia from the tenth century onwards enabled the ambitious Fatimid dynasty (909–1171) in Egypt to make their country a great centre of Islamic culture and to revive the Red Sea trade at the expense of the Persian Gulf.

Similarly, the migration of peoples into the Middle East often acted as a catalyst to new forms and directions of culture and maritime trade. Intrusions of peoples such as the Mongols have frequently been depicted as totally negative in terms of their destructive impact upon the great Islamic civilizations of the Middle East, but how true is this?

Before the Mongols erupted into the Middle East and other parts of Eurasia, there was a well-established pattern of Central Asian people moving into the sophisticated heartland of the Middle East. For example, from the ninth and tenth centuries, Turkish peoples had moved from their homeland along the Silk Route into the Islamic empire where they assumed the role of frontier mercenaries. Their movement undoubtedly caused political upheaval within the Arab Islamic empire, but it also added a new vigorous group of converts to the Islamic community who, in time, extended the boundaries of Islam into Turkey, Afghanistan and South Asia. In addition, these peoples reinvigorated the military prowess of the Arab empire, driving the Crusaders from Palestine, the Levant and Egypt, and establishing their own principalities in Egypt, Mesopotamia and Persia, which became flourishing centres of Islamic culture and commerce.

Even the Mongols, after their initial destructive explosion into Persia and Mesopotamia, established their own states across the Middle Eastern heartland and in Persia. At these new centres of power the Mongols attempted to re-establish classical Islamic culture, and eagerly sponsored international trade as a means of gaining access to luxury goods and the profits of Indian Ocean trade.

The maritime trade of the Persian Gulf had by now taken second place to that of the Red Sea. Nevertheless, the establishment of Mongol courts in the Persian highlands did something to revive the maritime trade of the Gulf. Both Mongol and Turk were initially disruptive, but once they had established themselves they ironically attempted to recreate much that they had destroyed and in the process subtly altered the rhythms of Indian Ocean trade. The establishment of the Turkish Fatimid dynasty in Egypt in the tenth century was to lead to a growth in Egyptian trade down the Red Sea, while the destruction of Baghdad and the foundation of Mongol dynasties in Persia was to lead to the eclipse of Basra and the revival of ports such as ancient Hormuz on the Iranian shore of the Persian Gulf. The fortunes of Hormuz received a further boost with the revival of Persian independence under the indigenous Safavid dynasty in the late sixteenth century, which led to an upsurge of economic activity.

Across South Asia from the fifth to the twelfth centuries there was a period of extensive agricultural colonization, particularly in southeast India, which led to an increase in agricultural production, the expansion of maritime trade and the formation of new states. Closer economic and political links were forged between coast and interior, intensifying coastal and trans-oceanic traffic, and shifting the focus of such trade away from ephemeral luxuries to hinterland staples, such as cotton cloth, grain and areca nuts. However, as earlier in the Middle East, the establishment of Muslim rule across northern and central India from the twelfth century led to considerable changes in the technology of warfare, and in bureaucratic organization, which were reflected in increases in the efficiency of revenue collection and changes in the nature of the maritime trade.

Technological changes prompted a massive upsurge in the ancient trade in Arabian and Persian cavalry horses into central and southern India from the twelfth century, as feuding states struggled for supremacy and each sought access to ports and the vital Middle Eastern trade. One of the results of bureaucratic change was an increase in the efficiency of revenue collection, the widespread substitution of cash for kind in revenue payments, and an increasing reliance upon precious metals and copper for coinage. To sustain imports of horses and precious metals and copper, southern and central Indian dynasties—the Cholas, Hoysalas, Pandyas, Pallavas, Bahmanis, Deccan sultans and Vijayanagara—had to take an active interest in the extension of arable land and the production of goods, and, from the thirteenth century, regimes in southern and central India were more than ever involved in encouraging long-distance maritime trade.

Further afield, Mongol depredation in the thirteenth and fourteenth centuries signalled the collapse of many Middle Eastern marketplaces and ancient Central Asian trade routes, which were replaced by sea routes through South East Asia and across the Indian Ocean to South Asia and the Red Sea. The decline in some Middle Eastern economic fortunes permitted South Asian merchant groups, many of them recent converts to Islam, to fill the breach in mercantile activity across the Indian Ocean. Finally, in South East Asia, more intensive attention by South Asian and Chinese merchants had profound effects upon political, cultural and economic life.

These effects were most marked in the Malay peninsula and the Indonesian archipelago, but also had an impact upon Thailand and Burma, which battled with one another for control of ports such as Mergui and Tenasserim and for domination of the northern reaches of the Malay peninsula. In Thailand the rulers of Ayuthia, and in the eighteenth century its successor state centred upon Bangkok, welcomed foreign merchants. Lacking a Thai merchant class, the rulers of Ayuthia (and also the rulers of Burma) had to rely upon royal agents—many of whom were foreign Muslims—and South Asian, Chinese and Japanese merchants and shipowners to export local goods and import foreign cargoes, as maritime trade became a lucrative source of profit to supplement taxes raised upon agriculture.

In East Africa the fate of ports and patterns of coastal trade were even more complex in the short term. The livelihood of East African ports depended upon their ability to collect goods from their immediate hinterlands and the interior: if either or both of these sources of export commodities were disrupted, ports could, and did, fall into decay. Political upheavals in the interior, epidemic diseases, ecological changes and the migration of peoples, were all factors which could spell doom for coastal settlements. Another factor influencing both the fortunes of ports and the direction of trade was the rivalry among the northern ports such as Mogadishu, Mombasa and Kilwa, which were linked into the monsoon system, for control of the southern ports which produced the bulk of the cargoes destined for overseas markets. Southern ports such as gold-exporting Sofala were tethered by coastal winds to the northern ports, but primacy among the ports varied according to the fortunes of economic rivalry.

Even more variations in the mechanics and direction of maritime trade could be detailed for all the areas. The main point is, however, that as important and fascinating as these variations were, they did not affect the long-term rhythms of Indian Ocean maritime trade. Rather, they caused subtle alterations to the volume, composition and direction of maritime cargoes within particular areas of the Indian Ocean but did not radically affect the broad flows of maritime commerce. These variations were unique historical events which had an impact upon the fortunes of individuals, communities and cultures across the Indian Ocean.

By the fifteenth century, Indian Ocean seaborne trade was marked by an increase in the carriage of staples between South Asia and the Middle East and along other routes. The trade in luxuries still thrived. Whatever the speculations about the essential characteristics of this trade, it represented a remarkably self-contained economic system that was only marginally dependent upon markets in the Mediterranean and East Asia, although the reverse was not necessarily true. Parts of the Mediterranean and China were increasingly dependent upon imports from the Indian Ocean by the fifteenth century. This was particularly true of Muslim trading cities such as Antioch, Sidon, Tripoli, Tyre and Haifa in the Levant, and Italian trading cities such as Venice and Genoa, whose prosperity was, to a large extent, based upon their role as marketplaces for Indian Ocean spices and pepper. Such imports were a response to growing demand in Europe, and were of sufficient importance to help determine the fortunes of mercantile communities in places around the Mediterranean and in the Middle East. The obverse was rarely true, with few Indian Ocean ports, apart from those in the Middle East and Melaka in South East Asia, dependent upon trade with regions beyond the Indian Ocean.

In the case of Melaka this dependency upon extra-regional trade was modified by its function as a transhipment port for South East Asia, as much as by its linkages with the China trade. In the case of ports on the Red Sea and the Persian Gulf (most particularly Aden and Hormuz), however, trade between the Indian Ocean and neighbouring regions was vital. In the Middle East the agricultural surplus needed to sustain internal demand and domestic market networks had declined considerably, and local commerce had become increasingly dependent upon the transit trade between expanding Mediterranean and western European economies, and the export commodities of tropical Asia. Increasingly, ports on the Red Sea and Persian Gulf were simply entrepôts for the passage of goods and bullion between the markets of the Christian Mediterranean, East Africa, South and South East Asia and China.

While it is relatively easy to sketch a general picture of Indian Ocean trade in the fifteenth century, it is much more difficult to give the story a human face. Who were the players? At one level one can argue generally that as most commerce, both maritime and landbound—in Europe as much as in Asia—during the centuries before the industrial revolution, was in the hands of small business partnerships, the number of merchant travelling on each vessel must have been high. There were very few merchants capable of filling all the cargo space for any trading voyage on their own account. Most cargoes comprised the belongings of a number of merchants, ranging from those of some substance to lesser characters more akin to peddlers. But there were merchant princes who were, no doubt, similar to the eighteenth century Muslim magnate of the Gujarati port of Surat, Mulla Abdul Ghaffur, who owned seventeen seagoing vessels with a combined deadweight of more than 5000 tonnes, trading extensively in the Red Sea and the Persian Gulf at a time when indigenous trade was supposedly in decline.[11] But men like Ghaffur were the exception rather than the rule, and most maritime merchants were of less substance.

Though it is difficult to quantify numbers of indigenous merchants travelling across the Indian Ocean in the pre-modern period, records do exist for some of the more famous ports at particular times,

[11] Ashin Das Gupta, 1967, 11–12.

notably Melaka. It has been estimated that in the fifteenth century there were some 1000 Hindu and Muslim Gujarati merchants resident in Melaka, while 1000–2000 were on the move across the Bay of Bengal at any one time during the sailing season.[12] In addition to the Gujaratis there were also Chulia (Tamil Muslim), Keling (Tamil Hindu), Bengali, Persian, Armenian and Parsi merchants travelling the same routes. It has also been estimated that in the early seventeenth century, immediately before the rise of Dutch power in insular South East Asia, 1500 Javanese merchants annually travelled to Banda in search of spices, which they carried to ports such as Melaka for purchase by Portuguese, South Asian and Chinese merchants.[13]

By the early sixteenth century Gujarati merchants were pre-eminent in the trade networks of the Bay of Bengal and were taking a greater share in the trade with East Africa and the Middle East. Lesser partners in this trade were merchants from the Malabar and Coromandel coasts and the ports of Bengal, such as Chittagong, and the many tiny ports which were dotted across the riverine web of the Ganges delta. Many of these South Asians were Muslims, but Hindus and Jains were also involved. Gujaratis were also prominent in the vigorous coastal traffic of the subcontinent and in the traffic linking southern India with Sri Lanka and the Maldives.

In Melaka the Hindu Gujaratis formed a self-governing community in the city and had an important voice in the running of the port and at the court of the Muslim ruler. Numerically, their Muslim compatriots were less important, but they too formed distinct legal entities within the port, occupied their own quarters, and had their own mosques which were distinct from those of their Malay co-religionists. In time, the common practice of Islam tended to blur the boundaries between South Asian and local Muslims, and many wealthy foreign Muslim merchants intermarried with local ruling families, leading to an intermingling of South Asian and Malay Muslim culture.

It is not possible to quantify maritime traffic for other parts of the Indian Ocean. Across the Arabian Sea, South Asians intermingled with Arabs, Persians, Armenians and Jews. Muslims from the Middle East

[12] B. Schrieke, 1966, 12; K.S. Sandhu & P. Wheatley, 1983, vol. 1, 181.
[13] B. Schrieke, 1966, 24.

formed diasporas along the western coast of India, but in time they merged in with local Muslim communities. Hindu Gujaratis regularly visited the Middle East and formed ephemeral communities at entrepôts such as Hormuz and Aden. In contrast to voyages from Gujarat to South East Asia, those westward across the Arabian Sea were short, and a return voyage was easily timed in one sailing season, so that there were less pressing reasons to maintain substantial South Asian communities in the Middle East.

Middle Eastern and South Asian traders were also regular visitors to East African ports. Arabs and Persians established settlements in many of these ports, but within a few generations, intermarriage and the conversion of some African coastal communities to Islam blurred the lines of distinction between foreign and local Muslims, although status remained associated with claims to foreign ancestry.

Apart from groups we would clearly describe as merchants, there were other groups of people also involved in trade who it is more difficult to categorize. Examples of these are the Orang Laut and the Bugis of South East Asia. As we have seen earlier, the Orang Laut were central to the economic fortunes of Srivijaya and later to Melaka, both of whom depended upon their peddling activities as a means of collecting goods for more central marketplaces. From the seventeenth century the Orang Laut were displaced by the Bugis who worked closely with the Malay sultanate of Johor, which provided a haven for many refugees from Melaka after its capture by the Portuguese in 1511.[14]

By the sixteenth century the Bugis were employed by the rulers of Ayuthia as trading agents and as mercenaries. Even later, the Bugis were deliberately incorporated by the British East India Company into the maritime commercial network of Penang when it was established in 1786, and then into Singapore's trade network by Stamford Raffles, when he founded the city in 1819 as an outpost for British trade in South East Asia. They were not ousted from the maritime trade of Singapore until the mid-nineteenth century, when new types of European shipping and new forms of European commerce made them

[14] V. Matheson, 1975.

redundant partners in European maritime enterprise in insular South East Asia.[15]

By the fifteenth century the trade of the Indian Ocean sustained a great variety of different ethnic, cultural and religious groups who mingled with one another in ports from East Africa to the South China Sea. Given the complex and sustained nature of trade across the Ocean from at least 2000 years ago, it can be argued that the Indian Ocean was a positive 'entity' which shaped the development of many of the locales which comprised it, by offering opportunities for ready communication and trade, and not simply an empty space which separated them. The complex maritime trading network was also the facilitator of cultural diffusion and interaction, and until the nineteenth century, when it was undermined by new patterns of commercial and economic activity, it was the binding factor between peoples and cultures around the Indian Ocean.

The Discovery of Europe

During the fifteenth century the Portuguese embarked on a great series of voyages seeking access to the fabled wealth of Asia. European trade with Asia was dominated by Italian merchants who monopolized the extremely profitable trade in Indian Ocean spices between the Levant and Christian ports on the Mediterranean. The Italian stranglehold, anti-Muslim sentiment in Portugal resulting from centuries of Muslim domination, and gold hunger, combined to spur the Portuguese on a quest to seek a maritime route to the mysterious 'Indies'.

Since at least the thirteenth century, European travellers such as Marco Polo had entranced Europeans with marvellous tales of fantastic wealth, mighty kingdoms and strange peoples somewhere to the east, but the overland route to the east was firmly in Muslim hands after they drove the last Crusaders from Palestine and the Levant in the thirteenth century. Both Portugal and Spain were on the edge of the world known to Europeans; both were poor; both were imbued with anti-Muslim zeal, and both were hungry for gold.

The Portuguese set the pace in the fourteenth and sixteenth

[15] L.K. Wong, 1960.

centuries when they fruitlessly sought glory and wealth in North Africa, and then more successfully sought a glorious future in the Atlantic, winning territorial empires in Brazil and West Africa, and then in 1498 finally reaching India by sea. Driven by the same imperatives, the Spanish sought a route to the east by sailing westward, where they created an empire in the Americas, and then crossed the Pacific to gain a foothold in Asia with the conquest of the Philippines.

The arrival of the Portuguese in the Indian Ocean in 1498 not only revealed the Indian Ocean world to Europe, but revealed Europe to a new world, provoking a variety of local responses. To achieve their goal of establishing a trade monopoly of the invaluable spice trade between the Indian Ocean and Europe the Portuguese, ironically, were forced to work within the old Indian Ocean trade network. Only incidentally did they begin the process of integrating the economies of the Indian Ocean world into an evolving global commercial economy, by linking in Indian Ocean trade with that of the Atlantic and the Pacific.

The Portuguese did not completely undermine the ancient mechanisms of trade between Mediterranean Europe and the Indian Ocean, via the Middle East, or completely replace it with a·system linking northern Europe, via the Atlantic, to the Indian Ocean. They singularly failed to re-orient intercontinental trade; this was to be the legacy of the Dutch and the English companies which arrived after them.[16] The major result of Portuguese intrusion was the integration of European enterprise into ancient indigenous commercial networks, opening up chinks in the system which the Dutch and English companies were later to exploit as a means of gaining a foothold in Indian Ocean trade.

With their discovery of the Cape route to the fabled Indies, the Portuguese hoped to eliminate both the Muslim-dominated Middle East and the Italian and Catalan merchants of the Mediterranean from the spice trade between Europe and the Indian Ocean.[17] Portuguese motivations were complex and by no means uniform. There was no pre-existing plan for imperial expansion, and once it was under way

[16] Niels Steensgard, 1972.
[17] T.F. Earle and John Villiers, 1990.

it was subject to constant inflections and improvisations in response to changing conditions and factions in both Portugal and the *Estado da India*.[18] Some Portuguese were imbued with a crusading zeal against the Muslims which coloured their approach to the commercial world of the Indian Ocean; some sought Christian allies in Africa and Asia, responding to ancient legends of Christian Ethiopia enshrined in the legend of Prester John, but others—perhaps the majority—were simply motivated by the desire to trade.[19] Nor was there agreement among the Portuguese concerning the conduct of Asian commerce: whether through the agency of a Crown monopoly, or by free-ranging merchants operating independently of royal bureaucrats in Lisbon and at the various strongholds in the Indian Ocean.[20]

The Portuguese used many devices to capture the lucrative spice trade, with a variety of consequences for Indian Ocean peoples. The newcomers had several advantages over the locals in their quest for wealth. For one thing, theirs was—initially at least—a united and co-ordinated enterprise under the control of the Crown. In addition, unlike indigenous traders and rulers, the Portuguese had developed aggressive naval tactics which they were prepared to use to further their commercial ambitions if indigenous commercial groups and rulers refused them the right to trade.[21] Some indigenous states, most notably Mameluke Egypt, had warships, but none of them possessed the Portuguese sense of naval strategy or maintained significant standing navies. Finally, the naval technology of the Portuguese was without parallel in the Indian Ocean.

In the century before the discovery of the Cape route, Portuguese shipbuilders had adapted the refined maritime technology of Mediterranean Muslims to their own ships in the Atlantic, and had armed their ships with cannon. The result was vessels technologically and militarily superior to those of any other peoples, with the possible exception of the Chinese, who had withdrawn from maritime adventures in the mid-fifteenth century. Although the Chinese invented ship-borne artillery in the thirteenth century, unlike Europeans they

---

[18] Sanjay Subrahmanyam, 1990 (c).

[19] T.F. Earle and John Villiers, 1990.

[20] L.F. Thomaz, 1991.

[21] Ibid., 6.

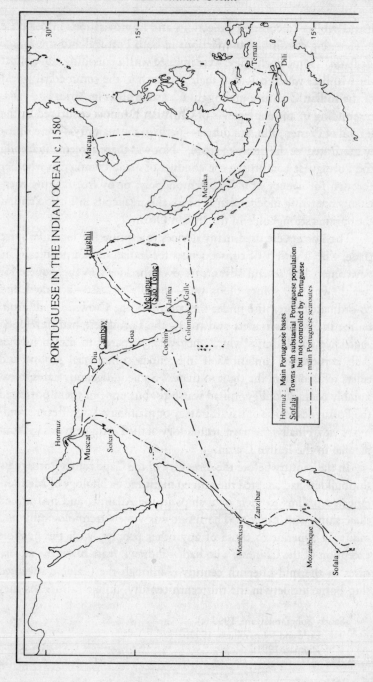

PORTUGUESE IN THE INDIAN OCEAN c. 1580

Hormuz : Main Portuguese bases
Sofala: Towns with substanial Portuguese population
but not controlled by Portuguese
-·-·-·- : main Portuguese searoutes

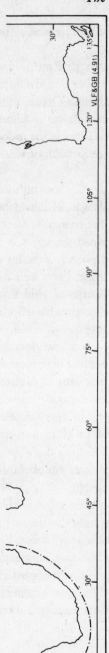

Map 10: The Portuguese in the Indian Ocean c.1580

never regarded it as a major part of the strategy of warfare, and all but abandoned its use in the late sixteenth century.

The superior maritime technology of the Portuguese must, however, be balanced against the shortfall in the number and condition of the ships they had available for service in the Indian Ocean. From the early sixteenth century there were constant complaints to Lisbon concerning access to careening and shipbuilding facilities in the Indian Ocean, as well as vivid accounts of the rapid deterioration of vessels in tropical and equatorial conditions.[22]

Using the advantages they possessed, the Portuguese captured strategically situated ports in a great arc from Sofala to Melaka, from which they hoped to dominate the sea lanes and the economic hinterlands of the Indian Ocean. The object of this broad strategy was to direct indigenous trade to Portuguese-controlled ports as a means of dominating the flow of spices and pepper to Europe. Ports were not chosen at random. Sofala was a prize as the source of gold from Zimbabwe which was used to pay for Portuguese cargoes from South and South East Asia; Hormuz was captured because it was linked, via Tabriz, to the markets of Central Asia, and also because of its location at the mouth of the Persian Gulf; Diu was seized because of its location close to the great cotton and silk textile exporting area of Gujarat; Goa because of its central importance in the maritime trade between the Deccan sultanates and the Middle East; Cochin because of its access to Malabar pepper; Colombo because of its cinnamon-rich hinterland and position astride a major sea route linking the western and eastern sectors of the Indian Ocean; while Melaka was obviously a key to the markets of South East Asia (See Map 10).

The Portuguese sense of purpose and will to violence would serve their ambitions well; however, it is wise not to draw the stereotype too far, for different strategies competed for ascendancy. Some, like Pedro Alvares Cabral in 1500, and the swashbuckling conqueror Albuquerque a few years later, set the Portuguese on a path of physical conquest.[23] Major Muslim ports from Sofala to Melaka were captured under such leaders, who envisioned a centralized mercantile and ter-

---

[22] T.F. Earle and John Villiers, 1990.
[23] Ibid.

ritorial empire operating within a Crown monopoly. Other Portuguese opposed Albuquerque's call for a territorial empire and sought a more cautious path to achieve their objectives. Such men invoked well-established Portuguese law which sanctioned mercantile cooperation with non-Christian peoples as an alternative to conquest and violence.

This latter group were pragmatists. The human and physical resources of the Portuguese were too limited to enable them to drive all Muslims from the high seas, or to create any sort of maritime trading monopoly. Practicalities alone forced the Portuguese into conciliation more often than violence in the trading world of the Indian Ocean. Furthermore, commercial exchange between Europe and the Indian Ocean remained limited until the eighteenth century, inhibiting the development of an overwhelming and stable system of Europe-Indian Ocean maritime trade.

The basic problem for the Portuguese, and later for the Dutch and the English, was that Europe had little to exchange for Indian Ocean cargoes except for bullion, and metals such as copper, which since ancient times had been in short supply in the Indian Ocean world. But contemporary European fiscal thinking was that bullion should, under all circumstances, be conserved.

The unleashing of the silver of the Americas and Japan upon world trade during the late sixteenth century in part resolved this problem, but it also encouraged inflation and so was to an extent, self-defeating. The more practical solution to financing imports was to work the Indian Ocean maritime commercial system as the locals had done for centuries—that is, to engage in segmented trading voyages within the Indian Ocean world in order to generate profit which could eventually be returned to Europe in the form of bulk cargoes of spices and other exotic goods.

In practice, this forced the Portuguese to undergo an apprenticeship in co-operation with indigenous mercantile groups. Although the religious and mercantile biases of the Portuguese and their failure to break into the indigenous pepper trade initially spurred them to attempt to brutally stifle the Muslim spice trade across the Arabian Sea, from Africa and South Asia to the Middle East, the realities of trade soon drove them into closer alliances with indigenous traders and rulers, which were sometimes closer than the authorities at Lisbon and Goa may have wished. In the Persian Gulf, most notably at Hormuz, along the East African coast and elsewhere, the Portuguese achieved a *modus vivendi* with Muslims, when it became possible for them to use their naval power to profitably participate in trade and to extract taxes from local traders and shippers, rather than to destroy them. In many parts of the Indian Ocean the Portuguese used the threat of their superior naval power to impose trading licences (*cartazes*) on local shipowners as a means of extracting profit from commercial systems they were unable to dominate. This produced revenue for the Crown, which in time came to exceed the profits of legitimate trade. But force and licences aside, the Portuguese still had to obtain cargoes for Europe, and to do this they had to work themselves into the interstices of local trade networks, where opportunities were offered by politics and diplomacy.

To turn a profit and secure cargoes of spices and rare goods for Europe, the Portuguese had to peddle goods and bullion from Europe and East Asia around the Indian Ocean, along with cargoes of local origin. They had, in effect, to secure a place in traditional trade. To do this, the *Estado da India* not only incorporated traditional networks but modified its monopolistic claims by developing a system of concessions which allowed some Portuguese private traders into the official enterprise, extending its tentacles deeper into the interstices of traditional trade. In this way they appropriated some of the trade between East Africa and South Asia in gold, ivory and textiles; between the Middle East and South Asia in pepper, textiles, bullion, cinnamon and horses; between South and South East Asia in cotton and silk textiles; and between South Asia, South East Asia, China and Japan in pepper, sandalwood, silk, ceramics, silver and copper. Locally they sought corners in the short-haul traffic, carrying elephants, areca nuts and cinnamon from Sri Lanka to the Malabar and Coromandel coasts; cowries from the Maldives to Bengal; and rice from Bengal and the Coromandel and Kanara coasts, to other parts of South Asia, the Persian Gulf and to insular South East Asia.

To survive, the Portuguese had to explore the nooks and crannies of the Indian Ocean, and to enlist local assistance. In doing so, they opened up the Indian Ocean world to the mind of Europe, beginning the process of breaking down its insularity and laying the foundations for its later integration with a multi-regional capitalist global economy.

The problems facing Portuguese enterprise were formidable. Force frequently proved inadequate to deal with the hostility of local merchants and sailors, and on land the Portuguese had to face the overwhelming power of indigenous imperial regimes such as the Ottomans (c.1453–1921) in the Arab Middle East, the Safavids (1501–1722) of Persia, the Mughals (1526–1857) in South Asia, and the Ming dynasty (1368–1644) in China, who could curb Portuguese excesses by closing off the ports which were central to the existence of the *Estado*. Thus, while the Portuguese may have controlled Hormuz, at the mouth of the Persian Gulf, and Diu, on the Gujarat coast, the exercise of power out of these bases was restrained by the knowledge that their prosperity depended upon access to hinterland markets which were controlled by strong Muslim dynasties (See Map 11).

Smaller states could also pose formidable threats. In South East Asia, the Muslim sultanate of Aceh in Sumatra used cannons supplied by its Ottoman allies to besiege Melaka on several occasions during the sixteenth century, while refugees from Melaka established a powerful trading state at Johor to the south of Melaka on the Malay peninsula. There, in alliance with the itinerant Orang Laut, they built up an aggressive mercantile force with whom the Dutch were to ally themselves in 1641 to drive the Portuguese from Melaka. In southern India too, much closer to the viceroy's seat of power at Goa, Muslims from the Malabar coast allied themselves with anti-Portuguese rulers in Sri Lanka and formed roving armed fleets which preyed upon Portuguese shipping. The Portuguese failed to wipe out these fleets, some of which were used by the Mughals out of the port of Surat to defend indigenous trading and hajj vessels from Portuguese attacks on the run between Surat and the Middle East.

Throughout the sixteenth century Portuguese ambitions in the Indian Ocean were also curbed by shortages of manpower, shipping and capital. The small nation's empire stretched from Brazil to the Moluccas, and its limited human resources were constantly depleted by the ravages of exotic tropical and equatorial diseases. Between 1580 and 1640 Spain controlled Portugal, dragging the nation into war with the English, and diverting much needed resources—in terms of

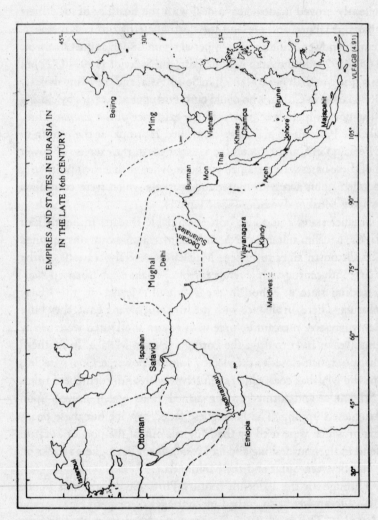

Map 11: Empires and States in Eurasia in the late 16th Century

men, ships and treasure—from the *Estado*. In time, the balance of Lisbon's interests shifted from the Indian Ocean to Brazil and Angola in the Atlantic, further undermining the ability of the *Estado da India* to extend its power, or even to exercise close supervision of its servants, private Portuguese traders and indigenous mercantile groups.

Portuguese pretensions to a monopoly of maritime trade were resented and challenged, where possible, by indigenous groups. Most galling of all, a growing number of Portuguese adventurers, merchants, renegades and corrupt royal officials either ignored official rules or moved beyond the authority of the *Estado da India* and the concession system. These mavericks traded on their own account, undermining the profitability of the Crown's operations and further integrating European trading enterprise into the traditional commercial system of the Indian Ocean world.[24] It was this unofficial Portuguese trade which in the long run was to enable a more thorough European penetration of local economies. The commercial successes of the English from the early seventeenth until the late eighteenth century were, in part at least, based upon the knowledge and co-operation of private Portuguese trading groups in South and South East Asia.

The Portuguese Impact

The intimacy of private Portuguese traders with traditional trading groups and practices belies the view that the Portuguese overwhelmed the indigenous world of the Indian Ocean as the Spanish did in the Americas in the sixteenth century, although it is true that they introduced new levels of violence and state interference in maritime affairs. However, they did begin the process of weaving economic linkages between the world of Europe and the Indian Ocean which would reduce the Indian Ocean world to a region of a much larger capitalist world economy in the eighteenth and nineteenth centuries, when economic changes in western Europe drastically changed the nature of European imports, and hence European economic interest in the Indian Ocean region.

This is not to suggest, however, that Portuguese activity had no

---

[24] Sanjay Subrahmanyam, 1990(a).

impact upon the indigenous maritime trading network. In the western Indian Ocean, Muslim shipping was badly mauled and the spice trade through the Red Sea and the Persian Gulf was slowly strangled; although this may have been due as much to the decline throughout the sixteenth and seventeenth centuries in the European price of pepper and spices, as to Portuguese violence. The resulting decline of the Middle East's ancient function as the pivot between the Indian Ocean and the Mediterranean was disastrous for the ports of the Levant and, in the longer term, for the Italian trading cities and the merchants of Catalonia.[25] Ironically, the commercial impact of the Portuguese in the Red Sea and the Persian Gulf was muted by the rise of the Ottoman and Safavid empires, which restored political and economic stability in the area and encouraged a partial revival of Middle Eastern ports and hinterland markets dealing in the imports of tropical Asia and Africa for local consumption.

But while the Portuguese precipitated a decline in the maritime linkage between the Arabian Sea and the Bay of Bengal in the sixteenth century, the snapping of this ancient linkage did not lead to Portuguese domination of either section of the Indian Ocean. Both sections developed their own indigenous systems in opposition to Portuguese ambitions.

In the Arabian Sea the Portuguese had insufficient power to seal off either the coast of East Africa, or trade through the Red Sea and the Gulf. Certainly, with the capture of Sofala the Portuguese fatally undermined the ancient flow of gold which they now appropriated, but elsewhere they were conspicuously unsuccessful in destroying Muslim enterprise. Even Albuquerque, with much Muslim blood on his hands, was driven to use Muslims in administrative posts and as middlemen in trade.[26]

In the mid-sixteenth century attempts were made to link up with the Coptic Christians of Ethiopia, on the Red Sea flank of the Muslim Ottoman empire. But arrogance, Roman Catholic intolerance of Coptic Christianity, the failure to capture Aden and control the Red Sea, and greed, disrupted this adventure and drove the Coptic Christians

[25] Niels Steensgard, 1973; C.H. Wake, 1979; E. Ashtor, 1980.
[26] T.F. Earle and John Villiers, 1990.

deeper into their ancient isolation in the mountains of Ethiopia. In the Middle East, although the Portuguese had restricted the Ottoman navy to the Red Sea and faced no maritime threat from the Safavids in the Persian Gulf, their presence was restricted to the ports of Muscat and Hormuz, indicating the limited nature of their military and naval resources; and in East Africa, to captured Swahili ports in a line south from Mombasa (which they seized in 1592) to the ports and river valleys of Mozambique.

In the Bay of Bengal the Portuguese had no more success in their early efforts to stifle local trading initiatives. On the east coast of India Muslim merchants from Masulipatnam (first the major port for the Muslim sultanate of Golconda, and then for the Mughal-controlled Deccan) established a thriving trade with South East Asia where, at the Thai court of Ayuthia in particular, South Asian Muslims played a prominent role in local trade and politics until well into the eighteenth century.

For other indigenous groups, and in other areas, the impact of the Portuguese was different. In Sri Lanka, Goa, and on the Malabar coast at Cochin they reduced many local rulers and merchants to subservience. But even in these areas Portuguese domination was readily challenged. In Sri Lanka the Portuguese controlled most of the coastal districts but failed to overwhelm the Buddhist mountain kingdom of Kandy, which retained its independence until conquered by the British in the early nineteenth century. This forced them to maintain a costly military presence which was engaged in long and fruitless wars with Kandy, although their resources were too limited to maintain a significant locally-based naval force which was needed to eliminate Muslim maritime commerce and to prevent Kandy trading in its own right. Along the Malabar coast Muslims developed very effective fleets of armed vessels to resist Portuguese pretensions, and in the Maldives, Portuguese control lasted barely a decade.

Generally in South Asia, where most of their human and military resources were located, the Portuguese could not play the overlord and were forced into more subtle diplomacies to survive. This was particularly true in areas such as the Indo-Gangetic plain, which was dominated by the expanding Mughal dynasty; central India, which comprised a constellation of powerful Muslim kingdoms (the Deccan sultanates) which fell to the Mughals during the seventeenth century; and the far south, which was held by vigorous Hindu warrior groups such as the Nayaks.

At the Mughal court Roman Catholic priests from Goa attempted to convert the great Mughal ruler Akbar (ruled 1556–1605) to Christianity, and into an alliance with the Portuguese, as he consolidated his hold over the northern reaches of South Asia from the Arabian Sea to the Bay of Bengal.[27] In central India the Portuguese supplied Arabian and Persian cavalry horses, Sri Lankan cinnamon, and other exotic imports through their port at Goa to various Deccan sultanates. Relations were generally good, given the dependence of local rulers for vital imports through Goa. On the Coromandel and Andhra coasts at indigenous-controlled ports such as São Tome and Masulipatnam, the Portuguese position was much more tenuous, for here they had to compete on an equal footing with indigenous traders who had established regular links with ports in Sumatra and on the Arakan and Tenasserim coasts, all of which lay outside the pale of Portuguese influence.

In the Hindu empire of Vijayanagara the Portuguese were cordially received, for they controlled the vital horse trade with the Persian Gulf. This cordiality was proffered, despite the fact that along the coasts of southern India Portuguese priests and officials interfered in local politics and the free flow of Vijayanagara's maritime trade. For example, on the Madurai coast—the 'Fisheries Coast'—the Portuguese encouraged the conversion of Hindu fishing and seafaring groups, such as the Paravas, to Christianity. Their objectives were not to undermine the authority of local potentates but to control the local pearl fisheries and to win allies against local Muslim trading groups. These groups were supported by well-armed Malabari Muslim fleets in the seas between Sri Lanka and western India, which threatened Portuguese access to local trade. Muslims held a major share of the maritime trade of the far south and were moving to exploit the rich pearl beds of the Gulf of Manaar which had previously been worked by Hindus Paravas. By converting and supporting various Hindu

[27] J. Correia–Afonso, 1991.

groups under economic pressure from Muslims, the Portuguese managed to gain a foothold astride the vital sea route between southern Indian, Sri Lanka and South East Asia, as well as a share in the coastal trade of the far south and control of the pearl fisheries.

At Melaka the Portuguese preferred to collaborate with Keling merchants from the Coromandel coast, driving Gujarati, Bengali and Chulia merchant communities from the city, although they encouraged Javanese Muslim merchants to remain, in recognition of their importance in accessing the ports of Java which were beyond Portuguese control. The expulsion of most Muslim merchants from Melaka encouraged the growth of the staunchly anti-Portuguese Muslim port of Aceh, on the northern tip of Sumatra, which was already expanding to control the rich pepper lands of western Sumatra, and minor alternatives to Melaka northward (at Kedah) and southward (at Johor) from the great entrepôt along the tin-rich Malay peninsula. From these ports, and others elsewhere in South East Asia, South Asian Muslim merchants continued to play a role in the maritime trade of the area until the early nineteenth century. In addition to South Asian Muslim merchants, indigenous itinerant trading groups such as the Orang Laut, and later the Bugis, continued to flourish, most notably out of the port of Johor.

On the more positive side, Portuguese purchases and new crops they introduced gave a boost to local economies. In southern India, potatoes, chilli, tobacco and pineapples were added to agricultural crops, while in Sri Lanka cinnamon production expanded greatly in the Portuguese-controlled lowlands. In southern Sulawesi the new port of Makassar flourished throughout the sixteenth and seventeenth centuries as an independent entrepôt for mace, nutmeg and cloves between the spice-rich Moluccas, the Portuguese at Melaka, Muslim-controlled Masulipatnam, China, and the English and Dutch companies.

Eastward from South Asia, Portuguese physical power was at its weakest. Mighty Melaka and lesser Portuguese outposts scattered throughout the Indonesian archipelago, where the *Estado* was present only as a mercantile force and not as a sovereign power, survived on the diplomatic wits of the Portuguese as well as their ability to trade with indigenous merchants and to divide their enemies. Ironically, given their physical weakness in this area, it was east of Melaka that the Portuguese were to have their greatest economic impact.

It was the Portuguese who opened up China to direct trade with Europe, when the Chinese imperial authorities granted them a trading base on the tiny island of Macao on the estuary of the Pearl river, in 1557. From Goa and Melaka came sandalwood, ivory, ebony and, above all, Peruvian silver, in return for Chinese silk thread, satins, copper, mercury, camphor and ceramics.

Some of these products filtered back to European and Indian Ocean markets, but others were carried in the annual 'Great Ship' which sailed from Macao to Nagasaki. There they were exchanged for silver and copper, which were fed back into the Chinese and Indian Ocean trading network. The Spanish, on the other hand, traded with China and insular South East Asia through Manila on the edge of the Pacific, which they occupied in 1571. In exchange for Mexican and Peruvian silver, brought across the Pacific from Acapulco in two great galleons annually, Philippine markets absorbed Chinese cotton cloth, while the Spanish loaded valuable return cargoes of silk thread, spices and pepper—with porcelain as ballast—for Latin America and Spain, via Mexico.

Until the latter half of the sixteenth century the Chinese imperial authorities remained hostile to maritime trade. They were affronted by the Portuguese occupation of Melaka, which they considered a Chinese protectorate, and were particularly concerned with the violence of the Portuguese, to the extent that they debated sending an expeditionary force to drive the Portuguese from Melaka and banned Sino-Portuguese trade between 1521 and 1557. China's demand for silver increased, however, following the adoption of silver coinage, from the fifteenth century, and by the late sixteenth century imports of silver from Japan had to be supplemented by imports of silver from Portuguese and Spanish sources. The need for silver also modified Chinese official attitudes towards Chinese civilian participation in maritime commerce, and the nature of Chinese imports and exports. Antipathy towards the Portuguese waned in official circles, and in 1567 Chinese civilians were permitted to trade overseas, although the export of silver was forbidden and foreign traders were restricted to specific Chinese ports. Chinese ships once more appeared in the South

China Sea, but shipbuilding in China had suffered from the imperial proscription of the late fifteenth century and never recovered to build great junks like Zheng He had sailed across the Indian Ocean.

Between them the Portuguese and the Spanish encompassed the world in the sixteenth century. Their impact was varied. In many places it was destructive—more so in Spanish dominions than in Portuguese—but it also began the slow process of opening up economies in Asia, Africa and the Americas to the direct influence of European economic rhythms.

The economies of the Indian Ocean world responded to this in different ways. Europeans were still on the periphery of Asian and African economic life, although during the sixteenth and seventeenth centuries they drew closer to the centre. The Portuguese, however, were never to overwhelm the centre. It was not until the advent of industrial capitalism, and the marriage of commercial and political interests in Europe in the late eighteenth century, that the English (or British as they should be called after the Union between the English and Scots Parliaments in 1707) in particular, were able, literally and metaphorically, to break out of the boundaries of the coastal enclaves they traded from in the Indian Ocean.

Overall, the impact of the Portuguese upon indigenous commercial networks must be assessed against a backdrop of an evolving and vital indigenous political environment, changing Portuguese official attitudes and the activities of private Portuguese traders. Portuguese official policy changed markedly from the sixteenth century, reflecting the rise and fall of many factions within the Indian Ocean and at the royal court. There was no stereotypical Portuguese policy or attitude, but rather a range of policies and attitudes reflecting the changing economic and political fortunes of Portugal on the world stage.[28]

Portuguese economic fortunes were intimately affected by the collapse of Vijayanagara and the consequent decay of its trade; by the rise of Masulipatnam as the gateway to the Deccan sultanate of Golconda; the presence of vigorous states on the Arakan coast, and in Burma and Thailand with an aggressive interest in trade; the expansion of Aceh and its direct pepper trade with the Red Sea; the

[28] Sanjay Subrahmanyam, 1988 (c) and in press.

rise to power of the Ottoman, Safavid and Mughal empires, all of which controlled major ports on the shores of the Indian Ocean; and the closing of Japan to Portuguese enterprise.

Similarly, the impact of the Portuguese upon the trade of the Indian Ocean cannot be considered solely within the confines of the operations of the *Estado da India.* By the middle of the sixteenth century Portuguese private trade, illegally or operating through the concession system administered by the *Estado*, was pushing European knowledge and experience well beyond the formal boundaries of Portuguese power. Private Portuguese trade, which increased during the seventeenth century as that of the Crown decreased, opened up new routes, penetrated indigenous systems and established a network of contacts and information that was vital to the daily existence of the *Estado*, and later to the Dutch, English and Danish companies who were far from loathe to use the services of the Portuguese private trader.[29]

And even more Europeans

During the seventeenth century various other European trading nations—most notably the Dutch, English and Danes—entered the maritime trading world of the Indian Ocean in search of the fabulous cargoes the Portuguese had introduced to Europe via the Atlantic.

In the first half of the sixteenth century the merchants of England and ports in the Low Countries—later to be known as the Netherlands and Belgium—obtained Indian Ocean goods via the markets of Lisbon. In the latter half of the sixteenth century, however, the English and the Dutch (the inhabitants of the northern half of the provinces which made up the Spanish-controlled Low Countries, the Netherlands) broke with Roman Catholicism to form various Protestant Churches which were bitterly hated by the Roman Catholic rulers of Spain and Portugal. Protestant traders were barred from the great markets of Lisbon and Cadiz in Spain, which were the main centres for the distribution of American, African and Asian commodities to ports in northern Europe.

[29] Sanjay Subrahmanyam, in press.

To survive, English merchants such as Francis Drake and Walter Raleigh were forced into preying upon the Spanish and Portuguese convoys bringing the exports of the Americas, Africa and Asia to Europe. The Protestant Dutch soon followed the English and by the 1580s had achieved their independence from Spain. By the 1590s both the English and the Dutch had moved beyond piracy in the Atlantic to forming companies of merchants who pooled their finances to outfit convoys which traded directly with the pepper and spice markets of the fabled 'Indies' as well as with West Africa, South America and the Caribbean: such were the origins of the Dutch and English joint stock companies which began to trade in the Indian Ocean in the first decade of the seventeenth century.

The English and the Dutch companies entered the trade of the Indian Ocean in search of pepper and spices. The economies of England and the Netherlands had taken on a mercantile flavour, with the growth of larger merchant marines and powerful merchant lobbies. Religious antipathy was compounded by growing economic rivalry, as the focal point of European economic growth moved from the Mediterranean to the Atlantic and North Sea. The English and the Dutch navies were initially weaker than either the Portuguese or Spanish, but their economies were to prove more efficient and durable.

This new European thrust into the spice trade was organized by national monopolistic companies. The most important of these were the English East India Company (EIC)(1600), the Dutch Vereenidge Oost-Indische Compagnie (VOC)(1602), the Dansk Ostindiske Kompagni (1616), and the French Compagnie des Indes (1664), which were made up of merchants who had invested capital in return for a share in exclusive national trade with the Indian Ocean world. During the eighteenth century several other companies were formed: the Ostend Company (1722–31), the Swedish East India Company (1731), two Prussian Asiatic Companies (1751 and 1753), the Imperial Austrian Company (1770s), and the Spanish Philippine Company (1784). With the exception of the Spanish Company, this last group simply comprised 'covers' for merchants attempting to infringe the monopoly of the big four in European trade with the Indies (See Map 12).

Unlike the *Estado*, the larger European companies were not state

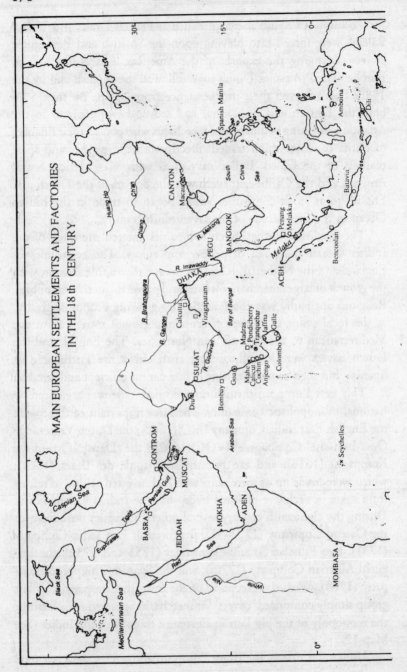

MAIN EUROPEAN SETTLEMENTS AND FACTORIES
IN THE 18th CENTURY

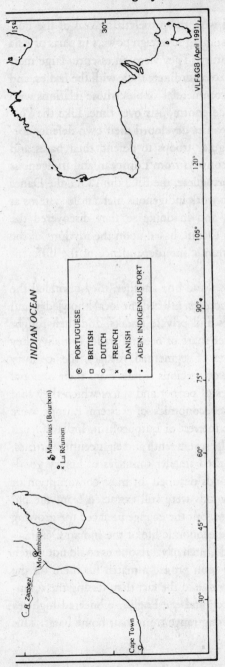

Map 12: Main European Settlements and Factories in the 18th Century

enterprises, were not imbued with the proselytizing zeal of the Portuguese, and did not begin assuming sovereign powers in parts of Asia
until the late seventeenth century. They were, in essence, large merchant corporations organized to co-ordinate trade with the Indies, and
were controlled by domestic commercial lobbies whose relations with
their home governments varied enormously over time. Like the Portuguese, however, these companies developed their own defence forces, comprising bodies of regular troops to defend their bases and
armed ships to protect their convoys from European and indigenous
rivals. In addition, like the Portuguese, the EIC, the VOC, the Danes
and the French were forced to work indigenous mercantile systems as
a means of securing profits, and in doing so they discovered the
structural unity of the Indian Ocean, based upon the rhythms of the
monsoon winds and the economic interdependence of the different
lands bordering the Ocean.[30]

Enemies of the Portuguese, and one another, they humbled the
Estado da India, copied its structures, utilized the local knowledge and
skills of Portuguese renegades and private traders, and then fought
among themselves for a greater share of oceanic trade. Initially, they
too participated in the system of segmented voyages, the 'country
trade', to minimize the drain of precious metals from their national
economies and pay for cargoes of pepper and spices which they sold
in northern Europe. But the economies of western Europe were
changing radically, as was the interest of Europeans in Indian Ocean
maritime trade. Throughout the seventeenth and eighteenth centuries,
Europe-bound cargoes comprised smaller tonnages of luxury goods
and increasing tonnages of goods destined for mass consumption or
processing in Europe. Such goods were still extracted from the old
Indian Ocean economic system, but the change prefaced the growing
role Europe was to play in the economic life of the Indian Ocean.

While initially English and Dutch naval resources could not match
those of the Portuguese, they soon proved a match for them on the
high seas. This was principally due to the fact that, during the seventeenth century, both the Dutch and the English pioneered high-sea
fleets capable of operating at long range from their home bases. This

---

[30] K.N. Chaudhuri, 1985, 83.

was a revolutionary development, for it also incorporated the concept of naval stations in various parts of the world, thus increasing the range of naval operations. The Portuguese did not develop this strategy, and consequently were at a fatal disadvantage when control of strategically important waters decided the balance of power among the nations of western Europe.

Like the Portuguese, neither the English nor the Dutch could match the land-based power of major indigenous states in either South Asia or the Middle East. Both the English and the Dutch were primarily interested in the spices and pepper of insular South East Asia and South Asia, and both began their commerce in these areas by courting the support of indigenous rulers. Embassies were sent to the Mughal court seeking trading privileges which both nations gained at Surat on the Gulf of Cambay, but advantages were easier to obtain in the islands of the Indies. Both the English and the Dutch established trading bases on Java in 1602, at Bantam, before moving to Jakarta. Unlike the English, however, the Dutch used their base at Jakarta, in the seventeenth century, as a springboard from which to capture Portuguese bases such as Melaka, Galle, Colombo, Jaffna and Cochin.

Outmanoeuvred by the Dutch in insular South East Asia, the English had to be content with various minor factories on Borneo and Sumatra, and a cluster of factories in Gujarat at Surat, Broach and Cambay until 1639. In that year a local ruler granted the EIC the obscure village of Madras on the central Coromandel coast as their first territorial possession in Asia.

Apart from insular South East Asia, vigorous indigenous states expanded on land during the sixteenth and seventeenth centuries and were assiduously courted by European embassies. The Ottoman empire increased its control over the waters of the Red Sea during the sixteenth century, following the conquest of Egypt in 1516 and the subsequent occupation of the Hejaz and Yemen, although the Mameluke navy had been driven from the Arabian Sea, following its defeat off Diu in Gujarat by the Portuguese in 1508; the Safavids secured Afghanistan, the Caucasus and much of Central Asia during the sixteenth and seventeenth centuries; and the Mughals moved out of the central Indo-Gangetic plain to occupy its extremities in Gujarat and Bengal from the mid-sixteenth century, and the Deccan and much of southern India during the seventeenth century. None of these empires had navies to match those of the European interlopers, but they were sufficiently strong on land to restrain any significant territorial European incursions into the Indian subcontinent until the mid eighteenth century, and into the Middle East until the late nineteenth century.

The EIC, VOC and the Danes were bitterly opposed by the Portuguese, and their entry into the Indian Ocean heralded an outburst of naval warfare which revealed a will to violence on the part of the newcomers, matching that of the Portuguese. The brunt of this violence was initially directed against the Portuguese, but the Dutch and English companies soon fell out among themselves over trade, and also turned upon their weaker indigenous rivals. The VOC effectively barred the EIC from any major share in the maritime trade of South East Asia, and in South Asia shadowed the establishment of English factories in Gujarat, as well as taking over Portuguese forts on the Malabar coast.

Apart from its greater financial and shipping resources, at least in the seventeenth century, the VOC differed from its English rival in one very important respect. Unlike the EIC, it was prepared to be deliberately and consistently aggressive to achieve its ends. The VOC was more willing than the EIC to expend considerable funds on military activity, and prefaced later European territorial expansion by seizing land in insular South East Asia to control the production as well as the distribution of goods. Key spice producing islands in the Moluccas were the first victims of Dutch expansion in Asia, which continued from the early 1600s to the early 1900s.

Initially weaker than the Portuguese, the English and the Dutch companies had to temper their naval resources with subtle diplomacy, currying favour with rulers disenchanted with the Portuguese. Thus, the VOC allied itself with the rulers of Johor and Kandy to drive the Portuguese from Melaka and Sri Lanka; the EIC and the VOC provided ships to defend Mughal hajj and cargo ships from Portuguese attacks and exactions on the run from Surat to the Red Sea and Persian Gulf; while the EIC formed an alliance with Persia, which resulted in the establishment of a Company trading post (known as a factory) at

Jask in 1616 and the eviction of the Portuguese from Hormuz in 1622..

Service for the Mughals, the Safavids, the sheikhs of the Persian Gulf, petty rulers on the Coromandel and Malabar coasts, and the embittered kings and sultans of Sri Lanka and insular South East Asia, insinuated the English and Dutch companies into local politics. Where their involvement in factional politics found them on the winning side, they were able to advance their trading interests at the expense of the Portuguese. However, like the Portuguese, neither the Dutch nor the English companies hesitated to attack weaker indigenous groups to enforce their mercantile demands. In this manner the Dutch insinuated themselves into the politics of Java where, during the seventeenth century, they brought key coastal areas under their control, eliminating indigenous opposition and isolating the English from any major share in the commerce of the island.

The French company followed a similar pattern of allying itself with local rulers to win trade concessions. In the eighteenth century the most spectacular area of such French activity was to be southern India, but in the previous century the French briefly entered into an alliance with the Thai kingdom of Ayuthia which was concerned about pressure from the VOC. The Thai alliance collapsed when the French became too insistent upon stationing troops at Mergui and Bangkok, and talked too openly of converting the king to Christianity. Some time before the Mergui and Bangkok incidents, a French company (the Societé de l'Orient ou de Madagascar) embarked on a futile attempt to establish settlements on the coast of Madagascar; this venture, along with plans to infiltrate Ayuthia, was abandoned after 1664 when the French government established the Compagnie des Indes Orientales to focus French ambitions upon India.

In the seventeenth century the VOC concentrated its efforts on taking control of the major spice-producing islands in the Moluccas; securing Java; gaining exclusive access to Chinese gold and Japanese silver and copper; and cornering the lucrative textile trade between South Asia and insular South East Asia. In insular South East Asia, by the late seventeenth century, they had driven out the Portuguese and their erstwhile rivals, the English, and were making handsome profits from the South Asia textile trade and the Japan trade. Indigenous merchants and producers were, where possible, subjected to restrictions aimed at undermining their independence and incorporating them into the VOC's commercial empire, as the Dutch attempted to extend a trading monopoly from the Moluccas to Sumatra. The VOC, for example, copied the hated Portuguese pass system in the Bay of Bengal in an attempt to increase its revenues and exercise some supervision over local shipping.

Unlike the Portuguese, however, the Dutch company refused to integrate the private trading activities of its nationals into its official system. By the eighteenth century corruption among company servants who were denied a legal trading status had reached such heights that it posed a serious challenge to the profitability of the VOC. In the long term this policy hampered the growth of individual Dutch mercantile activity and local knowledge, limiting the ability of the VOC to make the transition from company trade to capitalist entrepreneurial activity in the eighteenth century. The EIC on the other hand, solved the problem of errant servants and the poaching of private British merchants, often acting in co-operation with private and renegade Portuguese trading and shipping interests, by incorporating them into its official system during the eighteenth century. The EIC itself concentrated upon the Asia-Europe trade, leaving intra-Asian trade to private British traders whose remitted profits financed the Company's return cargoes. Such men were ideally equipped to further British commercial interests after 1813, when free traders in Britain managed to strip the EIC of its commercial monopolies.

Seeking a more efficient sea passage in the seventeenth century, the Dutch pioneered a more direct route to the spice islands, eliminating the long haul via South Asia. They established a revictualling base at Cape Town as the Portuguese had planned to do in the 1560s, and, using the Roaring Forties, they sailed from the Cape towards the western coast of Australia before turning north for Java. The ancient spice routes were, in part, neglected by the Dutch until they realized that they could not excise their interests from the inter-locking maritime trading world of the Indian Ocean. In addition, the Dutch soon found that, like the Portuguese, they could not so easily discount Malay and Chinese commercial activity in insular South East Asia. Despite occasional massacres, the Chinese were never to be eliminated from commerce in insular South East Asia, while Malay commercial activity was to survive the Dutch onslaught, until fatally undermined by the spread of capitalism in the nineteenth century.

In South Asia during the seventeenth century, the Portuguese, the VOC and the EIC struggled for access to the cloth and grain export trade to other parts of the Indian Ocean in order to accumulate profits for investment in cargoes of spices and pepper for Europe from South East Asia. During this century the VOC drove the Portuguese from the Japan trade (securing a vital source of copper and silver), Melaka, Sri Lanka and the Malabar coast, and established factories along the western and eastern coasts of India. The VOC moved beyond simply controlling ports, as the Portuguese had done, to establishing either direct or indirect control of spice- and pepper-producing areas in the Moluccas, coastal Sri Lanka and the Malabar coast, from strategically placed ports such as Makassar, Jakarta (Batavia), Melaka, Colombo and Cochin. They also briefly held the island of Taiwan as a means of gaining access to gold exports from China. The EIC, on the other hand, was almost entirely restricted to coastal India, in competition with the VOC, the weakening Portuguese official establishment and flourishing private Portuguese merchants.

Although the English and the Dutch began their ventures in the Indian Ocean as friends and allies against the Portuguese and Spanish, the relationship soon soured. The exclusive policies of the VOC in South East Asia angered the English, who found themselves edged out of the lucrative spice trade and physically driven out of some of their factories.

The success of the Dutch in evicting the Portuguese from so many of their possessions no doubt encouraged further Dutch arrogance and English jealousy. This was particularly true in South Asia, where their rivalry was only kept in check by the overwhelming presence of the Mughal empire. Anglo-Dutch rivalry was further compounded by events in Europe, where the two nations fought a series of naval wars in which France supported the Dutch, while the English sought allies in Spain and Portugal. By the 1660s any semblance of Anglo-Dutch accord was gone, wasted by conflict in Europe and Asia. The English moved into a formal alliance with Portugal, which was sealed by the marriage of Charles II to Catherine of Braganza and the transfer of

the island of Bombay to the English crown in 1661. This new alliance
isolated the Dutch in South Asia. It set them against the Portuguese
and English, who between them possessed a formidable string of
coastal factories from Gujarat to Bengal where the EIC established its
first factory at Hooghly in 1650, under agreement with the Mughals.

Against this background of intensifying rivalry, all the European
trading groups engaged in the intra-regional or 'country trade', seeking
a variety of cargoes in a bid to return a profit to crown or shareholders.
South Asian cotton textiles were hawked across the Indian Ocean by
European companies, who also edged into the rice trade of the subcontinent and the shipment of Maldivian cowries and cheap South
Asian cotton cloth to West Africa, as payment for cargoes of slaves
destined for the Americas. In the process, the VOC and the EIC found
themselves, as had the Portuguese, reliant upon the cooperation and
goodwill of indigenous merchants. Ironically, both companies—most
particularly the EIC—found co-operation with long established private Portuguese traders vital if they were to gain access to local
marketing networks. The trading activities of the EIC and the VOC
made the fortunes of many indigenous and private Portuguese merchants. This was especially true in southern India, where local merchants who held overlapping interests in overseas, coastal and inland
trade, as well as in local government and revenue collection, were well
placed to provide export commodities for the coast-based Europeans.[31]

By the mid-seventeenth century the VOC was leading all its
European rivals in Indian Ocean trade. Its fortunes were based upon
the trade in South Asian textiles from Gujarat, the Coromandel coast
and Bengal to South East Asia, and the Japan trade, in return for
cargoes of spices, copper and silver for other parts of the Indian Ocean
and for Europe.

The Dutch had successfully excluded the EIC from the spice trade
of South East Asia and had forced them to concentrate their activities
on the Coromandel coast, from where they attempted to compete
with the VOC in the export of South Asian textiles. Neither the VOC
nor the EIC had essentially altered the patterns of European mercantile

[31] Sanjay Subrahmanyam and C.A. Bayly, 1988, 401–24; Sinnappah Arasaratnam,
1986 (a) & 1989.

involvement in the Indian Ocean which had been established by the Portuguese. However, the VOC had extended the scope of inter-Asian trade by linking Japan more firmly into the trading networks of the South China Sea, and indirectly into the trade of the Bay of Bengal. But economic changes in Europe, the establishment of more European trading companies, and the expanding activities of British and Portuguese private traders were laying the foundations for the emergence of an overwhelming European commercial system, which preceded the domination of European capital in the Indian Ocean.

On a global level, from the late seventeenth century, the VOC and the Dutch state suffered a general decline in fortunes in contrast to the growing power of the English. In Angola, West Africa, North America, the West Indies and Brazil, Dutch treasure and manpower were drained by a series of military and naval defeats. This failure by the Dutch to create global political and marketing systems which they could dominate was reflected in the growing commercial conservatism of the VOC compared with the exuberant commercialism of the English, which was linked to their nation's growing power. The EIC did not readily reflect the vigour of individual English enterprise. However, unlike the VOC, it was carried along by a tide of general English commercial confidence which by the eighteenth century, cloaked the fact of its inherently conservative and inefficient commercial practices. By the end of the eighteenth century the finances of the VOC were further strained by the rising expenses entailed in maintaining a string of forts and standing fleets: burdens not borne to the same extent by the EIC.

By 1700 the Dutch were the dominant European power in the Indian Ocean judged in terms of bases and territory, but it was a flawed domination. The VOC was incapable of dominating the maritime trade of the region or of eliminating its major European and indigenous rivals. The EIC may have been pushed out of insular South East Asia, with the exception of insignificant Benkulu on the west coast of Sumatra, but it had significant trading bases in South Asia at Bombay (1661), Madras (1639) and Calcutta (1696), along with a string of minor factories such as Anjengo on the Malabar coast close to the Dutch at Cochin, Kasimbazar and Dhaka in Bengal, and Cuddalore and Fort St David on the Coromandel coast. In addition, the maritime trading network of the EIC was backed by a vigorous alliance of private English and Portuguese merchants and sailors across the Indian Ocean and by a global marketing network.

The VOC also faced stiff and continuing competition from indigenous merchants across the Indian Ocean. By 1700 the VOC may have been successfully carving out a territorial empire in insular South East Asia, but it failed to curb Chinese and South Asian commercial activity in the area. Like its European rivals, the VOC had to live with the daily reality of continuing indigenous competition: unlike its rivals, however, the VOC singularly failed to work with indigenous groups as a means of exploiting traditional maritime networks across the Indian Ocean. It was, therefore, singularly ill-equipped for changes in European economic and political fortunes which would dramatically alter relationships between Europeans and indigenous peoples in the Indian Ocean during the eighteenth century.

Of other Europeans, the Portuguese had lost their possessions in the Bay of Bengal, Sri Lanka and the Malabar coast, as well as chunks of territory associated with Goa. Bombay had passed to the English, and the Portuguese had been driven from the Persian Gulf and the East African coast north of Mozambique by 1700. The Danes had established a factory at Tranquebar on the Coromandel coast in 1620, while the French company established their main settlement at Pondicherry on the Coromandel coast in 1674.

By 1700 South Asia was emerging as the most profitable area for European commerce in the Indian Ocean. The produce and markets of South Asia were more varied and larger than those elsewhere around the ocean and, during the seventeenth century, the subcontinent had experienced a period of relative political stability as the Mughal empire expanded. Europeans of all nations benefited from this period of political calm and economic growth in most of South Asia, as did vigorous indigenous merchant groups whose involvement in maritime trade grew during the century.

In the Middle East and East Africa, both the VOC and the EIC made attempts to trade. Factories were established in the Persian Gulf and forays were made into the ports of East Africa but little came of these ventures. Despite the rise of Ottoman and Safavid power in the Middle East, which led to political stability and some economic recovery in the area, the Indian Ocean trade of the Middle East never recovered its former importance. Indigenous merchants out of west Indian ports maintained a minor but thriving trade with the Gulf, but neither the VOC nor the EIC managed to trade profitably in the area. On the other hand both companies did trade profitably in the coffee markets of Mocha in Yemen, from the 1620s, but this one instance of a profitable exchange simply highlights the failure of Europeans to trade profitably elsewhere on the Indian Ocean shore of the Middle East.

The story was much the same along the coast of East Africa. Merchants out of Oman, the Hadhramaut and Yemen traded profitably as far south as the Mozambique coast, having evicted the Portuguese, but European involvement in this trade was minimal. The gold trade of Sofala was a thing of the past, and there was little to attract Europeans until much later, when slaves and ivory drew their attention to the coast more firmly than ever before.

At the end of the seventeenth century European commerce involved many parts of the Indian Ocean. Such commerce, however, was still largely dependent upon working ancient trade networks and markets, and was further posited upon widespread co-operation with indigenous mercantile groups. Direct trade between the Indian Ocean and Europe still comprised mostly cargoes of spices, limited amounts of exotic goods, and some cotton textiles, alongside the remitted profits of trade within the boundaries of the Indian Ocean. Europeans were skimming profits off the top of an old economic system, and as yet had to fundamentally change the economic structures of the lands of the Indian Ocean and their relationship with the economies of Europe.

Workers of the Sea

The arrival of Europeans in the Indian Ocean in the sixteenth century quickened interest in the sea in many places. Europeans moved across the Ocean from one trading or mission settlement to another, attracting a growing number of indigenous peoples, such as merchants, sailors, artisans and mercenaries.

When the Portuguese attempted to establish a maritime empire in the Indian Ocean they were desperately short of manpower. Seamen were recruited from all the ports of Europe, as well as from many parts of the Indian Ocean, with the result that African and Asian Muslims crewed Portuguese vessels from Sofala to Nagasaki. The Portuguese sought a solution to their manpower shortage by encouraging coastal fishing communities to convert to Christianity. As previously noted, one such group was the Parava fishing community of the Madurai coast or 'Fishery Coast' on the Palk Strait.

The fate of the Paravas was not unique. Prior to Portuguese intervention Hindu rulers on the Fishery Coast controlled the activities of fishermen and pearl divers as a means of raising revenue. In addition they, and Hindu rulers on the Malabar coast, encouraged the conversion of fisherfolk by foreign Muslim merchants, to build a solid local base of seafaring skills and mercantile expertise, linked into the prosperous and expanding Muslim trading world.

However, attention rarely focused on fisherfolk simply because of their maritime skills. The Paravas, for example, attracted attention because of their multifaceted relationship with the sea. They lived at the junction of major trade routes between the western and eastern Indian Ocean, centring on southern India and Sri Lanka, and were involved in petty trade and fishing. In addition, they worked the valuable pearl and chank shell fisheries of the Palk Straits. Similarly, the Lakshadweep and Maldive islands, source of cowrie shells and dried fish, invited the attention of mercantile and political élites from southern India over the centuries. Elsewhere around the Indian Ocean, the pearl fishers of Bahrain; the Orang Laut of the Strait of Melaka; the trepang and trochus shell collectors of the Lesser Sunda Islands; and the Bugis of Makassar are examples of fisherfolk who at times came under the control of land-based merchants and rulers, and then of Europeans such as the Portuguese, British and Dutch.

In some instances external attention was attracted by the harvest of the sea. But in other instances, most particularly in the case of the itinerant Orang Laut and the Bugis, external attention was attracted by the piracy of these communities as well as by their skills as itinerant traders, seamen and fighting men. In the case of the Bugis the sea provided various means of survival: as pirates, traders and mercenaries. The less conspicuous Orang Laut were confined to the waters of the Malay peninsula, where they occasionally took to piracy, diverting looted cargoes to *ad hoc* beach markets. They were particularly active in the Strait of Melaka and around the island of Singapore, and over the centuries attracted the attention of indigenous and European powers determined either to incorporate them in their maritime enterprises or to halt their depredation.

The Portuguese were quick to make use of Muslim sailors, despite their antipathy towards Islam. The same pattern of recruitment was adopted by other European shipowners, and Muslims formed a major part of the muster on European ships in the Indian Ocean, from the sixteenth century.

While indigenous sailors and fishermen often found themselves incorporated in European shipping and mercantile activity, the fate of indigenous mercantile groups varied. Muslim Gujarati activity across the Bay of Bengal to Melaka was destroyed, although some compensation was found in diverting energies towards the Persian Gulf and East Africa. On the other hand, Hindu merchant groups from southern India and Gujarat, whose mercantile skills and local market knowledge were needed by the Portuguese, maintained their old links across the Bay of Bengal. However, on the fringes of Portuguese mercantile activity in the Bay of Bengal and South East Asia, Muslim mercantile groups from Bengal, Orissa, the Coromandel and Arakan coasts and from insular South East Asia, continued to operate successfully.

Indeed, in the sixteenth century the revival of the Persian empire under the Safavids and the establishment of the Ottoman empire was mirrored by an expansion of Persian, Armenian and Jewish mercantile activity. During the next century Persian Armenians and Muslims (encouraged by Safavid rulers) carved out a prominent position in the trade linking northern and central India with the kingdom of Ayuthia. From Masulipatnam, Persian merchants sailed across the Bay of Bengal to Tenasserim and Mergui, to service the Thai court at Ayuthia. At the same time Persian Armenian merchants established communities throughout Mughal India and South East Asia as far as Spanish Manila. Similarly, the Jews of Mesopotamia benefited from the partial restoration of prosperity that Ottoman rule brought to Iraq. They used links with co-religionists around the Mediterranean and in South

Asia to create small but flourishing maritime links between Bengal, Bombay, the Malabar coast, the Persian Gulf and the Levant.

Although the Muslim Gujaratis and Chulias were driven from Melaka when it fell to the Portuguese in 1511, their enemies were not able to complete their destruction. The Gujaratis found recompense in the lucrative trade between South Asia, the Middle East and East Africa. The Chulias worked a network of maritime trade—dealing mainly in South Asian cloth and tin from the Malay peninsula—between eastern India, Burma, Thailand and northern parts of the Malay peninsula, beyond the malevolent eyes of first, the Portuguese and then the Dutch. Northwards from Melaka, the Chulias formed diasporas at Mergui and Phuket, as well as at many smaller ports where they dominated the tin, cotton cloth and tobacco trade between mainland South East Asia and the Coromandel coast. Regular sailings between these ports and Nagore, Nagapattinam, Tranquebar and Madras on the Coromandel coast, kept the Tamil Muslim culture of these people alive, but there was also considerable intermarriage with local Muslim groups.

In the western Indian Ocean the realities of limited power forced the Portuguese to accommodations with Muslim mercantile groups. Hindu and Muslim Gujaratis still sailed to the Persian Gulf and the Red Sea, and to Portuguese-controlled ports such as Hormuz and Muscat, before they were lost in the 1620s, which had large South Asian populations. These merchants also continued to trade with East Africa where, ironically, they operated closely with the Portuguese to extract gold and ivory for the cloth and pepper markets of South Asia and the Persian Gulf. South Asian merchants remained prominent along the East African coast under Portuguese rule, throughout the sixteenth and seventeenth centuries. When the Portuguese lost Mombasa in 1698 to a revived Oman, and authority on the Kenyan and Tanzanian coast passed to Oman, South Asian merchants accommodated themselves without difficulty to the demands of the new rulers. Swahili sailors too, found a niche in indigenous and Portuguese maritime trade during this period, serving on ships sailing as far east as Gujarat and Sri Lanka.

Like other mercantile groups before them, the Portuguese formed trading communities in many parts of the Indian Ocean world. From

Sofala to the Moluccas, forts, trading posts and mission settlements were established by the Portuguese. The majority of these settlements—for example, Sofala, Kilwa, Mombasa, Hormuz, Cochin and Melaka—were small territorial enclaves, many seized by force, and administered by the viceroy of the *Estado da India* at Goa. The Portuguese carved out larger territorial bases only at Goa, on Sri Lanka and along the Mozambique coast. These Portuguese enclaves were unlike previous merchant settlements around the Indian Ocean. They were part of a new sprawling political entity and represented a new type of commercial organization in terms of scope and objectives. Most clustered around a fortress and church and frequently contained a mixed race population of Christians, resulting from the marriage of Portuguese soldiers, artisans and officials with local women.

In the sixteenth century the Portuguese did not, apart from renegades and corrupt officials,[32] operate as independent merchants within a relatively closely defined geographic area, but as representatives of a royal monopoly whose operations stretched from Lisbon to Nagasaki. But the Portuguese could not operate without local intermediaries, and their enclaves included majority populations of indigenous peoples drawn from all the traditional mercantile communities of the Ocean, as well as cosmopolitan European populations comprising Portuguese, Dutch, English, French, Spanish, Italians, Eurasians, New Christians (converted Portuguese Jews), local Christian converts and African slaves. By the seventeenth century the Crown, recognizing its inability to control and dominate maritime trade, accommodated private Portuguese traders into the mercantile activities of the Portuguese Indian Ocean establishment.

Portuguese attempts to compensate for their failure to attract large numbers of European settlers led to them placing an increasing reliance upon Eurasians and indigenous Christians, who became surprisingly mobile on the routes between Portuguese enclaves. Eurasian and indigenous Christian converts from South Asia formed a high proportion of Portuguese garrisons from Sofala to Timor, while Eurasians and indigenous Christian converts in South Asia provided a pool of settlers, albeit unwilling, used by the Portuguese to establish towns

[32] G.D. Winius, 1985.

and farms along the river valleys of Mozambique in a vain attempt to link the coast to the gold rich interior of Zimbabwe, where the Portuguese hoped to establish their authority.[33] These hopes were dashed by African resistance, but the legacy was a string of coastal and riverine Portuguese settlements in Mozambique populated by settlers drawn both from Europe and South Asia.[34]

Throughout the sixteenth century many Europeans were drawn to the new frontier of the Indian Ocean. Some operated within the system represented by the *Estado*, but others set up distinctive diasporas as private traders, missionaries, pirates and mercenaries serving local rulers. On the Arakan coast, for example, renegade Portuguese set up their own pirate state until they were defeated by a Mughal expedition which carried the survivors off to slavery in Bengal. Further to the east, Catholic missionaries created *de facto* Portuguese colonies around isolated settlements on Timor and other Indonesian islands, but frequently such missionaries found themselves at odds with the authorities of the *Estado* when official demands conflicted with the interests of their flocks. Even in India, the Portuguese at Goa found their authority flouted and challenged by missionaries and converts on the 'Fisheries Coast' who resented the financial exactions and interference in local affairs of Goa. Throughout the lands of the Indian Ocean European mortality rates were extraordinarily high, but each ship from Europe carried replacements heedless of the dangers and eager to make their fortunes in the Indian Ocean world.

During the seventeenth century, the English, Dutch, Danes and French entered the trade of the Indian Ocean. Like the Portuguese, they established trading settlements around the Indian Ocean. Unlike the *Estado da India*, these new companies were more firmly linked into international commercial networks stretching beyond the confines of the Indian Ocean. Many of their European employees moved around the globe from Europe and the Americas to Asia, and consequently often had a broader worldview than their Portuguese rivals, whose arena of operations shrunk drastically during the seventeenth century.

[33] K. McPherson, 1987.
[34] E. Axelson, 1969.

Given the small number of Europeans, indigenous co-operation was vital to their enterprise in the Indian Ocean. In some areas, however, the Dutch—like the Portuguese before them—moved to eliminate local merchants and shipowners as a means of furthering their mercantile monopoly. This was particularly evident in insular South East Asia, where the VOC vigorously prosecuted maritime trading groups in Java and attempted to extend a monopoly over the external trade of the Muslim sultanates of the Malay peninsula and the Thai kingdom of Ayuthia. In parts of insular South East Asia the Dutch were successful, but groups such as the Bugis of Sulawesi took to the seas as warrior traders and were able to avoid destruction as a merchant group until European technology, capital and fire power overwhelmed the world in the nineteenth century.

Indigenous mercenary soldiers also found niches in the changing world of the Indian Ocean from the sixteenth century. The Portuguese and other European trading groups were not only chronically short of sailors but were, from the beginning of their enterprise, short of soldiers; even Albuquerque used Malabari mercenaries to capture Melaka in 1511 and on other campaigns in South Asia and the Middle East. The same was true of many indigenous regimes, particularly in South East Asia. Muslim cavalrymen from Persia and South Asia found employment as élite guards in many royal courts throughout South East Asia, as did Japanese samurai, and exiled Japanese Christians who fled their homeland when Christianity was prohibited in the seventeenth century. In addition, the Portuguese regularly recruited Eurasians, indigenous Christian, and Hindu and Muslim mercenaries in South Asia for service at their bases scattered around the Indian Ocean. From the seventeenth century the English and Dutch companies also recruited indigenous soldiers in South Asia and in insular South East Asia to fight their wars against one another and against indigenous regimes from East Africa to the Moluccas.

Renegade European mercenaries also sold their services around the Ocean. European artillerymen and cannon foundrymen in particular, were in great demand at many larger indigenous courts in South Asia, while other European soldiers served as officers in indigenous armies. It is difficult to quantify European settlement around the Indian Ocean in the sixteenth and seventeenth centuries, but the numbers who survived the onslaught of new climates and diseases was probably very small. Despite the great mortality, however, the stream of Europeans continued to grow, as did the impact of European penetration upon many aspects of indigenous life. Europeans opened up the lands of the Indian Ocean to a much larger world. In the sixteenth and seventeenth centuries the cultural impact of Europe was limited to some innovations in indigenous shipping technology, stylistic additions to Persian and Mughal painting and architecture, but little else in concrete terms.

At a more intrusive level, however, the arrival of a combative Christianity in the wake of the Portuguese had a profound effect upon local religious practices and loyalties. In South Asia the Portuguese established small but vigorous Christian communities in Goa, southeastern coastal India, and on the Sri Lankan coastal plains. Adherence to Christianity did not necessarily mean loyalty to the political and economic ambitions of the Portuguese, but it did mean adherence to new philosophies by local converts, which inevitably set them apart as yet another distinct group within the complex human world of the Indian Ocean.

In East Africa, the Middle East and South East Asia, the Portuguese were singularly unsuccessful in spreading Christianity. In East Africa and the Middle East, aggressive Christianity came up against an equally vigorous Islam. The hold of the Portuguese on bases on the Swahili coast, north of Mozambique, and in the Persian Gulf, was too tenuous to propagate Christianity with any great success. The same was true in South East Asia. East from Melaka (with the notable exception of East Timor), Portuguese pretensions were muted by the realities of local power. Indeed, in the islands and on the mainland, the unfortunate association of Christianity with Portuguese ambitions counted against Christianity and, ironically, encouraged the spread of Islam among indigenous mercantile groups opposed to Portuguese economic and political expansion, as well as suspicions in staunchly Buddhist Burma and Thailand of Portuguese intentions.

While the flow of European ideas and knowledge to the lands of the Indian Ocean was relatively slow before the eighteenth century, the sixteenth and seventeenth centuries was a period in which the world of the Indian Ocean was opened to the European imagination.

European administrators, Roman Catholic missionaries, travellers, seamen, renegades and merchants produced an astonishing range of books and maps relating to the Indian Ocean, which fired the imagination of Europe. Fiction began to give way to fact and scientific observation, equipping Europeans with the knowledge and skills necessary to explore and exploit the littoral lands of the Ocean.

Portuguese crews and administrators were drawn from many parts of Roman Catholic Europe, and it was perhaps inevitable that reports would filter back to the great Renaissance cities of Europe such as Genoa, Antwerp, Amsterdam and London, concerning the wonders of the Indian Ocean world. Some medieval European travellers had prefaced this literary outpouring, but such accounts had entered the fable literature of the times. By the sixteenth century, travellers tales were being cast in a new mould shaped by the spirit of scientific inquiry which was abroad in much of Europe.

This new spirit of inquiry was driven by new approaches to mercantile activity, in which information had a real value in terms of shaping commercial decisions and improving profits. News from the Indian Ocean was news which could be turned to profit. While the Portuguese attempted to restrict the knowledge of maps and information about the Ocean they faced an impossible task, and by the mid-sixteenth century information concerning the Portuguese discovery of Asia was whetting the appetite of European trading communities as far afield as England and the Hanseatic ports of the Baltic.

Overall, the impact of Europeans upon the activities, beliefs and practices of local peoples who worked the Indian Ocean was surprisingly muted during the sixteenth and seventeenth centuries. European economic, political and religious activities may have disrupted and changed life for some indigenous peoples, but in general these disruptions and the changes wrought by Europeans have to be weighed against the changes taking place within indigenous societies, brought about by the spread of Islam and the expansion of great indigenous powers such as the Ottomans, the Safavids and the Mughals. European technology had little to contribute to the technologies of the Indian Ocean world, and Europeans remained largely peripheral to indigenous life and fortunes until the eighteenth century, when fundamental political and economic changes in Europe and Asia swung the balance of economic, and then political power, around the world in favour of the peoples of north-western Europe.

Until the eighteenth century European intrusion into the Indian Ocean world had remarkably little impact upon ancient civilizations and processes of cultural interaction. While the Portuguese, Dutch, English and French were attempting to establish commercial empires, Muslim civilization flourished from the Mediterranean to insular South East Asia under the patronage of the Ottomans, Safavids, Mughals and the rulers of ports such as Melaka. In mainland South East Asia, Buddhist culture prospered in the wealthy kingdoms of Thailand and Burma, and in insular South East Asia Islam continued to spread, as the Dutch and local sultans fought for control of the main islands of the Indonesian archipelago. Along the coast of East Africa, Swahili civilization flourished despite Portuguese occupation of major ports, and was to experience a resurgence when the Omanis drove the Portuguese from the Kenyan and Tanzanian coast.

Although Middle Eastern economies were in decline by the eighteenth century the previous two centuries had witnessed an efflorescence of Muslim cultural activity. From Turkey to Iran great public monuments were constructed, the plastic arts blossomed under imperial patronage and the great classical literary traditions of Islam continued. There had been some economic recovery under the Ottomans and Safavids, but not generally in their lands abutting the Indian Ocean. Consequently, there was no significant resurgence of ancient maritime links between the Middle East, South Asia and East Africa, apart from the extension of Omani interests into East Africa, and the brief flourishing of the Mocha coffee trade in the late seventeenth century, before coffee plantations appeared in Dutch Java and later in Portuguese Brazil.

In South Asia the Mughals constructed their greatest monuments during the sixteenth and seventeenth centuries, and created a brilliant court culture inspired by the civilizations of Iran, Central Asia and India. In central India, Muslim sultans, before they were overwhelmed by the Mughals in the seventeenth century, created equally vibrant centres of Muslim civilization, drawing upon local Hindu and Muslim genius and the inspiration of Muslim émigres from the Middle East. Mughal hegemony was accompanied by economic prosperity and a growth in foreign trade which benefited both indigenous and European participants.

In mainland South East Asia the royal courts of Ayuthia and. Burma remained centres of Buddhist culture and civilization. Rulers constructed temples and monasteries throughout their domains, and in their capitals cultivated all the traditional arts, ranging from painting to music. Foreign trade was still conducted through royal agents who dealt with the goods and merchants of all nations. Royal interest in maritime trade in fact increased during the seventeenth century, when the rulers of Ayuthia invested in western-style vessels and contracted Europeans to conduct trading voyages across the Bay of Bengal.

In insular South East Asia the conquest of Melaka by the Portuguese removed the most brilliant centre of Muslim culture, but elsewhere throughout the Indonesian archipelago other Muslim rulers in Borneo, Sulawesi and the Moluccas continued the traditions set by Melaka, as Islam spread throughout the islands. Indeed, despite Portuguese and Dutch inroads during the sixteenth and seventeenth centuries this was the period when the Islamic culture of modern Indonesia took shape. In form it combined both aspects of classical Islamic civilization and indigenous cultural traditions, as one-by-one the great inland centres of Hindu–Buddhist culture succumbed to Islam. This was particularly evident on the island of Java, which was the most populous and prosperous of all the islands of Indonesia. By the seventeenth century the last Hindu–Buddhist states on the island had been vanquished by Muslims from the coast, but in the process the culture and practices of these courts passed to the new rulers who maintained rather than disrupted Java's cultural links with its past. Ironically, this occurred at a time when Dutch expansion through coastal Java was beginning to seal off inland courts from contact with the outside world.

Throughout these centuries contact between these various civilizations was maintained by sea. At times, Europeans made such contact difficult, but the hajj continued to bind the world of Islam together, and Muslim merchants, intellectuals, divines and mercenaries still moved from one side of the Indian Ocean to the other, finding profit and employment at the many indigenous courts which continued to flourish within the Indian Ocean world.

4

From Commerce to Industrial Capitalism

Overview

European economic and political relations with the peoples of
the Indian Ocean world changed dramatically from the late
seventeenth century, leading eventually to the creation of European territorial empires. These changes resulted from developments
in western European economic life which gave rise to new forms of
overseas commerce. European interest in cargoes of rare and exotic
goods, exchanged for precious metals and the profits of European
trade within the Indian Ocean world, gave way to the pursuit of Asian
commodities for mass consumption in Europe, such as cotton textiles
and tea.

This change in European demand led to a more intensive European penetration of areas in the Indian Ocean world, where new
cargoes for the marketplaces of Europe could be found. This new form
of economic activity hastened the integration of Indian Ocean economies into an emerging capitalist global economy, and encouraged
European merchants to use political means and force to pursue their
economic goals. In this process many Indian Ocean lands passed under
European political domination. In addition, the relative economic
self-sufficiency of Indian Ocean economies was broken down, leading
to the transformation of the Indian Ocean world into a dependent
economic region of a capitalist-dominated global economy.

New forms of European economic interest and technology in the
eighteenth and nineteenth centuries had an adverse impact upon
indigenous economic, cultural and political fortunes. More intensive
European economic penetration coincided with the decline of major
indigenous states, such as Mughal India and Safavid Persia, creating
a power vacuum which was filled by European nations as they secured
their commercial and strategic interests by turning to military and

naval activity to carve out territorial empires. Indigenous seafarers and merchants were slowly edged out of their position of equality with Europeans in the maritime commerce of the Indian Ocean, to positions of subservience and collaboration in the pursuit of European economic interests. Age-old patterns of communication and interaction across the Indian Ocean were disrupted and destroyed.

In the nineteenth century the development of industrial capitalism in Europe fatally undermined many traditional manufacturing processes in the Indian Ocean region, making regional economies even more dependent upon Europe, which was both a market for regional raw materials and a supplier of manufactured goods. European investment capital moved into the region and, together with local capital, completed the integration of regional economies into a capitalist-dominated world.

By the late nineteenth century European economic and political activity and European-controlled technology had effectively brought the Indian Ocean region under European control. Most of the region was directly ruled by European states; European communications and military technology had overwhelmed indigenous shipping systems and indigenous political and commercial élites; while European medical technology made it possible for a greater number of Europeans to settle and survive in the tropics. In addition to dominating and reshaping indigenous economic activity, Europeans usurped indigenous political authority in much of the Indian Ocean region, and they imposed their own civilization as the model for behaviour and progress, destroying ancient processes of cultural interaction.

From the mid-eighteenth century, European activity had an impact upon the number of people travelling the Indian Ocean. The number of indigenous merchants on the high seas declined, but this decline was more than matched by the increase in the number of other types of maritime travellers. Between them, Europeans and Asians increased the movement of slaves to unsurpassed numbers, and this was followed by an equally massive movement of convicts, indentured and free migrants from Europe, South Asia and China to Africa, the Mascarenes, Australia and South East Asia. Along with these migrants there were colonial civil servants, European military forces (and their indigenous levies), pious Muslims on the hajj, European businessmen, free and indentured Asians migrating to the Pacific and the Americas, and, by the late nineteenth century, a growing number of European tourists, all of whom travelled by sea until the 1960s, when aircraft rather than ships became the major carriers of passengers across the Ocean.

In addition to altering human patterns of movement across the Indian Ocean, colonial rule destroyed old processes of cultural inter-action. New patterns of economic activity and colonial boundaries, drawn to suit European rather than local interests, disrupted ancient patterns of communication and exchange, ending various processes of cultural interaction.

By the end of the First World War the Indian Ocean was effec-tively a British lake, and a fully integrated and dependent region of the capitalist global economy. Although colonial rule had vanished by the second half of the twentieth century, economic dependency still exists, making the Indian Ocean a focal point of extra-regional interest and intervention. Colonial rule had destroyed ancient economic and cultural relationships, replacing them with extra-regional economic, political and cultural alliances and dependencies.

The Twilight of Traditional Trade?

By the last decades of the seventeenth century there were signs of significant changes emerging in the patterns of European commercial activity in the Indian Ocean. While traditional trade networks still flourished, and the carrying of what were essentially traditional cargoes still preoccupied the directors of the great European trading com-panies, there was a steady growth in direct trade with Europe. Until the late seventeenth century most European profits came from par-ticipation in the internal maritime trade of the Indian Ocean, but this was to change, with increasing profits being earned from the dispatch of cargoes of cotton cloth and other goods directly from South Asian producer to European consumer.

From Bengal, and to a lesser extent the Coromandel coast, the Dutch in particular were selling increasing amounts of South Asian cotton textiles in Europe as well as in West African markets. Initially the EIC lagged in this trade, but the English too were becoming enmeshed in the scramble for new cargoes for new destinations outside the Indian Ocean. The trade in South Asian textiles had originally attracted the attention of the VOC as a means of obtaining cargoes of spices from insular South East Asia, where imported cotton cloth was in great demand. But from the late seventeenth century European demand for South Asian textiles gradually reforged the nature of European commercial activity in the Indian Ocean. European trading companies, most particularly the VOC and the EIC, changed from uneasy partners in the traditional trade of the Indian Ocean to masters of that trade, which was redirected to supplying Asian and African goods to markets outside the Indian Ocean region.

These changes in trade can best be seen in the changes in the volume of company shipping on the route between northern Europe and the Indian Ocean. In the first decade of the seventeenth century, the Portuguese, English, Dutch and French sent 150 ships to the Ocean, the largest number of which were Portuguese; during the first decade of the eighteenth century, 461 European ships set sail for the Indian Ocean of which the largest number were Dutch, with the English rapidly catching up.[1] Also, throughout the seventeenth and eighteenth centuries, the range in tonnage of these vessels increased from 300–800 tonnes in the seventeenth century to 500–1000 tonnes in the eighteenth century, indicating a shift in cargo composition from relatively small consignments of spices, pepper and various luxuries to heavier and bulkier cargoes of cotton and silk cloth, porcelain and tea.[2]

This rapid growth in trade between the Indian Ocean region and the outside world resulted from several changes in European fortunes and markets beyond the Indian Ocean. Among these was an increase in the flow of gold and silver from the Americas, and rising demand in Europe and the Americas for large quantities of goods for mass consumption. Another factor was the decline of the pepper trade. By the late seventeenth century pepper was no longer at the centre of European interest in the Indian Ocean, and was reduced in cargoes to the function of a useful ballast. It was replaced by a range of other

[1] Niels Steensgard, 1970, 9; Holden Furber, 1976, 362, n. 32.
[2] Jean Sutton, 1981, 43, 46.

cargoes: indigo, saltpetre and most spectacularly in terms of profits, cotton textiles.

The decline in importance of pepper was associated with several factors. Over-supply by the VOC and the EIC led to a fall in price in Europe, compounded by changing dietary habits which undermined the importance of pepper in European cuisine. Improved agricultural technology and bumper harvests, in Britain in particular, in the eighteenth century had led to cheaper and more plentiful supplies of food. The range of foodstuffs also increased. Fresh food was now more readily available to a greater number of people than ever before, lessening the dependence upon pepper to disguise the unpleasant taste of poorly preserved foodstuffs or to titillate palates bored with bland diets.

While European demand was central to this explosion of extra-regional interest in Indian Ocean commodities, the influence of markets in other parts of the world was also important: the great slave markets of West Africa, and the European colonies in the Americas were also centres of growing demand for South Asian textiles which could be satisfied by the VOC and the EIC. But while the VOC initially took the lead in satisfying this new demand, it was the EIC which was to turn the greater profit in the long run, due to its more flexible organization, worldwide linkages to markets in English colonies in the Americas and the Caribbean, and the activity of private traders whom it incorporated into its operations. The VOC, on the other hand, retained an inflexible commercial structure, and had a declining hinterland of Dutch-controlled markets after losses of colonies in the Americas and West Africa. In addition it continued to restrict the activities of private traders and to concentrate primarily upon the South and South East Asian spice trade.

Ironically the EIC, which could not compete with the aggressive Dutch in the spice and pepper trade, developed its interests in the South Asian textile trade, placing itself in an excellent position when cloth replaced spices and pepper as the most profitable commodity to sell in Europe. In excluding them from the maritime trade of South East Asia the VOC had forced the English into an early development of their interests in South Asia, so that when Indian textiles became the most profitable item of European trade in the eighteenth century, the EIC was ideally situated to turn its exile from South East Asia to its advantage.

Neither the EIC nor the VOC, throughout the seventeenth and eighteenth centuries, could discount the activities of indigenous and private European traders in the movement of cotton textiles and other goods across the Indian Ocean. For example, English private and indigenous mercantile activity in cotton textiles throughout mainland South East Asia undermined Dutch attempts to monopolize the trade. Muslim and Hindu merchants from Bengal and the Coromandel coast, alongside the EIC, the British and Portuguese private traders, competed successfully against the VOC in South East Asian markets with cargoes from South Asia. Similarly, in the western sector of the Indian Ocean, cargoes of South Asian textiles from the great Mughal Gujarati port of Surat returned handsome profits on the runs to the Gulf, the Red Sea and East Africa. Textiles were carried in the ships of indigenous and European private traders, and—to a lesser extent— in ships of both the VOC and the EIC, until that port declined in the 1750s.

Overall, wider entrepreneurial activity favoured the EIC. Like the VOC, the major part of its activities were concentrated in one part of the Indian Ocean, in this instance, South Asia rather than insular South East Asia. But it had access to a growing number of British-dominated markets elsewhere in the world, as well as to a growing volume of gold and silver. In addition, trade with South Asia provided the EIC with a far greater range of profitable commodities than the VOC obtained out of insular South East Asia.

In contrast, the VOC's fortunes weakened during the eighteenth century. From the late seventeenth century the Company's access to East Asian copper, silver and gold bullion declined, most particularly when the Chinese authorities once more prohibited foreign maritime trade between 1655 and 1684 and drove the Dutch from their base in Taiwan. Also, access to Japanese silver was lost when Japan all but closed its doors to foreign trade in the late seventeenth century. Gold was still available to the VOC from Japan until the mid-eighteenth century, but in general, by the late seventeenth century, the Dutch were not getting enough bullion out of their Asian trade to pay for the vital cargoes of South Asian textiles they needed for Europe, and to support their spice trade. Increasing amounts of bullion had to be imported from the Netherlands to sustain Dutch trade in South Asian textiles. At approximately the same time, the profits of the VOC's spice trade were declining, and the company faced increasing competition for its Asian imports in Europe from the EIC and European private traders. By the 1740s the days of heady profits were over, and the VOC lurched into permanent deficit until it was liquidated in 1799, shortly after the same fate befell the French company.

In at least one other important aspect too, the British had an advantage over their Dutch rivals. The VOC vigorously fought the growth of Dutch private trade—thereby ironically encouraging the growth of widespread corruption among its servants—whereas the EIC, initially no less hostile to the activities of private traders, proved incapable of stifling private initiative and eventually permitted company servants to trade on their own account, as well as incorporating some private traders into its network as Free Merchants. In collaboration with indigenous and Portuguese private traders, particularly after the English and Portuguese resolved their differences in the 1660s, English private traders pioneered new markets inside the Indian Ocean. By the late 1680s English and Portuguese merchants had overhauled the Dutch in the China trade, while Chinese and Portuguese merchants controlled the trade between China and Java.[3] This Anglo-Portuguese commercial activity built up an infrastructure of English free trade, which was to serve the interests of that nation well when the EIC collapsed, alongside the VOC, in the late eighteenth century. In contrast, private trade within the central core of the VOC's empire in the Indonesian archipelago passed into the hands of Chinese traders, upon whom the Dutch became increasingly and very grudgingly reliant.

During the seventeenth century and into the early decades of the eighteenth century, the trading activities of the EIC and the VOC mirrored those of the Portuguese who, despite a string of defeats at the hands of their enemies, were to maintain a considerable renegade commercial presence until well into the next century. Trade with Europe still largely comprised the luxurious and the exotic, while

[3] J.E. Wills, 1974.

European trade within the Indian Ocean centred increasingly on staple cargoes.

As the EIC and VOC engaged in a desperate bid to wring profits from the dwindling spice and pepper trade, private European traders made considerable inroads into maritime trade at the expense of the companies and indigenous traders. To maintain their profits, European ships (belonging to the EIC, the VOC and the less important French and Danish companies, as well as to private traders) carried cargoes for local merchants, who found them both cheaper and more secure than indigenous craft.

In addition, the EIC and the VOC scoured the Ocean for new cargoes and explored the possibility of new exports from Europe—ranging from re-exports of West Indian sugar, to English copper and broadcloth (which found favour as tenting material). More importantly, the interest of the European companies shifted from spices and pepper to more complex cargoes, including the newly fashionable coffee from Yemen; porcelain and silk from China (to satisfy the European vogue for *chinoiserie*); copper from Japan; as well as South Asian saltpetre for the manufacture of gunpowder, dyestuffs, raw silk and cotton textiles; and Maldivian cowries as currency for the slave markets of Africa. Some of these commodities were undoubtedly luxuries, but the majority were now considered bulk staples which previously had been carried as low value ballast.

This export activity was underpinned by an even more intensive working of the 'country trade', particularly by British private traders, and by continual attempts to introduce new imports from beyond the region. Both the VOC and the EIC traded spices, pepper and textiles extensively, if in the end unprofitably, in the Persian Gulf, extracting gold and silver from the contracting markets of the now declining Ottoman and Persian empires, to finance trade elsewhere in the region. Similarly, both companies, along with the French, Arabs, Persians, South Asian Hindus and Muslims, jostled for a share of the lucrative coffee trade of Yemen on the Red Sea and the spice trade between insular South East Asia and South Asia.

In mainland South East Asia there was also vigorous competition as merchants manoeuvred against one another to gain access to the trade of the Thai kingdom of Ayuthia. The Thai king's commercial

agents played off one European faction against another and against
Chinese and Japanese merchants, to secure the best deals on luxuries
such as horses, Persian carpets, Chinese brocades and Indian tapestries.

The VOC was also quite ruthless in guarding its Taiwanese and
Japanese trade, which provided silver and gold in exchange for Chinese
and South Asian imports, until it lost Taiwan in 1662, and the export
of silver from Japan was banned in 1688. The EIC, on the other hand,
continued to obtain Mexican silver by trading South Asian textiles
through Armenian intermediaries, with the Spanish at Manila. The
success of the British in increasing their access to silver increased their
purchasing power and facilitated the expansion of their trading networks.

By the beginning of the eighteenth century western Europe was
undergoing a commercial revolution which led to major social, economic and political changes. This was reflected during the late seventeenth century in major changes in the composition of Indian Ocean
cargoes destined for Europe and the Americas, when South Asian
textiles replaced pepper and spices as the main cargoes. Western
Europe was emerging as the fountainhead of commercial capitalism,
and rising prosperity was creating new markets for bulk commodities
for mass consumption. The focus of European rivalry in the Indian
Ocean switched from the Indonesian archipelago to Bengal in South
Asia, the great producer of cotton textiles: the key trading commodity
around the Indian Ocean and the most profitable cargo to sell in
Europe.

The development of European domination over Indian Ocean
trading routes was not the result of the triumph of the European
trading companies, which did not maintain their profitability in intra-
Asian trade, but of the activities of private European merchants, many
of whom worked hand-in-glove with indigenous entrepreneurs. Increasingly more and more of the trade between the Indian Ocean and
external markets, as well as maritime trade within the Indian Ocean
region, was dominated by private European traders. The EIC frequently operated in deficit, while the VOC faced declining margins on a
dangerously small range of increasingly unfashionable commodities,
with the result that it was bankrupt by 1799.

However, while European merchants were busy achieving domination of maritime trade, many indigenous economies still flourished during the eighteenth century. Only in the nineteenth century did European economic and political domination adversely effect the growth and development of indigenous economies. But if the economic impact of European enterprise upon indigenous economies during the seventeenth and eighteenth centuries was muted, there was a more immediate human impact relating to the world of force and to the world of the mind.

It has been argued that 'the principal export of pre-industrial Europe to the rest of the world was violence, and that the *fidalgos*, the *conquistadores*, the *vrijburghers* and the *nabobs* were (in effect) warrior nomads who differed little from the Mongols or the Mughals'.[4] Such an argument goes a long way towards explaining the very real extension of European political power in the eighteenth century, when the great European trading companies were lurching towards bankruptcy. The independent European trader, the European military and naval officer, and the errant company servant, were quite prepared to use force and the claim of 'national interest' to further their financial interests in a way which was quite foreign to the world of the Indian Ocean. Comparable groups or attitudes were not present in the indigenous world. Force, avarice and ambition were not unique to Europeans, but their attachment to national interests and the concept of national naval strategies were.

European penetration of the Indian Ocean impacted more subtly and selectively upon the human mind. The Indian Ocean world was linked into an expanding worldwide European cultural system. Europeans operating within the Indian Ocean regarded themselves as members of nation states whose interests they promoted. In this sense they had a different view of the world from their indigenous counterparts, the greater number of whom still saw the world in terms of ancient cultural, religious and economic boundaries which largely coincided with the geographic confines of the Ocean. In economic terms this restricted the mercantile possibilities for indigenous merchants, while in political and cultural terms it encapsulated ruler and subject alike in a fragile system, unprepared for the looming confron-

[4] Geoffrey Parker, 1988, 115 & note.

tation with European nationalism, capitalism and political and cultural imperialism.

The Commercial Revolution

During the eighteenth century there was a commercial revolution in the Indian Ocean which resulted in the British (both the EIC and British private traders) dominating the major trade routes of the Indian Ocean, as well as its external maritime linkages. In addition, the British established a major territorial empire on the shores of the Ocean in South Asia, as did the Dutch in the Indonesian archipelago. This revolution was based upon three commodities: South Asian cotton textiles and opium, and Chinese tea.

In the course of the eighteenth century the markets for South Asian textiles in Europe expanded rapidly, but Europe had acquired a taste for another even more profitable Asiatic commodity: tea. There was a reorientation of South Asian exports by indigenous and European traders eastward across the Bay of Bengal, to markets in South East and East Asia. Paralleling this development there was a very rapid growth in the export of cotton textiles, and a new commodity—opium—from Bengal. The value and volume of textile exports from Bengal by the 1720s, outstripped those of both the Coromandel coast and the great Gujarati port of Surat.[5]

As we have seen, both the EIC and the VOC established factories in Bengal in the seventeenth century, and it was here, more than on the Coromandel coast, that the private British trader was to give the EIC the edge over its rivals. By now the pursuit of private interest had become an integral part of British commerce, and private trading interests were a force to be reckoned with in the formulation of British national policy. The EIC encouraged private British enterprise as a supporting arm of its own activities. This was particularly true from the mid-eighteenth century, when the EIC emerged as a major, if unwilling, territorial power in South Asia, with the conquest of the Mughal province of Bengal, following the battle of Plassey in 1757, and of much of the Coromandel hinterland out of their base at Madras.

[5] Susil Chaudhuri, 1975.

The tail was now wagging the dog, as servants of the Company assumed military functions and dragged it into the political turmoil of South Asia in search of personal glory and untold wealth. Their cry was national glory, indicating a shift in perceptions about their reasons for being in the Indian Ocean: the desire to trade was replaced by the desire for territory (See Map 13).

As Mughal power waned during the mid-eighteenth century, Anglo-French rivalry, already burning bright in the Mediterranean and the Atlantic, spread to the waters of the Indian Ocean, and then to the decaying Mughal empire. In the twilight of imperial authority provincial governors and warlords established their independence, setting up petty states which struggled over the carcase of the empire. From their coastal enclaves the British and the French took military action to protect and advance their interests in this political interregnum and to trounce one another. Naval warfare between the British and the French across the western Indian Ocean and in South Asian waters began a process which ended with great military clashes in various parts of the decaying Mughal empire between the EIC, French forces and the indigenous allies and agents of both. Such wide-ranging and co-ordinated naval warfare between rival European powers marked a new development in the geopolitics of the Indian Ocean, and from the eighteenth century until the present it has remained an arena for the extension of extra-regional rivalries and conflicts.

The Directors of the EIC may have been loath to risk its commercial fortunes for military glory, but statesmen in western Europe thought otherwise. In 1760 the French chief minister, the Duc du Choiseul, put it most succinctly when he declared 'it is colonies, trade and, in consequence, seapower which must determine the balance of power' in Europe.[6] Such sentiments were no doubt shared by his British counterparts, particularly after they had lost their American colonies and were desperately seeking to vanquish the spectre of French naval superiority in the Atlantic and Indian Oceans.

With hindsight, for the Anglo-French struggle over South Asia was to continue into the 1790s, the conquest of Bengal marked the

[6] Geoffrey Parker, 1988, 82.

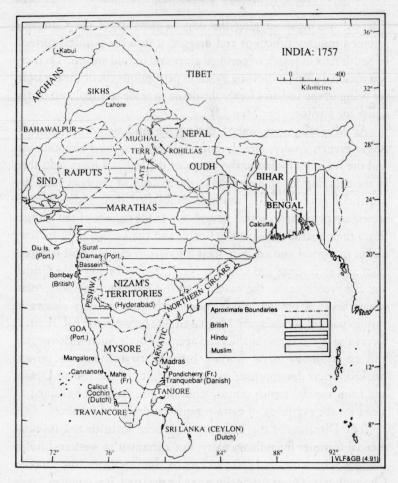

Map 13:   India: 1757

triumph of the EIC over the VOC and the French company. It was not simply a triumph of one commercial company over another, but was rather the triumph of British political interests over those of the French, when they wrested political authority and territory from the decaying Mughal empire. The EIC now received an income from the territories it had conquered which was to become more profitable than the returns from trade. Following the establishment of the EIC's empire in South Asia, British merchants were, in effect, in alliance with the British government whose global aims of asserting national power suited their activities and interests. A similar relationship had existed between the French company and the French government, from the late seventeenth century. In this instance, the nexus led to the downfall of French commercial ambitions in the disastrous Anglo-French wars of the eighteenth century, which broke French naval, military and commercial power in the Atlantic and Indian Oceans.

Indigenous merchants in South Asia, in contrast to their European rivals, did not have the support of a sympathetic government. Those who had structured their commercial life around the purchases of local rulers suffered oblivion if they were unable to adjust to the decline in fortunes of the aristocracy and the emergence of European commercial domination. Increasingly throughout the eighteenth century successful South Asian merchants retreated from direct participation in foreign trade to concentrate their energies on mass domestic markets, and as agents and financiers for European enterprise within South Asia.

Trade with China was, by the eighteenth century, shaping the major directions of Indian Ocean maritime trade. For the past three centuries the most conspicuous feature of that trade had been the Gujarat-Coromandel-Melaka axis, at the centre of which were the great import markets and export production areas of South Asia. By the mid-eighteenth century export cargoes from China were being sought more eagerly by Europeans than ever before. South Asian cargoes, particularly from Bengal, were now directed more frequently eastward at the expense of trade with the less profitable markets of the Middle East, Africa, the Americas and Europe, where South Asian textiles were now being replaced by factory produced European textiles. China had become the major focus of Indian Ocean maritime trade by the late eighteenth century, as European demand underwent yet another change.

Bengal, through ports such as Calcutta and Dhaka, provided the main cargoes for the China trade. With the assistance of indigenous merchants and financiers, South Asian textiles and opium were sold in South East Asia, primarily for silver and pepper, which were then shipped to China to finance purchases of tea. For much of the eighteenth century, however, Bengal's trade with South East Asia was directed principally towards the Indonesian islands, and had to face the unremitting hostility of the Dutch, who frequently allied themselves in Europe with Britain's French enemies. The EIC was cautious not to provoke the Dutch and left British trade with insular South East Asia in the hands of private merchants who were prepared to risk their fortunes by trading in areas which the VOC regarded as within its sphere of influence. British private traders were particularly active along the eastern shore of the Bay of the Bengal, between southern Burma and northern Sumatra. Such private traders worked the 'country trade', dealing in any and all cargoes and building up a considerable body of intelligence concerning the coast, its people, politics and trade goods. Information of this sort was passed to the EIC's officials in India, who came under increasing pressure to protect British private trade from Dutch arrogance and depredations.

While Europeans, especially the British, came to dominate much of the Bengal-China trade, they did so in co-operation with indigenous merchants and shipowners who controlled significant areas of trade until the last decades of the eighteenth century. In the South China Sea during the eighteenth century, for example, Chinese and Thai merchants established the lucrative rice export trade to China. Europeans were never able to break into this trade, which flourished into the early twentieth century. Chinese entrepreneurs and shipowners also dominated trade between Dutch territories in insular South East Asia and China.

The eighteenth century was the golden age of the Bengal textile trade, with cargoes sent to all corners of the Indian Ocean region and to Europe. The British, with a substantial territorial base in Bengal, were the major beneficiaries in this development. The VOC, with bankruptcy looming, could only look on as a jealous observer. The

Danes tied their interests to those of the British and eventually wound up their company in 1808. It was only the French who seriously attempted to challenge the extension of British commercial and political interests in South Asia in the late eighteenth century, masked behind the ambitions of indigenous rulers such as Tipu Sultan of Mysore and the Nizams of Hyderabad, who fought the British for control of southern India. Such meddling precipitated a final confrontation which lead to the destruction of French political and commercial interests in South Asia, by the late eighteenth century, following a series of Anglo-French wars across southern and central India.

British expansion in South Asia was encouraged by the decline of the Mughal empire, which gathered pace from the mid-eighteenth century, and the volatile nature of successor states across the subcontinent. At the same time, the economic importance of South Asia in the whole maritime trading system of the Indian Ocean was heightened by the rapid decline in Middle Eastern economies. The decline was evident by the late eighteenth century, as the Safavid empire collapsed in chaos, the Ottoman empire began to weaken and the Red Sea and the Persian Gulf became commercial backwaters.

Ironically, the EIC would emerge as victor in the struggle over Mughal India in the late eighteenth century, between a shifting spectrum of British, indigenous and French interests, at a time when the South Asian mercantile activity still flourished, and the agricultural economy was both prosperous and still the source of much mercantile capital and profit.

By the last decades of the eighteenth century the EIC was not only master of much of what is now northern and eastern India and Bangladesh, and the major supplier of South Asian textiles to Europe, but it was also busy extracting a valuable agricultural surplus and indigenous capital from its South Asian possessions. In addition, and most importantly, it had found even more profitable markets for South Asian textiles and opium, through which it was possible to dominate the China tea trade, just as the European and American demand for South Asian textiles began to decline with the development of cotton textile production in Britain.

The attempts of the British, both the EIC and an increasing number of Free Traders who were hostile to the monopolistic claims of the EIC, to sell South Asian cargoes in South East Asia, brought them into bouts of conflict with the exclusive trading claims of both the VOC in the Indonesian islands and the Spanish in the Philippines.

Apart from the hostility of their rivals, the British faced the hostility of the Chinese authorities who opposed the sale of opium and were concerned about a drain of silver to pay for imports. To break into the China market, the EIC had to trade opium and textiles in insular South East Asia in return for silver, tin and pepper which were then shipped to China. The VOC resented this renewed British interest and, along with the Spanish, resisted the attempts of British traders to move into insular South East Asia beyond the one remaining EIC outpost at remote Benkulu (Bencoolen), on the west coast of Sumatra. Manila was briefly occupied by the British, and inconclusive warfare erupted between the British and the Dutch.

Eventually the EIC obtained a central foothold in South East Asia when they leased the island of Penang from the sultan of Kedah in 1786. Penang was established as a free port to attract indigenous traders from all over South East Asia and from southern India. Through it, South Asian textiles and opium were funnelled into South East Asia, in exchange for goods and silver which were then traded with China for tea and silk for Europe, along with very large consignments of Chinese porcelain used as ballast. The EIC's agent in Penang deliberately encouraged the settlement of Chinese, Chulia, Javanese, Bugi and Sumatran merchants in the port as a means of gaining access to indigenous trade networks. Penang's attraction for indigenous merchants was based on the fact that in creating a free port the EIC provided a happy alternative to the exactions of the VOC, which was moving to monopolise the tin trade of the Malay peninsula and to tie local sultans into exclusive trading agreements.

Ironically, the British occupation of Penang contributed to the decline of many, although not all, indigenous ports. For a century or more the VOC had been attempting to curb the activities of ports such as Johor, by force. Where Dutch force failed, British commerce succeeded. Against a background of conflict between Burma and Thailand, and Dutch depredation, Penang was an oasis of commercial security, attracting indigenous merchants away from the string of indigenous ports which stretched along the eastern shore of the Bay of Bengal. In fact Penang was not a spectacular success in terms of its original charter as a halfway house to China: increasingly from the early 1800s the British found cargoes elsewhere to finance the China trade. However, Penang did flourish as a sub-regional entrepôt, serving a range of secondary ports between southern Burma and Sumatra, and providing a base from which Chinese merchants were able to control a major share of indigenous maritime trade of the area.

At the moment of its apparent triumph, however, the days of the EIC were numbered. Throughout the eighteenth century, cargoes of spices to Europe had been replaced by much larger cargoes of cotton cloth and tea for a rapidly expanding consumer market. Changes in the British economy had ushered in the age of the individual capitalist entrepreneur who, as a Free Trader, co-operated with, and then replaced, the antiquated and inefficient company system, the antithesis of the new capitalist ethos. By the late eighteenth century, British merchants around the world had espoused the principles of Free Trade. They now rejected the Company's mercantilist trading monopoly of the Asia–Europe and China trade, and launched an attack on its privileges which was to eventually result in their abolition. In 1813 the EIC lost its monopoly of the Asia–Europe trade, and in 1833, of the China trade.

While the British were busy constructing a convoluted series of trading systems to extract tea from China, the French and the Dutch were experimenting with a new type of economic and trading activity. In the Mascarenes—Mauritius, La Réunion and the Seychelles—during the eighteenth century, colonies of French settlers and slaves from Madagascar and West and East Africa were established to work plantations: initially of spices, and then of sugar, coffee, vanilla and coconuts for export to Indian Ocean and European destinations. Similarly, in Java, the VOC established successful coffee plantations to supply Indian Ocean and European markets, following the collapse of the coffee trade with the Yemeni port of Mocha in the early eighteenth century. Neither the Dutch nor the French, however, established a private trader presence in the Indian Ocean on the scale of the British, consequently, neither were prepared for the transition of European economic activity from commerce to capitalism.

The slave-based settlement and exploitation of the Mascarenes

highlights a darker trade, whose thread runs through the history of
Indian Ocean trade from earliest times. The slave trade was practised
in all parts of the Indian Ocean world, with the exception of Australia
(until the nineteenth century when 'Kanaks'—Melanesians—were
kidnapped to work sugar plantations in Queensland, and Aboriginals
worked as virtual slave labourers in pearl fisheries off Broome and in
cattle stations across northern Australia), but with the arrival of Europeans it grew rapidly. From the late seventeenth century Europeans
transported slaves from Mozambique and Madagascar to the plantations of the Mascarenes and the Americas.

The bulk trade in South Asian cotton textiles and Chinese tea,
and the establishment of plantations in the Mascarenes and Java to
produce tropical commodities for European consumption, heralded a
major change in the economic relationship between Europe and the
Indian Ocean, which was to gather momentum during the nineteenth
century. It also marked yet another change in the general direction of
Indian Ocean maritime trade. The Gujarat–Melaka axis had been
replaced by the Bengal–China axis in the eighteenth century. In the
nineteenth century, however, this gave way to a general Asia–Europe
axis, directed after 1869 through the newly opened Suez canal.

Commercial Capitalism—Integration or Change?

Until recently, many European scholars, though sympathetic to non-
European civilizations, have tended to view their histories simplistically as relatively uncomplicated and unsophisticated, compared with
the progressive civilizations and economies of Europe, which struggled
out of medieval chaos through the Renaissance to create a modern
capitalist world. In this evolutionary struggle non-European civilizations and economies are seen as the losers, and consequently as the
weaker partners in the battle between European enterprise and charm-
ing but antiquated Asian, African, Australian and American native
civilizations and economies.

Such arguments are typified by the writings of the American
sociologist and historian Immanuel Wallerstein, who has attempted
to explain world history against a central theme based on the development of an overwhelming western European capitalist system which

integrated a number of isolated 'world systems', including the Indian Ocean 'world system', in the eighteenth and nineteenth centuries into a European-dominated capitalist world economy.[7] Wallerstein claimed such integration could only occur when trade between two 'world systems' was based on the exchange of necessities (basically articles for mass consumption), and this was clearly the case by the nineteenth century.[8]

With respect to Wallerstein's arguments concerning the integration of the Indian Ocean world system into a European-dominated world system, there are problems relating to prerequisites and timing concerning the process of integration. While western Europe undoubtedly did develop an overwhelming capitalist system in the eighteenth century, it is simplistic to relegate all trading systems outside Europe until then as necessarily isolated from one another, apart from the limited exchange of luxury goods. To argue such a situation is to ignore the ancient and vital economic exchanges which linked Europe, Africa and Asia for the last 2000 years, and reflects a simplistic view of the nature of that trade.

Wallerstein viewed trade between the Indian Ocean world system and other world systems as minimal, unsophisticated and based largely upon luxuries. He defined the pre-modern trade between the Indian Ocean world system and other parts of the globe in spices, pepper, precious metals, textiles and ceramics as a trade in 'luxuries', and therefore he argued that the Indian Ocean world system operated largely in isolation. Wallerstein also ignored trade between the Indian Ocean world system and East and Central Asia, which was not based exclusively on what he defined as luxuries, but which included commodities such as cotton and silk textiles, pepper, foodstuffs, cowries, ceramics and copper: all of which were considered necessities by certain classes of people.

Wallerstein's argument is based upon a simplistic interpretation of 'necessities' and 'luxuries', as well as an imprecise knowledge of the economic history of the Indian Ocean and early European enterprise

[7] Wallerstein, 1987.
[8] I. Wallerstein, 1979, 16 and 1987, 222–253. For a critique of Wallerstein see Michael Pearson, 1987 (b), 23–31 and 1988, 455–472.

in the area. He singularly failed to address the problem of differentiating luxuries and necessities. Although Wallerstein qualifies his description of pepper as a luxury, it was clearly a necessity for many in Europe, the Middle East and North Africa, who were consuming a growing proportion of Indian Ocean production by the fifteenth century. In Europe, for instance, its widespread use as a payment in kind for rent and as a dietary supplement, as well as its general acceptance as an item of regular consumption by mercantile and land-owning classes, challenges any attempt to classify it as a universal 'luxury'. Similarly, as we have already seen, precious metals imported from beyond the Indian Ocean were a necessity for the Indian Ocean 'world economy' by the ninth century where, as coinage, it underpinned the operation of complex indigenous states.

Wallerstein is on firmer ground when he argues that the overwhelming economic expansion of the British in the Indian Ocean—and the integration of the Indian Ocean world system into a global economy—in the eighteenth century, was based on their command of commercial capitalism; to which I would add the fact of their military superiority. The economic domination of the British began in the eighteenth century, with a commercial revolution based on the capture of Asian maritime trade and their domination of European-Asian trade, which were facilitated by politicians who moulded national objectives to the furtherance of trade.[9]

In this process the British utilized the skills and money of indigenous merchants in South Asia. It was only in the wake of this British commercial victory that industrial capital from Europe began to change the economies of the Indian Ocean into servants of a capitalist European-dominated global economy. The development of industrial capitalism certainly forced the pace of imperial expansion, but it was not the primary cause. The commercial revolution came about in no small measure as the result of co-operation between private British and indigenous merchants. Such co-operation was to extend into the nineteenth century and underpinned the growth of capitalist enterprise in the Indian Ocean region.

European consumer demand changed rapidly during the late

[9] Pamela Nightingale, 1970, 236.

eighteenth and early nineteenth centuries. The development of industrial manufacturing increased the market in western Europe for obvious mass consumption necessities such as unprocessed raw materials and for foodstuffs to feed an urbanized labouring class. In Britain, for example, during the late eighteenth and early nineteenth centuries, the development of a cotton textile industry based on imports of raw cotton from the USA challenged and then severely reduced imports of South Asian textiles. Cotton yarn for English textile mills replaced cotton textiles as the major export from South Asia to Britain. At the same time, the rapid growth and urbanization of the population of western Europe encouraged the importation of foodstuffs from areas beyond Europe. Commodities such as tin, timber, raw cotton, jute, rice, sago, palm oil, sugar, hides, skins, wool, iron, copper, lead, zinc, silver, gold, mica, indigo, wheat, fruit and meat—and later plantation-grown rubber, tea and coffee—became the major objects of European commercial activity in the Indian Ocean region during the first half of the nineteenth century, replacing the more exotic and glamorous cargoes of previous centuries.

Import cargoes into the region also changed dramatically. The ancient drain of gold and silver from the West was halted when industrial manufactures of the West flooded the markets of the Indian Ocean region, displacing many of the local cottage-industry manufactures, including textiles. The South Asian textile industry which had expanded rapidly to satisfy European demand, contracted, while other local industries collapsed in the nineteenth century as Europe flooded the region with cheaper factory-produced goods. Other victims were the European monopolistic trading companies. Having outlived their usefulness and profitability, they were now replaced in a free-wheeling capitalist world by individual European entrepreneurs.

It was in response to such developments that the maritime trading economy of the Indian Ocean began to react to external rather than internal market demand. It was not simply a matter of being integrated into a global capitalist economy as the Wallerstein school has argued, but was more precisely, a process whereby the economies of the Indian Ocean 'world system' were made peripheral to, and dependent upon, the economies of western Europe with the evolution of industrial capitalism. Western capitalism had triumphed and had destroyed the relative economic self-sufficiency of the Indian Ocean world. The process had begun in the eighteenth century, as Indian Ocean cargoes began to be distributed outside Europe, particularly to the Americas, where there were considerable markets for cheap South Asian cloth, pepper from Sumatra and slaves from Madagascar and East Africa. This was paralleled, as we have seen, by changes in the content of European trade. Relatively small cargoes of goods such as pepper and spices were increasingly replaced by bulk cargoes of more mundane staples such as textiles, tea and various tropical raw materials.

South Asia, South East Asia and China were central to these changes as they were the greatest suppliers of raw materials and staple manufactures. The economies of the Middle East and East Africa were either in decline or were so structured that initially they were of marginal interest to European merchants and investors. Not until the late nineteenth century were they to be fully exposed to the workings of foreign capitalists.

The growing concentration of financial resources in European hands, and the sheer size of their commercial purchases, which tied regional supplying markets much closer to extra-regional consuming markets, were vitally important to changes in patterns of European economic activity in the Indian Ocean. As European political control expanded, maritime trade was increasingly directed towards serving European economic interests, and the economies of the region were laid open to the ambitions of European entrepreneurs. Maritime trade began to operate along new routes, leading to the rapid decline of many traditional maritime trading routes, as commerce within the Indian Ocean took second place to trade between the Indian Ocean and the rest of the world.

During the nineteenth century there was a decline in the fortunes of indigenous mariners and merchants. There were many reasons for this. Until the eighteenth century the technological and commercial gap between Europe and the great civilizations of Asia was relatively small. In the first half of the nineteenth century this gap widened enormously, enabling Europeans armed with a range of new technologies, both scientific and commercial, to overwhelm the rest of the world. Communication technology was revolutionized, quickening the pace of mercantile activity and tying production areas outside

Europe even more closely to European markets. New medical technology increased the survival rate among Europeans and hence their human resources. None of this technology—which was a form of capital—was controlled by non-Europeans, and little of it was available to indigenous entrepreneurs, who could no longer seriously compete with their European rivals in the new economic order.

Scientific technology aside, there were other reasons for the decline in indigenous mercantile activity. European commercial technology, in the form of global banking and finance institutions, overwhelmed non-European monetary and finance networks. With the decline and collapse of indigenous states such as the Mughal and Safavid empires in the eighteenth and nineteenth centuries, and the growing exclusion of indigenous merchants from profitable markets, major sources of local finance evaporated. The spread of exclusive European banking systems, and the increasingly monopolistic activity of well-financed groups of European shipping and trading companies, further undermined indigenous economic activity.

The development of indigenous merchants and investors was further restricted when colonial regimes legislated to restrict activity by indigenous merchants, shippers and industrialists who, given access to adequate capital, might have competed with European merchants and investors. In British India, for example, attempts by Indian investors to establish an Indian-owned steamship company were thwarted until the twentieth century. On the other hand, Indian investors were more successful in establishing modern cotton, coal and steel industries, initially to supply local markets.

European capital in the Indian Ocean region from the 1830s was directed towards the control of the production of raw materials as well as into trade, and in this process independent action by local merchants, shippers and investors were marginalized. The European preoccupation with trade, which had been the driving force behind their overseas expansion since the fifteenth century, was expanded to include new economic interests based on the investment of capital.

Although European colonial governments, merchants, bankers and investors combined to restrict the development of an indigenous class of capitalists who might have threatened European economic and political power, some of the capital utilized by Europeans to develop plantations, mines and public works came from indigenous investors. Ironically, therefore, local money was used to further the expansion of European-controlled economic activity and contributed to the evolution of a capitalist economic system in the Indian Ocean region. Indeed, indigenous capital, particularly Indian capital, was vital to the development and expansion of European capitalism throughout the Indian Ocean region, and remained so until the late nineteenth century, when Western money markets came to dominate world finances.

Indian merchant capital led to the economic penetration of the East African and Somali interior in the eighteenth and nineteenth centuries, financed the sugar industries in Mauritius and Natal, modern textile production throughout South Asia, the slave and clove trade of Zanzibar, the ivory trade of Mozambique, pearling in the Gulf and Red Sea, the Mocha coffee trade, trade in the Gulf and between South and South East Asia, the opium trade between South Asia and China, and performed myriad functions for European economic interests. Indian mercantile and banking groups dominated the trade of the western Indian Ocean as financiers, merchants, investors and commercial agents, throughout the eighteenth century and well into the nineteenth century. By the late nineteenth century Indian capital even began to challenge European investment in some areas, most particularly in the coal, iron and steel industries of British India.

Until the twentieth century, however, these Indian groups were never able to expand their activities outside the Indian Ocean region, where they remained essentially middlemen in the financing and collection of export cargoes for the West. Some of them followed the British to Hong Kong, the West Indies and Canada, but in all these areas they remained on the periphery of major capitalist enterprise.

In the late nineteenth century the establishment of colonial rule throughout East Africa, and the resurgence of Ottoman authority in Arabia, alongside the revival of Arab trading groups in Aden and Oman, led to a decline in Indian mercantile pre-eminence and curtailed the range of their economic activities. Much the same happened in Singapore, founded by the British in 1819, and the Malay peninsula. There, both Indian and Chinese economic activity was initially restricted by the establishment of European rule, and the increasing power of European capital determined to reduce indigenous co-operation and confine indigenous economic activity, if possible, to select areas such as petty trade and commodity collection.

These changes in the sources and structures of capital were underpinned by a series of technological developments, giving further impetus to the economic penetration of European investors in the region.

By the late eighteenth century European maritime technology had overtaken its indigenous counterparts in the Indian Ocean region. With the invention of the steam vessel in the early nineteenth century, this victory was absolute. The all-weather European vessels were larger, faster, safer and more reliable than indigenous craft on long-haul coastal and trans-oceanic voyages, especially with the development of more cost-efficient steam-driven and iron-constructed vessels in the 1860s and 1870s. But the victory was less clear on short-haul marginal and feeder routes, for example, between India and Sri Lanka and along the East African coast, where a symbiotic relationship evolved between European steam vessels and indigenous sail. Also, in the Persian Gulf, Indian-owned vessels flying the British flag maintained a small but profitable trade out of ports such as Bombay, to Muscat, the Trucial Coast, Bahrain and Basra.

By the late nineteenth century the region was also reeling from the impact of European manufacturing technology, and a rising barrier of protective tariffs in Britain which replaced the doctrine of Free Trade and which reduced the import of better-quality manufactures from Asia. Mass production and the factory system enabled Europeans to flood Indian Ocean markets with cheaply produced manufactured goods which undermined the products of indigenous cottage industries. The region's high-quality ceramics, for example—apart from Chinese export ware which retained its markets in South East Asia— was replaced by the products of Scottish, English, Dutch and German factories. In the same way, cheap textiles, woven out of American and Egyptian cotton and Indian yarn in British and US mills, displaced Indian cotton textiles from domestic, regional and international markets, when they were unleashed upon the world.

Europe was paying for its imports from the Indian Ocean region with a flood of manufactures which led to a change in the nature of local markets. Increasing populations around the Indian Ocean resulted in the expansion of local markets which were now locked into the worldwide movement of raw materials and manufactures dominated by European and North American economic interests. In addition, the capital goods supplied by Europe and North America, such as machinery and railway equipment, facilitated the extraction of raw materials to further fuel the factories of the industrializing West. In British India railways gave rise to an indigenous-financed coal industry, and then to iron and steel industries. But such industries remained servants to the imperial economy, and their activities were limited by the realities of imperial rule which placed British interests above those of colonial peoples.

The development of the telegraph in the 1840s bound local economies even more tightly to the wider world. Economic demand in Europe could now be transmitted almost instantaneously to the markets of Asia, Africa and Australasia, where economic activity became more thoroughly subordinated to the will of industrialised Europe. Railway technology, developed at the same time as the telegraph, provided yet another means of penetrating and controlling hinterlands and their economies. Railways revolutionized the pace and cost of commodity movement, directing a growing volume of goods to European-dominated markets. Railways not only displaced indigenous vehicular and porter traffic on many routes, they also attracted cargoes away from coastal shipping. In the twentieth century the revolutionary impact of the railway on trade was matched by the introduction of the motor lorry, which linked even more markets and production centres into the major regional markets controlled by European colonial powers.

The impact of new transport, communication and medical technologies, and the spread of European political control, was also felt in the centralization of port activities. As an increasing volume of trade was funnelled through a smaller number of channels, many formerly prosperous ports vanished or were turned into backwaters. Others, particularly those which had been the earliest seats of European power in the region, became centres of the new transport, communication and medical technology. They became great entrepôts serviced by a declining number of out-ports. Mombasa, Karachi, Bombay, Colombo, Madras, Calcutta, Rangoon, Singapore and Jakarta were the heirs to the great ports of the pre-European period. Unlike their predecessors, however, they tended to drain the mercantile lifeblood of lesser ports in the Indian Ocean region.

Capitalism Triumphant?

The opening of the Suez Canal in 1869 tethered the maritime trading network of the Indian Ocean even more closely to European markets and suppliers, reducing both travelling time and cargo costs. Such costs were further reduced as steam vessels became more efficient. Steam vessels were the major beneficiaries of this new route, and sailing ships were left to hauling low-value bulk cargoes and emigrants around the Cape of Good Hope, and, in the early decades of the twentieth century, to extinction.

The changes wrought by Europeans in the Indian Ocean region between the seventeenth and nineteenth centuries integrated four new areas—southern Africa, the Mascarenes, western Australia and eastern Africa—into both the regional and international economies. European settlement in the first three areas produced colonial economies moulded by European investors. All three became suppliers of raw materials and foodstuffs for Europe, but none were encouraged to develop a major manufacturing base: this was the prerogative of Europe, the US and, later, Japan. But while these colonies were created to serve industrialized Europe, and indirectly other industrialized nations, they were not initially isolated from the rest of the Indian Ocean region and all developed trading links with other parts of the region.

The Dutch settlement at Cape Town was closely linked to other Dutch establishments in insular South East Asia and South Asia, while the French Mascarenes had intimate trading links with French outposts in India. Regional trade was also important for the survival of the British colony on the Swan River on the west coast of Australia. In the early decades after settlement in 1829, Swan River colonists built their own ships and traded foodstuffs, timber (both jarrah or 'Swan River Mahogany' and sandalwood), and horses as army remounts, with British India, Singapore, Jakarta (Batavia), Mauritius and the Cape Colony. At the same time, fishermen from Sulawesi were regular visitors to the north-west shores of Australia, gathering trepang and trochus shell for export to China. This activity was curtailed as Europeans took over control of the western third of Australia, only to be revived in the twentieth century.[10]

The fourth area drawn more closely into the trading world of the Indian Ocean was the East African interior, stretching from Kenya and Uganda in the north to Zimbabwe and Malawi in the south, and the southernmost stretches of Africa from Mozambique to the Cape. In the seventeenth century the VOC settled farmers at the Cape, just as Portuguese and Indian Christian settlers were moving inland along the Zambezi valley towards the uplands of Zimbabwe. Nearly 200 years later, European intrusion into the southern hinterland increased as British settlers and Boers moved from the Cape and the Natal coast into the interior. From Mozambique northward, from the early eighteenth century, Muslim traders from the East African coast, financed by Indian Hindu bankers, pushed inland in increasing numbers. No longer content to wait on the coast for cargoes from the interior, Muslim traders now responded actively to the rising demand for slaves in the expanding plantation economies of Zanzibar and Pemba, off the coast of East Africa, the Mascarenes and the Americas, and for ivory universally. This intrusion into the African interior linked into local trade networks, paving the way for European economic and political penetration in the latter half of the nineteenth century, in the footsteps of Muslims from the coast.

Apart from these four areas, by the early nineteenth century the southern waters of the Indian Ocean (between Africa, Australia and Antarctica) were opened up to exploitation. European and North American whalers chased their prey across the southernmost reaches of the ocean, setting up temporary bases on Kerguelen and other islands and preparing the scene for the exploration of the world's last uninhabited continent, Antarctica, in the early twentieth century. In addition to whalers, fishing industries were established by European colonists in southern Africa and western Australia, based primarily on the exploitation of continental shelf fisheries.

[10] C.C. Macknight, 1976.

Although the domination of European capitalism in the Indian Ocean region can be partially explained by technological and commercial changes, these went hand-in-hand with increasing European political domination. At the end of the eighteenth century European territorial control in the region was limited. The British controlled parts of South Asia and had outposts in South East Asia at Penang and Benkulu (Bencoolen). The Dutch held Cape Town, coastal Sri Lanka, Java, Melaka and scattered enclaves throughout the Indonesian archipelago. The French held the Mascarenes, Pondicherry on the Coromandel coast and several minute enclaves elsewhere in coastal India. The Danes had the decaying port of Tranquebar to the south of Madras; while the Portuguese clung to shrinking territory on the Mozambique coast, around Goa, Daman and Diu in India, and on Timor.

Following the defeat of the French and their allies in 1815, after a worldwide war which lasted more than twenty years, there were changes in European territorial possessions in the Indian Ocean region. The British emerged as the dominant power in South Asia, gaining Sri Lanka from the Dutch, along with Melaka and Cape Town, as well as the major part of the Mascarenes from the French. The French presence was restricted to the island of La Réunion and minor Indian enclaves, the Dutch were contained within the Indonesian archipelago, and the Portuguese were tolerated in their Indian enclaves, on the Mozambique coast and on Timor (See Map 14).

The French wars had also drawn the attention of both the British in Westminster and India back to the Persian Gulf. French intrigues at the court of the Shah of Persia, Napoleon's Syrian campaign, and the southward extension of Russian power into Central Asia and the northern border lands of Persia, alerted the British to potential threats to India from the direction of the Middle East. In addition, British Indian vessels and merchants came under attack from various groups in the Gulf. To counteract these strategic and commercial threats the British in India began to take a closer interest in the affairs of the Gulf during the 1820s and 1830s. Treaties were signed with local rulers which in effect guaranteed their status in return for British protection and an end to attacks on British Indian shipping. Throughout the nineteenth century, these concerns dragged the British deeper into the

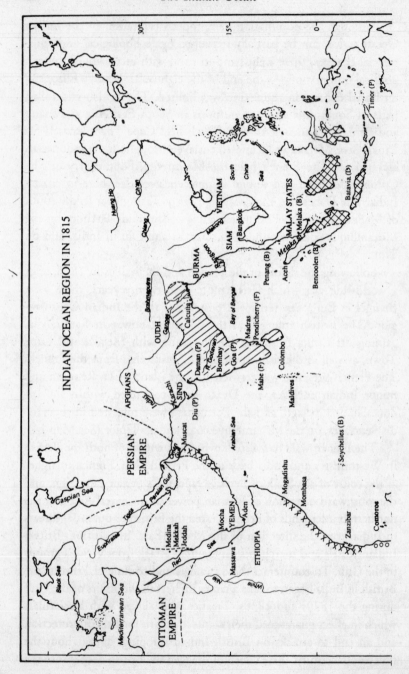

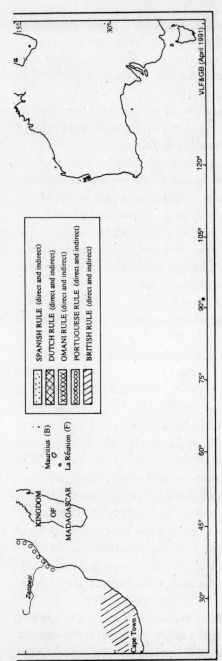

Map 14: The Indian Ocean Region in 1815

affairs of first the Gulf states, and then Persia and Afghanistan, creating a sub-imperial sphere of influence based on British power in India.

It was also the French threat that first drew the British into establishing a permanent presence to guard the entry to the Red Sea. In 1799 they occupied the island of Perim off the coast of Yemen, followed in 1839 by the occupation of Aden, when they became concerned about the expansionist policies of a potentially hostile Egypt under Mahomed Ali and his French advisers.

During the nineteenth century the British completed their control over South Asia. In the first two decades of the century central India and the Ganges valley came under British control and, by the 1850s, Sind and the Punjab had been incorporated into British India. Disastrous attempts were made to curb the independence of Persia and Afghanistan where there were fears of growing Russian influence, although in the early twentieth century a *modus vivendi* was achieved with respect to both countries and British India.

By the 1880s the British had gained Burma, the Maldives, most of the Malay peninsula, and had moved out of the Cape to seize the major share of southern Africa. By 1900 they were the dominant power in the Red Sea and the Persian Gulf, controlling the Suez Canal and the Red Sea from Egypt and Aden, and the waterways of the Persian Gulf from Bahrain to Oman. In addition, by 1829 they held the Australian continent from the Pacific to the Indian Ocean. Also, during the nineteenth century, the Dutch consolidated their control over the Indonesian archipelago, while the French, Germans and Italians followed the British into Africa during the 1880s and 1890s. The French took control of Djibouti on the Red Sea, Madagascar and the Comoros (where they had maintained a presence since the 1840s), and the Germans carved out a colony in Tanganyika. The Italians took Eritrea on the Red Sea from Ethiopia and occupied the ports of the Benadir coast, creating the colony of Italian Somaliland next door to the British, who were alarmed by the Italian move and created the colony of British Somaliland on the coast, opposite their port at Aden, to secure their control over the entrance to the Red Sea.

Much of this expansion can be explained in terms of economic interests and to an extent the flag did follow trade; but it was also due to fears of the growth of rival European interests into the Indian Ocean region. The intrusion of rival European powers into the Indian Ocean pushed the British to secure their domination of the region by seizing the Sudan, with its ports on the Red Sea, as well as Zanzibar, Kenya, Uganda, Zimbabwe, Malawi and Zambia, creating a swathe of British-controlled territory from the Cape to the Mediterranean, once Egypt had been occupied in 1882. Similar fears drove them to proclaim protectorates over the Arab sheikhdoms of the Persian Gulf, the Muslim sultanates of the Malay peninsula and the Cocos (Keeling) Islands, ruled by a Scots merchant family as a private estate until the 1970s.

By the end of the nineteenth century—in political and strategic terms—the Indian Ocean was a British lake dotted with Dutch, French, German, Italian and Portuguese enclaves. Ethiopia remained in landlocked isolation after losing coastal Eritrea to Italy, and was briefly occupied by the Italians in the 1930s. Iran and Thailand maintained their independence by adroitly playing off one imperial power against another. The Iranians lost much territory in Central Asia to Russia, but ultimately preserved their independence by setting the Russians against the British in their struggle for influence over the country. Similarly, the Thais lost territory in the Malay peninsula to the British, and in Laos and parts of Cambodia to the French, but they were able to pit the conflicting interests of these powers against one another to retain their independence.

Western commercial power—both European and North American—was now backed by European political and military power, and indigenous merchants and investors now responded to European commercial and industrial demands, rather than to locally-generated needs.

While there was some industrial development in the Indian Ocean region from the late nineteenth century which involved indigenous capital, the greater part of industrial output was directed towards the extraction and partial processing of export commodities—jute, cotton yarn and cloth, minerals, foodstuffs, rubber, tea, coffee—destined for markets in the industrialised West. The smaller part of industrial activity was directed towards the service sector, and most manufactures were imported into the region from Europe, North America and later, Japan.

By the First World War European control over the major maritime trading routes of the Indian Ocean region was complete. Oil from the Gulf, Burma and Indonesia; minerals from South Africa, Zimbabwe, Zambia and Australia; tea from India and Sri Lanka; rubber and tin and a range of tropical products from Malaysia and Indonesia; wheat, wool, fruit, wine and gold from Australia and South Africa; sugar from the Mascarenes; phosphate from Christmas Island; minerals, tropical raw materials, cotton yarn and foodstuffs from India and many more mundane staples, were moved in the direction of Europe. The trade in luxury goods and staples had been largely replaced by a plain but profitable trade in raw bulk commodities for the industrial economies of the West.

Indian Ocean cargoes were not only prized by Europeans for their worth in Europe, but they were also the currency of very profitable trade with other parts of the world. Goods from British India were sold in China, once foreign trade had been forced upon that country by the British in 1842. Similarly, we have seen that in the early nineteenth century, cargoes of cheap Indian cloth and Sumatran pepper, along with cargoes of slaves from East Africa, found profitable markets in the USA. By the twentieth century the raw materials and manufactures of India and of other countries of the region were traded around the world. Following World War I, however, the European share of India's seaborne trade declined sharply and there was a growth in India's trade with other parts of Asia, Africa, Oceania and the Americas.

Hand in hand with European domination of regional markets and means of production, was an equally exclusive control of communications and transport systems, and new medical technology. Railways were entirely European-controlled, either directly through private ownership or through colonial state-ownership. The same held true of telegraph and telephone systems, air transport and, above all, modern shipping, until the emergence of the Japanese after World War I.

New scientific technologies in the nineteenth century were also the exclusive domain of Europeans. Medical discoveries throughout the nineteenth century, along with improvements in diet, helped Europeans live longer in the tropics and the equatorial zone, encouraging the settlement of European women, the raising of European families, and an increasing separation between European communities and indigenous populations. European medical science only slowly permeated among indigenous peoples, whose mortality rates continue to be greater than those of Europeans to this day.

Beneath this awesome edifice of Western science and technology, some of the ancient maritime trading structure survived. On many short-haul routes indigenous craft still operated: as collectors of cargoes to be gathered at large ports for dispatch on foreign vessels; as carriers of local produce for indigenous consumption; and as distributors of manufactured goods which filtered into the smaller markets of the region.

It was also true that many indigenous mercantile groups survived the impact of western economic and political penetration. In the nineteenth and twentieth centuries, as in the seventeenth and eighteenth centuries, European trade within the Indian Ocean region depended upon indigenous collaboration. While many merchant groups were eclipsed—including the famous Muslim merchants of the Gulf and western India, the fleets of Gujaratis who had made Melaka great, and the Persians and Armenians who had sustained trade with Thailand and the Philippines in the eighteenth century—they were replaced by new diasporas of indigenous merchants and entrepreneurs, who worked within the European-imposed economic system, both as intermediaries in the collection process and as financiers of capitalist enterprise. The economies of colonial India, Burma, Mauritius, Singapore, Aden, Malaya and Indonesia were sustained by the intense and vital activity of indigenous mercantile groups engaged in the age-old commercial activities of their ancestors, as well as in the new forms of capitalist investment and speculation.

Some indigenous mercantile groups managed to penetrate the world of modern finance. In South East Asia, Chinese settlers developed a wide-flung and very successful banking network, as did the Hindu Chettiars in Sri Lanka and South East Asia. Although severely restricted, the access of indigenous entrepreneurs to venture capital had not entirely vanished.

Not only did the Europeans need indigenous collaborators, but there remained areas of maritime trade where indigenous interests could secure a comfortable profit, even at the height of European political and economic hegemony in the region. Indigenous vessels continued to ply the seas between India and Sri Lanka—and along myriad minor feeder routes of the Persian Gulf, the Bay of Bengal and East Africa—which sustained great European-controlled entrepôts. Their cargoes were small when compared with those carried by the large European-owned vessels; however, on lesser routes they were more profitable. They gathered commodities both for domestic consumption—for example, foodstuffs from coastal South Asia and insular South East Asia—and for transhipment in foreign-owned vessels through the great ports. In addition, these indigenous vessels carried foreign imports deeper into the domestic markets of the region.

It was in this way that the Omanis, in the eighteenth and early nineteenth centuries, were able to establish a small maritime trading empire on the ruins of Portuguese settlements on the Oman, Kenyan and Tanzanian coasts, which were controlled from Muscat and Zanzibar. The Omanis captured control of seaborne trade within this area, providing export cargoes of ivory, slaves and cloves to South Asian intermediaries, in return for European, North American and South Asian manufactures. These commodities were then re-distributed into the African interior and to other parts of the African littoral which they controlled.

In the nineteenth and early twentieth centuries British Indian financiers and Hadhramauti, Persian Gulf and Indian vessels displaced Omani interests, until Middle Eastern oil exports through the Persian Gulf introduced new and dominant types and patterns of shipping in the twentieth century.

Eastward from South Asia, traditional Indonesian and South Asian vessels survived in the Bay of Bengal and the waters of Dutch-controlled Indonesia. If the great steam-driven, foreign-owned vessels—cargo ships, liners and oil tankers—were the behemoths of long-distance trade, then indigenous sailing craft were their attendants, who, in conjunction with land-based transport systems, collected export commodities and distributed import cargoes to the many markets of the Indian Ocean region.

However, even where indigenous maritime mercantile activity survived into the twentieth century, its geographic range was limited. The imposition of colonial boundaries, and the regulation of colonial economies ensnared indigenous merchants and mariners in new bureaucratic restrictions. Territorial and sea boundaries, customs posts and naval patrols, passport restrictions and national tariffs disrupted traditional lines of communications. Age old sea and land routes were disrupted by colonial bureaucratic and fiscal impositions which placed many maritime mercantile groups in the category of 'foreigners', 'pirates' and 'aliens' in ports and waters their ancestors had worked.[11]

By the beginning of the twentieth century Europeans owned nearly all the steam vessels active across the Indian Ocean and had achieved a near monopoly of trans-oceanic and long-distance coastal and inter-island trade. Nevertheless, into the twentieth century, sail continued to compete successfully with steam on marginal and feeder routes. From East Africa to the Indonesian archipelago, indigenous craft, the relics of a pre-modern world, still managed to find a niche in the new European-dominated economic order.

Despite a degree of indigenous mercantile survival on land and sea, the essential patterns of trade within the Indian Ocean region changed dramatically from the eighteenth century. Until then the 'volume and composition of Indian Ocean trade were conditioned to a great extent by the ability of . . . farmers to create a surplus' of food and cash crops.[12] The monsoons controlled agriculture and trade, determining their temporal rhythms and economic relationship. But with the increasing power of European markets, old economic rhythms, along with the region's self-sufficiency, were modified. Indigenous economic activity was subordinated to external demands, and even where an indigenous capitalist class emerged the range of its economic activity was restricted by extra-regional groups whose interests were invariably those of the colonial regimes.

There are indications, however, that a degree of readjustment was beginning to take place by the twentieth century. In British India signs of adjustment were evident by the end of the nineteenth century and, by the time of the First World War, nearly a quarter of its exports comprised manufactures. At the same time, British domination of India's seaborne trade began to decline rapidly. To an extent, other

---

[11] Michael Pearson, 1979, 15–42; Esmond Bradley Martin, 1979; M. Al-Qasimi, 1988.

[12] K.N. Chaudhuri, 1985, 27.

industrialized economies—in continental Europe, Japan and North America—filled Britain's niche in the Indian market. On the other hand, India's seaborne trade with other parts of the Indian Ocean region increased at the same time, as did the ratio in value of raw materials for manufacturing in India's total of imports.[13]

At the end of the First World War Britain rounded out its empire in the Indian Ocean region with the seizure of the German colony of Tanganyika. However, within thirty years, almost immediately following the end of the Second World War, a rapid process of decolonization began in the Indian Ocean region.

Mariners, Merchants and Ports

The human world of the Indian Ocean in the seventeenth century was largely unchanged from previous centuries, despite the scattered presence of Europeans. Indigenous maritime merchants and sailors flourished alongside their European counterparts and indigenous passengers still travelled on ships of all nations. But in the eighteenth century age-old indigenous relationships with the Ocean began to change, as European commercial activity began integrating the economies of the Indian Ocean world into a global economy dominated by European commercial interests, and in the nineteenth century by the rise of European and North American industrial capitalism.

All indigenous workers and travellers of the Ocean were affected by the development of European global hegemony. Indigenous sailors were reduced to labourers on European-owned shipping, with the decline in locally-owned shipping which occurred during these centuries. Indigenous maritime merchants were transformed from rivals and partners of European enterprise to collaborators in the expansion of Western capitalism throughout the Indian Ocean region of the global economy.

In the nineteenth century, with the triumph of European-owned shipping, the employment and recruitment patterns of indigenous sailors underwent drastic changes. As sail gave way to steam, new skills were required. Engineering skills were the exclusive domain of Euro-

[13] Vera Anstey, 1929.

pean sailors, with indigenous sailors recruited as deckhands, stokers, cooks, launderers and stewards. The political division of the Indian Ocean region among European powers changed recruitment patterns of indigenous sailors, as the new rulers recruited cheap maritime labour exclusively from their areas of influence within the region to serve on their ships around the world. For example, British shipping companies recruited lascars from Bengal and Bombay, as well as Goan cooks and stewards from the Konkan coast and Bombay. Singapore was another source of cheap labour, providing imported coolies from China for service as carpenters, cooks and launderers, employed at rates much below those of their European counterparts. In Indonesia, the Dutch recruited local sailors in much the same way. Indonesians provided unskilled labour on many ships, with Chinese occupying middle-rank skilled and semi-skilled jobs as they did on British ships.

The losers in these changing patterns of recruitment and work were indigenous sailors, confined to the lower paid jobs, and the fishing communities which had provided sailors in pre-modern times. Recruitment by the nineteenth century was from port-based communities of seafarers, through the agency of communal and village intermediaries with links into depressed rural areas.[14]

By the late twentieth century patterns of recruitment and work had changed yet again for indigenous sailors. New maritime technologies and vessel types, alongside the decline of maritime passenger traffic, led to a fall in the number of sailors. There was some compensation in the growth of national navies, created in the region since the late 1940s when decolonization began. However, these navies remain small and their pattern of recruitment tends to be universal within their respective states, with an increasing emphasis upon technical skills. Sailors as 'littoral communities' have largely vanished from the Indian Ocean region, as the shipping industry has undergone profound changes affecting the number and types of sailors it needs.

Ironically, indigenous fisherfolk have fared better than indigenous sailors as an occupational group, although they remain impoverished and socially marginalized. Their links with the sea remain strong, but they are being challenged, as fishing becomes a multi-national industry

[14] Frank Broeze, 1981; Conrad Dixon, 1980.

financed by industrialised nations from outside the region. In many parts of the Indian Ocean region, traditional fishing groups have been drawn into what is an increasingly commercialized industry, financed by outside interests. This has resulted in many, often adverse, changes in some places in traditional social, cultural and economic linkages and values. In both South Africa and Australia, European colonization led to the development of new maritime industries worked by European settlers alongside indigenous peoples. Examples of these new industries included fishing fleets out of ports such as Cape Town, Durban, Fremantle and Bunbury; whaling out of South African and Western Australian ports; guano mining on off-shore islands; and pearling out of Broome on the north-west coast of Western Australia.

The fate of indigenous sailors was, in part, shared by indigenous maritime mercantile groups, many of whom were badly affected by changing patterns of trade which occurred from the eighteenth century. As we have seen, the economic integration of the Indian Ocean 'world' as a region of a global economic system, dominated by the industrializing nations of the North, reduced indigenous merchants from partners to collaborators in the expansion of European capitalist enterprise.

At a most obvious level, European hegemony in the region from the eighteenth century was reflected in changing patterns of port activity, in which many ancient ports and merchant groups faded into oblivion. Along the coasts of South Asia through to insular South East Asia, Europeans created new ports—Bombay, Madras, Calcutta, Chittagong, Rangoon, Penang, Singapore and Jakarta—where fort and factory defined European-controlled marketplaces around which indigenous merchants, artisans and coolies settled, often abandoning more ancient marketplaces. The European quarters of such settlements were frequently microcosms of European towns, with their populations of European artisans, shopkeepers, servants, soldiers, clerics, lawyers, doctors, prostitutes, innkeepers, and merchants. They were a new type of marketplace associated with a new type of power, which transformed and subjugated traditional economic and political practices to the furtherance of extra-regional interests.

Even more significantly, the growth in economic and political importance of these new ports, which were the beachheads for European territorial expansion, resulted in a shift in power from hinterland cities to those on the shores of the Ocean. This was particularly true in South and South East Asia where power and wealth moved from ancient cities of the hinterland—for example, Lahore, Delhi, Lucknow, Kandy, Murshidabad, Mandalay and Jogjakarta—to European-controlled ports such as Karachi, Bombay, Colombo, Calcutta, Rangoon and Jakarta. In East Africa and the Red Sea, European-controlled ports such as Durban, Maputo, Dar es Salaam, Mombasa, Mogadishu, Djibouti, Massawa and Aden became major centres of European economic, technological and political power during the eighteenth and nineteenth centuries, dominating, not serving, their hinterlands as had the ancient Swahili ports.

The changing role of indigenous mercantile activity from rivalry and partnership to subjugation and collaboration was rapid. In the eighteenth century, for example, there was a free and vigorous migration of Chinese into South East Asia. They came as merchants to Java, gold and diamond miners to Borneo, as tin miners to the Malay sultanates, and as general merchants to Thailand, particularly after the restoration of the Thai state at Bangkok, following the destruction of Ayuthia in a war with Burma in 1767. By the late eighteenth century Chinese merchants in Thailand had built up great fleets of junks which traded throughout South East Asian. Also, as the VOC declined in the same period, there was a revival of Indonesian short-haul cargo and passenger traffic in the twilight years before armed steam vessels reasserted European mastery of South East Asian waters.

Other groups survived into the eighteenth century by playing upon European rivalries and attaching themselves to one group or another. For example, as we have seen, the EIC established a base at Penang in 1786, on the correct calculation that local rulers and merchants would use the entrepôt to avoid the exactions and pretensions of the VOC. Penang attracted Chulia, Bugi, Thai, Burmese, Chinese, Keling, Javanese and Sumatran merchants and sailors. Its European population remained small, but it soon contained a large resident population of South Asian and Chinese merchants, craftsmen and labourers, prefacing the fortunes of Singapore, founded thirty three years later.

By the late eighteenth century the number of indigenous merchants travelling by sea began to decline. The reason for this was two-fold. In areas such as the Coromandel coast, merchants began placing their cargoes in European vessels under the charge of agents, and this led to a rapid contraction of the local shipbuilding and shipping industry, as well as to the eclipse of many indigenous-dominated ports in favour of European-controlled ports. Madras became the major port on the Coromandel coast, establishing a primacy which has yet to be challenged; ancient ports such as Nagore, Nagapattinam and Masulipatnam became minor anchorages serving mainly coastal traffic. A similar decline was evident elsewhere in South Asia. These changes relate specifically to rising political chaos in the subcontinent and a shortage of investment capital, much of which had been provided by the now vanishing Mughal élite.

The decline of the Mughals was mirrored by the collapse of Safavid Persia in the eighteenth century; the slow death of the Ottoman empire, which lingered on until the First World War; the decline in power and wealth of Muslim states in South East Asia; and the establishment of major European colonies in Asia. The *Dar al-Islam* was sundered by these developments, and there was a contraction in the range of Muslims travelling by sea. The hajj traffic survived and expanded, but the Muslim mercenary, the travelling divine and intellectual, and the ship-owning merchant prince vanished. Important parts of the interlocked economies of the Indian Ocean were undergoing major changes, as a result of internal decline and the adverse impact of European commercial activity, from the eighteenth century.

But as we have seen, the pace and scope of the decline in indigenous maritime mercantile activity can be exaggerated. Certainly, indigenous maritime commerce shrank in the western Indian Ocean, leading to the eclipse of once-great ports such as Hormuz, Muscat, Bahrain, Aden, Mogadishu, Mombasa and Surat—although Bahrain, Aden, Mogadishu and Mombasa were to gain a new lease of life when they became springboards for European colonial and political activity in the late nineteenth century.

Afro-Asian, Arab and South Asian merchants did, however, remain active in the flourishing slave and ivory trade across the Arabian Sea. In addition, Hadhramauti merchants found a niche in the economy of Dutch-controlled Indonesia. On routes across the Bay of Bengal and in South Asian and Malayan ports, traditional craft and indigenous merchants still comprised a considerable portion of the traffic, with Chulias, Gujaratis, Bengalis, Jains, Kelings and Parsis deserting indigenous and Portuguese ports for British ports, from the eighteenth century. Generally, however, the picture is one of slowly shrinking indigenous maritime mercantile traffic in the years before the formalisation of European imperial control, and the triumph of the steam vessel.

During the nineteenth century fewer and fewer indigenous maritime merchants travelled the Indian Ocean. An increasing number of them adopted European mercantile principles and organization and remained landbound, using the telegraph, European banking facilities and corresponding agents in foreign ports. The creation of colonial states and economies set the final seal upon indigenous maritime mercantile activity, replacing the travelling merchant with settled communities of merchants—indigenous and European—who used new exclusive technologies to transport their cargoes and convey information and money, eliminating the tyranny of sail and the monsoon winds.

All these changes undermined the vitality of ancient merchant communities around the Indian Ocean. While indigenous merchants, artisans and labourers may still have travelled the high seas, they now tended to travel as migrants, moving on a more permanent basis to foreign ports and settlements. More significantly, the creation of the centralized colonial state undermined the ancient function of foreign merchant communities as possible intermediaries between different cultures. The new type of state interrupted traditional processes of cultural and religious interaction with its intervention in indigenous social and economic life. For its own purposes, the colonial state now became the intermediary between cultures, as the foreign rulers defined and moulded colonial societies to suit their own economic, political and cultural objectives.

In all European colonies, dominant indigenous groups were influenced by the cultural mores of their foreign rulers, leading to a disruption of ancient cultural interaction within the Indian Ocean region. In this process, the linkage between merchants, trade and cultural interaction was broken, to be replaced by a linkage between colonizers and the colonized.

New patterns of cultural life and cultural interaction were established as a result of European political domination. At an obvious level, the breaking of ancient maritime linkages between cultures around the Indian Ocean disrupted traditional mechanisms of cultural diffusion and interaction. At a less obvious level, the eclipse of many traditional élites destroyed patronage systems which had sustained many of the values and practices of indigenous civilizations: architecture, music, painting, sculpture, dance, literature.

The new rulers fostered the cultural, linguistic and philosophical values of their own societies in colonial Asia and Africa. The language of administration, education and commerce was the language of the colonial power, with indigenous languages relegated to secondary status. Colonial peoples were inculcated with the values of their masters who, by the nineteenth century, were imbued with the belief in the supremacy (both moral and technological) of European civilization. Intellectually indigenous élites were incorporated into the value-system of their European rulers and culturally oriented towards Britain, France, The Netherlands or Portugal. Europeans were pre-eminent in recording the form and history of indigenous civilizations, but in practice, colonial regimes did not patronise or encourage such civilizations, preferring instead to create colonial élites, who in culture and philosophy were tied to their European rulers.

At the most extreme level this meant that some indigenous peoples were expected to become carbon copies of their masters in language and life-style, while others were expected to re-shape their societies, having absorbed the best that Europe could offer. In Portuguese, French and Dutch colonies the emphasis was upon assimilation, the creation of carbon copies; in British colonies the process was less assimilationist and more by the example of good works and deeds which would be evidence of the superiority of British ways.

In all European colonies Christian missionary activity propagated the values of Western civilization, from the nineteenth century. Missionary schools, orphanages and hospitals were focal points for the dissemination of European cultural and technological values and tended to dismiss the indigenous heritage of their followers. Christianity made some converts in Africa, South Asia and South East Asia, but overall it remained the religion of a very small number of people. The small number of converts should not, however, lead us to underestimate the impact of Christian schools which, by the late nineteenth century, had replaced foreign merchant communities as the mechanism for the transmission of foreign cultural values throughout the Indian Ocean region. In addition to missionary schools, universities were founded in British India in the late nineteenth century to train an indigenous westernized bureaucratic and professional class. Early in the twentieth century, European settler communities in the British Dominions of South Africa and Australia also established universities, but these institutions were intended to preserve European cultural values in diasporas far from Europe and were not open to indigenous participation.

No colonial ethos was essentially better than the others, for they were all based on the belief in the superiority of European civilization and the inferiority of native ways. All discounted indigenous civilization, all anticipated remoulding indigenous societies, and all were concerned with the extension of European, rather than indigenous, interests. Colonial regimes were posited on the dependence of indigenous peoples, not on their independence. The irony was, that many of the European values taught to indigenous peoples, particularly those relating to liberal philosophies and the value of individual enterprise, rebounded on the teachers as indigenous peoples came to expect equality of treatment and freedom of action. The seeds of nationalism were unwittingly sown by European colonizers, whose rule was ultimately challenged by many of the élite groups they had so carefully cherished and instructed in the values of European civilization.

The centralized state which was created in the colonial period was an entirely new political innovation in the Indian Ocean region. Until the establishment of colonial regimes, political units in the region cannot be regarded as strongly centralised. Pre-modern communication systems, military technology, the strength of local élites and traditions, and fractionalised economies, were all factors which inhibited the development of strongly centralized political regimes. During the nineteenth century, however, all this changed. New communication and military technology, and fundamental economic changes which led to the creation of a 'world economy', facilitated the evolution of centralized colonial states in which cultural and economic variations were subordinated to an élite cultural and economic ordering, dictated by the needs of colonial rulers. In this process cultural and economic variety, as well as the freedom to make cultural and economic decisions based on local imperatives—rather than based on the imperatives of the colonial regime—were subordinated to the decisions of central authorities. Ancient patterns of cultural and economic interaction were disrupted by the growth of the centralized colonial state in the nineteenth century, as freedom of action and choice was subordinated to the needs of new ruling élites.

Travellers Old and New

European intrusion and the establishment of European trading bases gave rise to new forms of passenger traffic, as well as reinforcing the traffic of slaves across the Ocean.

The Portuguese moved numbers of Indian Christians, *Canarins*, to Mozambique as settlers, while the VOC despatched troublesome Javanese and Malabaris to distant parts of its trading empire, particularly Cape Town and Colombo. Under the Portuguese in the sixteenth century, the traffic in mercenary soldiers also increased. The Portuguese, and later the Dutch, French and British, used Ethiopian, African, Malay and indigenous *canarin* troops (also known as *lascarin* and *sipai*) as well as German and Swiss mercenaries, in garrisons stretching from Mombasa to Melaka. Overall, their traffic was irregular and related to the vagaries of political events, until the eighteenth century, when the British built up a considerable reliance on South Asian troops for use within their expanding Indian empire, and to oust the Dutch from Sri Lanka and the Indonesian archipelago. In the nineteenth and twentieth centuries South Asian troops were shipped around the world to fight British imperial wars on nearly every continent: in the 1914–18 war, for example, British Indian troops fought on battle fields in France, Tanganyika, Mesopotamia and Gallipoli, while levies from Africa and Indo-China fought for France in Europe as soldiers and as front-line labourers.

There was also a steady movement of European troops into and across the Indian Ocean from the early eighteenth century. The armies of the EIC in South Asia contained European officers and regiments, as did the French forces in the Mascarenes and India. The Dutch maintained European garrisons at all their major outposts. Mortality rates among these Europeans were extremely high, but the reservoir was large.

By the late nineteenth century colonial armies in the region comprised both numbers of European regiments on temporary rotating service and European officered regiments of indigenous troops. The European regiments were the visible symbol of European domination, while the indigenous regiments were more frequently the workhorses of imperial control and expansion. Troopships regularly carried European regiments between Britain, France and the Netherlands to colonial bases in the Indian Ocean region, and also served to shuttle colonial levies from one European colony to another on garrison duty. Indian troops garrisoned Bahrain, Kuwait, Aden, Suakin, Berbera, Mombasa and Dar es Salaam, and fought for their imperial masters in China, the Sudan, Afghanistan and Persia. Dutch colonial levies were central players in the expansion of Dutch authority throughout the Indonesian archipelago, and in the late nineteenth century were central to the Dutch conquest of Aceh and Bali.

Paralleling changes in the traffic of indigenous merchants and soldiers in the eighteenth century, there was a steadily growing flow of free and indentured indigenous craftsmen. This began from the French port of Pondicherry on the Coromandel coast, to the Mascarenes in the 1760s, heralding the establishment of a large South Asian population on Mauritius.

The phenomenon of free indigenous and 'contract' labour migrating by sea to centres of European activity in the Indian Ocean region, developed steadily throughout the eighteenth century, prefacing the great movement of indentured people in the nineteenth century. Apart from the eighteenth century Chinese settlement in Dutch-controlled Java and Borneo and on mainland South East Asia, South Asians moved to the Mascarenes and to South East Asia, providing European settlements with much needed skills and brawn.

During this same period European settlement increased slowly. In the French Mascarenes for example, there was a small but steady flow directly from France, with an upsurge in the 1790s of refugees from the Antilles, when several hundred people settled the islands. Elsewhere in the Indian Ocean prior to the eighteenth century, European settlement remained equally small, given the appalling death rate among Europeans in the tropics. In the western half of the Indian Ocean, Europeans numbered no more than 30,000 as late as 1800. The Dutch settlement at Cape Town accounted for about 17,000 Europeans, the Mascarenes for 10,000, with Portuguese settlements along the coast of East Africa containing perhaps no more than 1000 Europeans, with larger numbers of *mesticos.*[15] British, French, Portuguese and Dutch settlements elsewhere around the Indian Ocean probably accounted for a somewhat larger number of Europeans. These European communities were incredibly polyglot, including representatives of the great trading companies, alongside Swiss, German, Greek, Danish, Swedish, Italian, Spanish, Jewish and Armenian mercenaries, artisans, shopkeepers, merchants, musicians, priests, scientists, teachers and artists.

Overall, the European component among maritime passengers was increasing. European merchants were joined by greater numbers of European administrators and soldiers, as colonial empires evolved during the eighteenth and nineteenth centuries. Following merchants, administrators and soldiers, came a host of imperial camp followers, ranging from wives to clergymen, and last of all the very first trickle of permanent European settlers: the harbingers of what was to be a great flood in the nineteenth and twentieth centuries.

In the nineteenth century European activity fundamentally altered traditional patterns of human movement across the Indian Ocean. This was the century in which the British, Dutch, Portuguese, French, Germans and the Italians consolidated their territorial empires around the Indian Ocean. This formalization of European territorial power was reflected in a great increase in the number of people moving by sea into and out of the Indian Ocean region, and to a major reorientation of the number and types of indigenous peoples using the Ocean.

Perhaps the most spectacular example of Europeans impinging

---

[15] A. Toussaint, 1977; P. Curtin, et al., 1982.

upon traditional passenger traffic across the Indian Ocean during the nineteenth century, was in the slave trade. Until the eight and ninth centuries, this traffic was intermittent. Between the ninth and eleventh centuries, when the Arab empire was at the peak of its power, the black African slave trade flourished. In the following centuries a regular network of slave routes developed across the Indian Ocean, from Madagascar in the west to the Moluccas in the east. The two major supply areas of the trade were Africa and the Indonesian archipelago. East Africa, Madagascar, the Sudan and Ethiopia supplied slaves via the Red and Arabian Seas to Egypt, Arabia, Mesopotamia, Persia and India; elsewhere a similar traffic existed, centred upon the Indonesian archipelago, which involved the movement of enslaved peoples from one part of the archipelago to another.

The volume of this early traffic is difficult to quantify. An annual figure of 10,000 slaves carried from East Africa, the Sudan and Ethiopia has been suggested.[16] Following the decline of the Arab empire the trade declined, but in the mid-seventeenth century it began to grow again, initially in response to increasing demand in the Ottoman and Mughal empires. In the 1700s, Kilwa and Pate dominated this trade, exporting slaves from the coast and Madagascar to the Gulf, the Makran coast and Gujarat, where they were distributed among the north Indian élite, and to European settlements as far afield as Bengal.

In South East Asia a traffic of comparable volume existed. Bali and the eastern islands of the archipelago, as well as South Asia to a limited extent, were sources of slaves for markets in Java, Sumatra and the Malay peninsula. In addition, the Muslims of Sulu conducted a flourishing slave trade centred upon Borneo and the southern Philippines.

European involvement in this traffic was intermittent until the mid-seventeenth century, with the occasional Portuguese vessel carrying slaves from the Mozambique coast to South Asia, Brazil and Portugal. The Dutch were the most vigorous European pioneers of this trade. In insular South East Asia they conducted a flourishing slave market at Jakarta (Batavia), dealing annually in several thousand

[16] André Wink, 1988, 14.

indigenous slaves destined for the Philippines, Melaka, Sri Lanka and Cape Town. In 1673 the population of Batavia was about 27,000, of whom more than 50 per cent were slaves.[17] In Cape Town, the growing Dutch settler community imported skilled slaves from South Asia, Sri Lanka, Java, Madagascar and East Africa. In toto, this Dutch traffic in slaves was considerably less than the indigenous-controlled traffic from the Swahili coast: the slave population of Cape Town, for example, was only 29,000 in 1800, some 148 years after initial settlement.[18]

In the late 1600s and early 1700s European slaving activity in the western Indian Ocean was dominated by freebooters, most of whom were French and who pioneered the regular movement of slaves out of the Indian Ocean to other parts of the world. These slavers were centred on Madagascar and carried slaves both ways across the Mozambique Channel, to Batavia, La Réunion, England and the West Indies. French slaving activity increased after their settlement of the uninhabited Mascarenes and various Indian ports. Initially, the French in the Mascarenes imported only small numbers of slaves from West Africa, Madagascar, and South and South East Asia as farm labourers. During the 1730s, however, the slave plantation complex common to European-dominated tropical lands in the Americas, expanded to the Mascarenes. In 1735, Mauritius had some 600 slaves, by 1739 this had risen to about 3000.[19] In subsequent decades the slave population expanded even more rapidly, as European freebooters and Mascarene merchants developed a regular link with slave markets on Madagascar, the Comoros islands and the East African coast.

Paralleling the upsurge in European participation in the slave trade, the number of slaves carried from East Africa by indigenous slavers to plantations on Zanzibar and the markets of the Middle East, increased steadily from about 4000 in 1800 to 6000 annually in the 1870s, when it declined sharply.[20] The traffic to South Asia, however, vanished in the eighteenth century with the fortunes of the indigenous élites who had purchased African slaves.

[17] S. Abeyasekere, 1987, 19, 28.
[18] P. Curtin, et al., 1982; R.M. Martin, 1839.
[19] R.R. Kuczynski, 1949, 752–53, 755, 787–9.
[20] W.G. Clarence–Smith (ed.), 1989 (a).

The massive changes in volume and direction of the slave trade which occurred in the eighteenth and nineteenth centuries were due to several factors, most notably the expansion of plantation economies in Brazil, the United States and the Mascarenes, and to a sharp rise in the price of West African slaves. These factors encouraged the slave trade out of Mozambique, Kilwa, Madagascar, and the Comoros by French, Brazilian, Spanish and Portuguese slavers, to the Mascarenes and the Americas.

By the late eighteenth century, Madagascar and the Portuguese-controlled Mozambique coast were the major export areas for slaves in the western Indian Ocean. During the 1780s and 1790s more than 5000 slaves annually were carried officially from Mozambique island alone, in French and Portuguese vessels.[21] Probably about half the slaves carried off were destined for the Americas, with the rest destined for the Mascarenes. Kilwa also provided slaves for these markets, but the majority of slaves from there were directed towards Zanzibar and the Middle East. Rulers of various Malagache states were also active in the slave trade, enslaving members of rival tribes and raiding the Comoros and the East African coast for slaves who were sold mainly to the Mascarenes.

The slave trade from East Africa and Madagascar continued long into the nineteenth century, accounting for some 200,000 transported in that century alone to plantations of the western Indian Ocean.[22] In insular South East Asia the traffic of slaves flourished in the hands of Dutch, Spanish and various indigenous groups who transported several thousand slaves annually by the beginning of the nineteenth century.

Slaves comprised the greater part of human traffic across the Indian Ocean until the 1850s, when the trade began to decline. This was largely due to the activities of the British government, which had embarked on a worldwide campaign to secure the abolition of slavery, following the emancipation of slaves within the British empire in 1833. In South East Asia, however, the slave trade was not finally extinguished until the first decade of the twentieth century.

Ironically, the slave trade precipitated new processes of cultural

[21] E.A. Alpers, 1975, 185.
[22] William Gervase Clarence-Smith, 1989, 10.

interaction within the Indian Ocean region. In the Middle East and South East Asia, slaves appear to have been integrated into local society and culture without transforming such societies and cultures to any marked degree. But in European colonies, most particularly the French and British Mascarenes where slaves formed the majority of the population, they evolved a vibrant Afro-European culture blending African, French and British themes into the Kreol language and culture.

Following the abolition of slavery in the British empire, and the decision of the Merina rulers of Madagascar to restrict the export of slaves who were now needed for a rapidly growing domestic sugar plantation economy, convict and indentured labour provided a modern system of bondage. This new form of slavery involved the movement of millions of people by sea within the Indian Ocean region and beyond.

Indentured South Asian labourers and craftsmen followed the British flag to Sri Lanka, Malaya, South Africa, Mauritius, the Seychelles, Kenya, Uganda, Tanzania, Singapore, Aden and Burma and even further afield to Fiji, the West Indies and British Guyana, as plantation and construction labourers. Indentured labourers, *engagés*, from South Asia and Mozambique also moved in their tens of thousands to the French island of La Réunion from the late 1840s, as slave substitutes, following emancipation on the island in 1848. The movement of indentured South Asians was matched by indentured and free Chinese who came as cheap labour, mostly to Singapore, Malaya and Indonesia—and to a lesser extent to the Mascarenes—to work rubber plantations and tin mines, as well as labouring in dockyards and on railways.

Few of these indentured labourers returned to their homelands and they formed distinctive communities in their host countries. In South East Asia, and East and southern Africa, strong links were maintained between the migrants and their homeland, reinforcing the group boundaries of these migrant communities, but in the Mascarenes, links with the homeland were not so strong, and, in time, the South Asian migrant communities adopted and adapted aspects of British and French culture, to the extent of linguistic affiliation and the blurring of traditional internal divisions such as caste and language. Convict labour was less widespread, but Indian convicts were transported by the British to Mauritius, while English, Welsh, Irish and Scots convicts were transported to Western Australia in the mid-nineteenth century to provide cheap agricultural labour.

Between the fifteenth and nineteenth centuries there were major changes in the nature and direction of maritime trade and passenger traffic. At the beginning of this period maritime routes were dictated primarily by inter-regional economic and political factors, but in the course of the eighteenth century European activity in the region became increasingly important and led to the sundering of the ancient unity of trade and shipping across the Indian Ocean. By the nineteenth century the growth of European economic and political interest in the Indian Ocean region had altered traditional patterns of passenger movement across the Ocean, and introduced new motives and incentives for travel which were not necessarily associated with trade. European interest and involvement prompted an increase in the number of people travelling by sea, and broke the nexus between maritime trade and maritime passenger traffic.

Although European intervention may have irrevocably changed old patterns of trade and passenger movement by the nineteenth century, the majority of maritime passengers were still from within the region and represented a major continuity which reinforced the ancient cultural panorama of the Indian Ocean region. But the nineteenth century also saw a dramatic increase in the number of Europeans travelling the Indian Ocean.

In European colonies in Africa and Asia, transient military, administrative, planter, mining and commercial communities increased in size, as did permanent communities of Europeans in major administrative centres. Also, in some parts of the Indian Ocean region, Europeans established permanent settler colonies. The oldest of these was at the Cape of Good Hope and dated from Dutch and Huguenot settlement in the seventeenth century. In the 1820s the British began settling the Natal coast of southern Africa and the Swan River area on the western coast of Australia. By the middle of the century, British colonies in southern Africa and Australia attracted thousands of European settlers—some free, some bonded and some convicts—annually, setting a new pattern of passenger traffic which was to last into the 1960s. During the late nineteenth century and following the First

World War, British, French, Portuguese and Italian settlers also moved into Kenya, Tanganyika, Zimbabwe, Madagascar, Eritrea, Mozambique and Italian Somaliland, although in much smaller numbers than to South Africa and Australia.

During the nineteenth and twentieth centuries indigenous involvement with the sea underwent major structural and quantitative changes which were to fundamentally alter age old patterns of working and using the Indian Ocean. Also, the discrete Indian Ocean world of the mind and the workplace was integrated into a capitalist world culture and economy. In the same period, economic changes and the transport revolution profoundly affected the nature of human interaction with the sea. European-controlled steam vessels were central to these changes in human movement, insofar as they eliminated ancient sailing skills and sailing schedules based on the rhythm of wind systems, and undermined the role of indigenous shipping and sailors.

A study of the workers of the sea to the twentieth century has much to tell us about the economic and cultural history of the Indian Ocean region. Maritime workers and travellers were critical to economic activity and cultural interaction, and were central to the evolution and shaping of many Indian Ocean societies. However, by the end of the nineteenth century there were signs that the age-old physical intimacy between people and the sea was fast loosening and would, in the twentieth century, be effectively broken.

The Twentieth Century

At the beginning of the twentieth century the Indian Ocean was very clearly a British Lake. British steamships—and their European rivals—linked the ports of the region with the outside world; British troops and their imperial levies garrisoned hundreds of bases; and British merchants, administrators and missionaries were active and pre-eminent in a curve of colonies from South Africa to Hong Kong. Each year thousands of settlers from Britain and Ireland made new homes in South Africa and Australia, as well as on the expanding African colonial frontier in Zimbabwe, Zambia and Kenya. In both South Africa and Australia, by the first decade of the twentieth century, new states had been formed in which white settlers had created a Westminster type parliamentary democracy for themselves, to the exclusion of the indigenous inhabitants. Both countries created flourishing economies based upon mining (primarily gold in both South Africa and the Australian state of Western Australia) and rapidly expanding white-owned farming of wheat, sheep and cattle. British capital flowed into both areas, helping create an urban and transport infrastructure which supported a 'European' lifestyle and the extraction and removal of raw materials and foodstuffs for European markets.

In South Africa the white population—comprising both the Afrikaans- and English-speaking communities—remained a minority. In Australia the indigenous population was almost exterminated by deliberate massacres and introduced diseases. In Zimbabwe (Southern Rhodesia), Zambia (Northern Rhodesia) and Kenya, British settlers were far less numerous and remained a land-owning élite on vast estates and plantations.

Elsewhere, French, Portuguese and Italian settlers also moved into Madagascar, Mozambique, Eritrea, and Italian Somaliland, although not in large numbers. In Mozambique the Portuguese settlers ranged from poor farmers to members of a large urban bourgeoisie concentrated primarily in Maputo (Lourenço Marques). In Madagascar and the Italian colonies, on the other hand, Europeans tended to form a small class of wealthy plantation owners, entrepreneurs and bureaucrats, located mainly in urban areas.

In both South Africa and Australia the early years of the twentieth century saw the formation of white-dominated states tied to the British Empire. Both states were vital sources of minerals, wool and foodstuffs and their economies were firmly wedded to the economic interests of Britain. While the white inhabitants of these states certainly regarded themselves as part of the imperial élite their relationship to the British economy was essentially the same as that of other British colonies in the Indian Ocean region. Neither South Africa nor Australia were to establish major manufacturing bases until World War II, and even then remained reliant upon the continuous inflow of capital from industrialized nations eager to secure their resources of raw materials.

In the early years of the twentieth century European interest was drawn to the southern reaches of the Indian Ocean. Australia, Britain, France and Norway mounted expeditions to Antarctica, with each claiming a slice of the empty continent. These expeditions continued throughout the twentieth century but were not considered of vital interest until the late twentieth century. From the 1960s the possibility of massive coal and oil deposits and extensive marine resources attracted increasing competition from the original explorers of the continent, as well as from other nations concerned to gain a share of its wealth. This rush to gain a foothold in Antarctica was only resolved when the international community agreed to leave it an unspoiled natural reserve, as part of humanity's effort to avert global environmental disaster.

The era of triumphant European imperialism was brought to an abrupt end during World War II. Until then there had been no serious threats mounted to European hegemony, although in British India and the Dutch East Indies, westernized colonial élites were beginning to agitate for democratic rights and self-government. In the Indian Ocean region India remained a British military fortress and the seas were secured for British commerce by the imperial naval presence in the Atlantic and the Pacific. The rise of Japan in the Pacific in the 1920s caused some alarm in Britain, and led to the slow construction of a mighty naval base at Singapore to guard access to the Indian Ocean from the South China Sea and the Pacific. Elsewhere in the Indian Ocean region, however, little was done to upgrade decayed British naval facilities in India, Sri Lanka and South Africa. By the 1930s the British had established an airforce presence in the region with small bases stretching from Egypt, the Persian Gulf, British India and Singapore. In addition, British Imperial Airways, the Australian airline Qantas and the Dutch airline KLM established the first commercial flights between the region and Europe, supported by government subsidies for the rapid transport of mail.

This nascent air power was a little too late to avoid the catastrophe of World War II which shattered the myth of European military superiority. The Japanese occupation of British, Dutch and French colonies in South East Asia encouraged nationalist movements across Asia to seek freedom from foreign domination. Following the defeat of Japan in 1945, Indonesian nationalists refused to accept the re-imposition of Dutch rule, and the same problem faced the French when they attempted to re-establish their authority over Vietnam. The exhausted British were forced to concede independence to Burma and India in 1947, although British India was divided between the two nations of India and Pakistan.

In 1948 Sri Lanka achieved independence from Britain, and during the 1950s and 1960s, nationalist movements rapidly gained strength in the remaining British, French and Portuguese colonies in Asia and Africa as well as among the islands of the ocean. By the 1980s, all European colonies (with two major exceptions), were politically independent. The two exceptions are the French island of La Réunion which has been absorbed politically into metropolitan France, and the British Indian Ocean Island Territory (the Chagos Archipelago).

La Réunion and several smaller islands (for example, Mayotte in the Comoros) have been incorporated into metropolitan France, with the territory a *département* of France having representation in the National Assembly. The French retain a naval presence on the island. The Chagos Archipelago was excised from Mauritius when that island gained its independence. The inhabitants of the archipelago, the Ilois, were deported to Mauritius, so that a naval communications base could be constructed on the central island of Diego Garcia. The British disposed of two other tiny island communities in a more gracious manner: sovereignty of phosphate-rich Christmas Island was transferred to Australia, while the inhabitants of the Cocos (Keeling) Islands voted to be incorporated into Australia after a UN organized plebiscite. The mixed Asian populations of both territories became full citizens of Australia.

The last two European colonies to gain independence were Mozambique and East Timor in 1975. Both were former Portuguese colonies: Mozambique became a republic, East Timor was occupied by Indonesia in 1976.

Many of the newly-independent nations exist within boundaries created by their former rulers; boundaries which cut across ancient linguistic, cultural, ethnic and economic entities. Thus, ironically, freedom from colonial rule helped further cement the regional fragmentation brought about by European imperialism.

Despite the fact that, by the late 1960s, the British were fast leaving their colonies east of the Suez canal over which they had lost the last vestiges of control in 1956, maritime power had not passed back to the peoples of the Indian Ocean region. The Communist insurgency in Malaya in the late 1940s, the development of the Cold War, and the Communist victory in China in 1948, continued to focus the attention of the Great Powers on the region. Their interest was due both to global strategic considerations and the rise in importance of Middle Eastern oil to western economies from the 1940s. To protect this oil the British and the US interfered in Iran in 1952 to destroy a nationalist regime. In 1956 Britain, France and Israel invaded Egypt in an attempt to force the collapse of Nasser's nationalist government and to recapture control of the Suez canal; the invasion failed, but it exacerbated a conflict between the Western allies and Arab nationalism which has led to continuing confrontation in the Middle East.

The Cold War, Western concern over increasing Communist influence in the so-called 'developing world', and Middle Eastern oil forced the British to maintain a naval and airforce presence in the Indian Ocean region until the 1960s. Initially the British maintained major naval and airforce facilities in Sri Lanka, Singapore and Aden, but by the 1960s had abandoned Sri Lanka to develop an airforce base on the Maldivian atoll of Gan, and were in the process of evacuating Singapore and Aden. By the late 1960s Gan was relinquished and Britain left the Indian Ocean region. But the Cold War demanded a Western presence in the region and the British created the base at the pseudo-colony of Diego Garcia (the British Indian Ocean Islands Territory) which they leased to the USA as a major communications and naval base. Diego Garcia was created to match the increasing naval presence of the USSR in the former British colony of Aden and in the Somali port of Mogadishu. As in the eighteenth century European and American rivalries spilled over into the Indian Ocean, dragging newly independent nations into the global divisions and rivalry spawned by the Cold War.

The move towards political independence was frequently accompanied by attempts to restructure economies warped by imperial economic demands. Such moves, often anti-capitalist in character, exacerbated Western suspicions of the political nature of many regimes in the Indian Ocean region and led to instances of blatant interference to destroy overtly nationalist governments. In 1952 the Mossadegh government in Iran was destroyed when it attempted to nationalise the oil industry, and, as we have seen, in 1956 attempts were made to invade Egypt and destroy Nasser's government after it nationalised the Suez canal. In addition, India and Indonesia were treated as pariahs by many Western governments on suspicion of being pro-Soviet. Under Nehru, independent India had attempted to establish its own socialist model of economic development which alarmed the capitalist West, while in Indonesia the nationalization of Dutch investments in the 1950s, and the Non-Aligned Movement which Nehru—and the Indonesian leader Sukarno—supported, created even more suspicions in the West that both India and Indonesia had fallen under the sway of the Soviet Union.

In the Middle East, Suez, a successful anti-western revolution in Iraq, and Arab-Israeli conflict added to Western fears and fuelled the battle for influence between the US and the Soviet Union. The same pattern of interference was played out in Africa, and from Ethiopia to Mozambique there was a general tendency to move towards socialism, with only Kenya and South Africa maintaining an attachment to Western capitalism. By the 1970s and the Middle Eastern 'Oil Crisis', the greater number of Indian Ocean states were involved in some variety of socialist experiment to restructure the damaged economies they had inherited from their colonial masters. Against them stood the interests of the West represented by the naval power of the United States and capitalist bastions such as Malaysia, Singapore, Australia and South Africa.

Both Australia and South Africa stood out as enclaves of European capitalist enterprise. Australia, after the shock of near-defeat during the Second World War, was firmly wedded to an alliance with the USA, while South Africa had secured the domination of its white minority behind apartheid, which condemned non-Europeans to second rate citizenship and poverty, and barred them from any participation in the political life of their country. The nature of the South African regime cut it off from direct contact with most of its Indian Ocean neighbours, but Australia's position was less clear.

Until the 1960s Australia firmly excluded any non-European settlement and the Aboriginal peoples were excluded from political life and citizenship. Internationally Australia was wedded to the worldview of the USA. During the 1970s, however, Australia's perceptions of its place in the world began to change. The exclusive immigration policy was abandoned, the first substantial groups of non-European settlers began to arrive from South East and South Asia, and Aboriginals were granted full citizenship. Australia continued to support many of the international initiatives of the USA—as in Vietnam—but diplomatically it began to take a more independent line in its relations with Indian Ocean neighbours such as Indonesia and India, after nearly three decades of tension and neglect. In part this was driven by economic need as Australia lost markets in Europe with the formation of the European Economic Community (EEC), but in part it was also driven by the growing realization among many Australians that they were politically and physically part of the Indian Ocean region.

By the late 1980s changes in the international environment leading to the end of the Cold War and the collapse of the Soviet Union had effectively removed overt extra-regional military influence from the Indian Ocean region (with the exception of the French at La Réunion and the US at Diego Garcia), but the demise of the Soviet Union also included the eclipse of socialist economic policies, and the 1990s is witnessing a rapid change in the direction of economic development in most Indian Ocean economies. Another great change has been the death of official apartheid in South Africa and the renewal of that country's links with its Indian Ocean neighbours.

In the 1990s most economies of the Indian Ocean region are still attempting to undo the economic effects of colonialism. The economies of the region are now firmly part of a global economy, yet they remain in a subsidiary position, reflecting Wallerstein's concept of the core and the periphery in terms of economic relationships. For the most part they have limited manufacturing bases, and continue to be economically dependent upon industrialized countries as purchasers of their raw materials and suppliers of investment capital. There has been some resurgence of regional trade and shipping, and countries such as Singapore and Malaysia have expanding manufacturing bases, but most other countries in the region have yet to break out of the economic mould cast during the colonial period. The traditional self-sustaining trading world of the Indian Ocean is gone forever, and there are few possibilities of its revival.

Just as the old trading world of the Indian Ocean has vanished, so too have traditional civilizations and patterns of cultural interaction. Many of the forms of those civilizations had been destroyed by the colonial experience or (in countries such as Thailand, Ethiopia and Iran which avoided direct European political domination) by the march of capitalism which undermined traditional cultural practices, as Western technology, manufactures and commercial activity permeated the Indian Ocean region. Factory-produced goods replaced local handicrafts; films and records undermined indigenous theatre, dance and music; and the colonial élites (European and non-European) patronized the forms of European civilization.

Not all the old values were lost, but the linkages between the various civilizations of the Indian Ocean region were broken. These linkages had been a major force for change and innovation as cultures interacted with one another, but in the wake of colonial rule these civilizations were isolated from one another and interacted with the civilizations of the industrialized West. The legacies of colonial rule in the Indian Ocean region are economic underdevelopment and cultural confusion, as indigenous societies attempt to establish individual identities in a world fragmented into nation states and dominated by the major industrial powers.

This cultural confusion is exacerbated by the concept of nationalism which is another Western legacy. In the pre-modern Indian Ocean world, cultures and civilizations were not bounded by the nation state but had porous and elastic boundaries which encompassed enormous internal variation. There was no sense of belonging to a nation which had a distinctive and exclusive 'national identity', rather, one belonged to particular overlapping 'worlds' defined in various ways: by religion, by cultural practice, by geography, by language, but not by affiliation to a particular political unit and identity.

With independence, however, indigenous peoples inherited the nation state which had to construct and legitimize a clear cultural identity to mark it off from its neighbours. Frequently this identity was defined by particular readings of history which suited élite groups and was physically defined by colonial boundaries, but it was often constructed on the basis of the dominant religion, language or culture within the legal boundaries of the new state. For religiously, linguistically and culturally homogenous states this did not present a major problem, but most colonial states were pluralistic in all these categories, leading to struggles for domination among the various groups comprising the state. Frequently this has led to civil war and the creation of new states. This was the fate of Pakistan, where the linguistic divisions between Bengali- and Urdu-speakers overwhelmed their common adherence to Islam and resulted in the Bengali-speakers seceding to form Bangladesh. Such tensions remain a major problem in India, Sri Lanka, Burma, Kenya, Tanzania, Ethiopia, Somalia and South Africa and reflect the continuing legacies of colonialism: cultural fragmentation and isolation, exacerbated by continuing underdevelopment and economic deprivation.

In the last decade, however, there have been some moves towards collective action in the region, based on groupings of countries. In South East Asia, Indonesia, Singapore, Malaysia, Thailand and Brunei have formed an economic and cultural association, the Association of South East Asian States (ASEAN); in South Asia, India, Pakistan, Sri Lanka, Bangladesh and Nepal, have formed a similar organization known as the South Asian Association for Regional Co-operation (SAARC); and in the Middle East the Gulf Co-operation Council provides a forum for united action on the part of the smaller states in the Persian Gulf. At the international level Indian Ocean countries in the UN have been discussing for a decade or more the question of establishing an Indian Ocean Zone of Peace, with little immediate success. None of these organizations have a regional focus, but collectively they represent the first stirring of an attempt on the part of inhabitants of the Indian Ocean region to seek to resolve their problems through collective action rather than perpetuating national differences.

While independence may have made possible some reforging of regional linkages, the colonial experience resulted in indigenous involvement with the sea undergoing major structural and quantitative changes, which were to fundamentally alter age-old patterns of working and using the Indian Ocean. Also, the discrete Indian Ocean world of the mind and the workplace was integrated into a capitalist world culture and economy. In the same period, economic changes and the transport revolution profoundly affected the nature of human interaction with the sea. European-controlled steam vessels were central to these changes in human movement, insofar as they eliminated ancient sailing skills and schedules based on the rhythms of wind systems, and undermined the role of indigenous shipping and sailors.

By the mid-twentieth century there was a noticeable decline in the interaction between people and the sea in the Indian Ocean region. Ancient coastal societies and polities had their relationship with the sea altered, as European rulers and technologies shaped new land–sea relationships. Even when they gained their independence, new transport and communication technologies prevented any return to ancient intimacies between human beings and the sea. Fishing still involves many people, as do the growing indigenous merchant marines and navies of the region. But modern technology and business methods have reduced the number of people who need to travel as seaboard passengers or who depend for their livelihood directly upon the sea. The aircraft, the bulk carrier cargo vessel, containerization, space satellites, radio, television and the facsimile machine led to a decline in direct contact between people and the sea across the Indian Ocean, although modern tourism provides a new means of intra-regional contact.

During the late twentieth century ports have undergone major changes in their functions. The development of bulk carriers, the emergence of 'container ports' and containerization, and the decline of passenger traffic have reduced the port workforce associated with maritime activities. The intimate interface which existed in most ports between the harbour and the surrounding population has declined, leaving the harbour and its functions distanced from the daily lives of most inhabitants of ports. Ports as urban phenomena have lost their cosmopolitan character and are now little different from any other urban setting. Durban, Mombasa, Aden, Karachi, Bombay, Colombo, Melaka, Singapore, Jakarta and Fremantle are no longer shaped by their role as ports but are essentially cities on the sea, part of whose economic activities includes a harbour.

Despite losing its importance as the most common highway between the peoples of the Indian Ocean region, the Ocean has retained a central role in their lives, albeit in a quite different sense from its earlier function as a highway. Growing environmental consciousness, and the awareness of the value of the Ocean's food and mineral resources have combined to give the Ocean a new value to the people who live on its shores. Offshore oil and gas fields now engage national attentions in India, Bangladesh, Thailand, Malaysia, Indonesia and Australia, as do seabed mineral resources for a range of other nations in the region. National boundaries have been pushed further out to sea and Exclusive Economic Zones have been declared: such actions represent attempts to secure new mineral resources and also to protect the vital fisheries resources of the Ocean. The Indian Ocean has been divided politically by the nations on its shores, and currently attempts are underway to develop legal regimes to take into account this new area of political and economic activity.

For much of human history the Indian Ocean has been used and viewed solely as an entity which helped bind distant communities into various complex economic and cultural relationships. But by the late twentieth century, the Ocean was viewed increasingly as a vital environmental and economic entity in its own right, central to the sustenance of human life.

Conclusions

In this history I have traced the evolution of the relationship between people and the Indian Ocean. It is a relationship which began millennia ago when the ancestors of the first Australians crossed narrow seas, passing from South East Asia into an Australian continent which at that time included what are now the islands of New Guinea and Tasmania. The first of these migrations probably occurred at least 75,000 years ago: perhaps there were earlier seaborne migrations in other parts of the Indian Ocean region, but they have left no trace.

In succeeding millennia, human beings around the Ocean began to utilize the sea as a source of food and as a means of communication. These first mariners were simply engaged in survival, using the harvest of the sea as an adjunct to hunter-gathering and the earliest forms of agriculture. In time, as human beings developed a more complex sedentary existence, their relationship with the sea became more complex. The Ocean became a common highway linking scattered communities. For some it was a highway which facilitated the evolution of barter networks, for others it facilitated the extension of more sophisticated land-based trading networks onto the high seas, to link up with distant markets and sources of luxury goods.

Five millennia ago the Ocean linked the world's earliest urban civilizations—in Mesopotamia and the Indus valley—in a maritime traffic which dealt in luxury commodities. In succeeding centuries, such traffic increased to encompass luxuries and staples along a crescent of lands stretching from Somalia to Indonesia by the beginning of the present era.

The development of this expanded network of maritime trade routes was a response to the needs of land-based peoples. The rise and fall of states, the random impact of natural disasters, climate changes, epidemic diseases and technological advances, combined to shape the history of people's intimacy with the Ocean. The discovery of the

monsoon wind systems opened up the high seas to sailors and merchants who had been confined to restricted coast-hugging voyages
until the first millennium BC. By the early centuries of the present
era, maritime trade linked Africa and Asia across the Indian Ocean in
a tightening embrace which was to facilitate processes of cultural and
technological diffusion and exchange.

Until the twentieth century the Indian Ocean was to remain a
major arena of human activity. Not only did it link a range of
economies and cultures physically, but it was a great highway travelled
by fishermen, sailors, merchants, pilgrims, slaves, artisans, mercenaries,
artists, scholars, migrating peoples, tourists, and conquering armies
and navies. Such travellers helped mould and shape the cultures on
the shores of the Ocean. Hinduism, Buddhism, Judaism, Islam and
Christianity spread along maritime highways, leading to a diffusion
of religions, and an intermingling of cultural forms which gave rise
to complex civilizations from East Africa to the shores of the western
Pacific. Until the establishment of modern colonial states, communities of merchants acted as intermediaries between different cultures
around the Indian Ocean, but from the eighteenth century the colonial
state became the intermediary, dissolving ancient maritime-based cultural linkages.

Maritime highways were an extension of land-based and riverine
highways, with each linked to the other by myriad ports and marketplaces where cargoes of goods and ideas mingled. Long-distance trade,
by land and sea, was a cornerstone of international relations in the
pre-modern period. So important was the trade that it fostered the
exchange of envoys, the extension of privileges to select mercantile
groups, and was protected by military expeditions. For example, the
Chinese garrisoned the Silk Road deep into Central Asia 2000 years
ago to protect the caravans moving between the Middle East and East
Asia; the Byzantine emperor, Justinian, courted the Christian ruler of
Aksum as a means of circumventing the Sasanian domination of the
trade of the Arabian Sea 1400 years ago; the states of South East Asia
at the same time began a 1000-year-long diplomatic relationship with
the Chinese imperial court; the Cholas, Burmese and Srivijayans
campaigned against one another over the issue of trade across the Bay
of Bengal; and at the port of Melaka in the fifteenth century, South

Asian mercantile communities were granted, what were in effect, extra-territorial privileges to secure their participation in the trade of the port.

The distinctive Indian Ocean maritime world which evolved during these millennia was remarkably self-contained until the eighteenth century. At least 2000 years ago goods from the lands of the Indian Ocean—pepper and spices in particular—were eagerly sought in marketplaces of the Mediterranean and China, but the reverse was not true. In 1498 the Portuguese became directly involved in the maritime trade of the Indian Ocean, and were joined in the seventeenth century by other Europeans. Until the eighteenth century, however, European trade was largely integrated into traditional networks within the Indian Ocean, and was based upon the carriage of traditional cargoes and collaboration between European and indigenous merchants. But in the eighteenth century, European maritime trade overwhelmed indigenous maritime trade, laying the foundations for European colonial empires, although it was not until the nineteenth century that cargoes other than bullion from the west, and ceramics and silk cloth from the east, began to impact upon the peoples and economies of the Indian Ocean region, breaking down its ancient economic cohesion and self-sufficiency.

The eighteenth century also marked the beginning of the integration of the Indian Ocean into the arena of world geopolitics. During that century, the British, French and Dutch continued their rivalries across the Indian Ocean in what was, in effect, the first world war, involving them in military and naval confrontation from the Americas to the Pacific.

During the nineteenth century European political and commercial domination of the Indian Ocean region—accomplished in the eighteenth century—facilitated the triumph of capitalist enterprise and the completion of colonial empires, which made regional economies dependent upon a global capitalist-dominated economic system. This triumph not only subjugated colonial economies to extra-regional economic and cultural imperatives, but also limited the range of economic opportunities available to indigenous merchants and entrepreneurs. The physical range of their activities was severely curtailed, and they became enmeshed in a developing capitalist system which was driven by extra-regional market forces. In previous centuries mercantile activity in the Indian Ocean region had been shaped by regional market systems and random events, but from the nineteenth century, such mercantile activity either vanished or was integrated into a global capitalist economic system, driven by the market forces of core industrial economies in western Europe and the USA.

But while developments during the nineteenth century dissolved old trans-oceanic linkages and reforged regional economies, undermining age old dependencies upon the Indian Ocean, new lands became more than a geographic part of the region. Until the nineteenth century neither southern Africa nor western Australia were more than a geographic part of the region, but European settlement, the development of intra-regional trading linkages and intra-regional migration—which has continued into the twentieth century—have made the modern nations of South Africa and Australia more active participants in the affairs and fortunes of the region.

These are the bare bones of my story, but it is a story without an end. The Indian Ocean remains an entity which determines basic rhythms of human life, and its impact upon people in the past remains a subject of debate among historians.

During the last two hundred years the writing of history has been profoundly influenced by European scholarship. The economic and political domination by Europe of the rest of the world has encouraged an intense preoccupation with European history as the central driving force of modern world history. The history of Asia, Africa, Australia and the Americas has been divided into pre- and post-European history, with the divide determined by the chronology of European supremacy over these continents, and pointing to fundamental differences between 'them' (the conquered) and 'us' (the conquerors). The expansion of Spain, Portugal and later European imperial powers beyond Europe, has been seen as determining the creation of a modern integrated world which overwhelmed and replaced an archaic and fragmented world.

There have been many European critics of this process and the horrors and injustices that it involved, but there has been a general acceptance of the basic thesis, that an essentially modern European economic system pushed aside an essentially primitive non-European conglomeration of fragmented and primitive economic systems: a division of the world based on historical differences between 'them' and 'us'. Western European romantics may have mourned—in poetry, painting, the novel and histories—the passing of the noble savage, but in the imagery of their mourning they compounded the belief of their more arrogant peers, that even the most noble non-European was an exotic savage defined by her or his difference from the European observer.

There is even a thesis within the larger thesis. This sub-thesis also divides Europe into 'them' and 'us', with particular reference to the modern histories of north-western Europe and southern and eastern Europe. This attitude is clearly reflected in Anglo-American responses to the history of Portuguese expansion. The Portuguese are presented as the last of the medieval crusaders—fanatical Roman Catholics, Don Quixotes of the high seas, and as violent anachronistic Latins—in contrast to the essentially modern and measured English and Dutch who followed them into the Indian Ocean in the early seventeenth century. The contrast was in fact not all that stark, and is to a large extent the fanciful product of an Anglo-American arrogance, forged out of their economic and political hegemony achieved during the nineteenth and twentieth centuries.

The French *philosophes* of the eighteenth century; Karl Marx in the nineteenth century; and many liberal, socialist and Marxist historians of the twentieth century (along with their conservative peers), have tacitly accepted this duality of world history, with its European-dictated chronology and belief that European violence, capital and technology inevitably overwhelmed the rest of the world, because the rest of the world was not 'modern', hence unlike 'us'. By accepting the duality of world history, even the most trenchant critics of imperialism, ironically, subscribe to the more chauvinist view that the world beyond Europe was underdeveloped, historically moribund and different. The temptation for many of these scholars has been to develop apparently new models and theories to encapsulate and explain world history: but many of these simply dress old paradigms in new clothes. However, an increasing number of scholars around the world are now challenging such a view of world history, by exposing the workings of non-European societies before they came into contact with Europe. In doing so they are revealing the bankruptcy of the many assumptions underpinning the divide between the 'modern' and 'pre-modern' world, between 'them' and 'us', and the development of modern imperialism.

Before the eighteenth century European commercial enterprise in the Indian Ocean region, from East Africa to South East Asia, depended for its success upon participation in ancient economic networks and systems. Undoubtedly, European enterprise worked some major changes upon the volume and direction of Indian Ocean maritime trade, by opening it up to European, American and Pacific markets, but Europeans did not overwhelm and dominate such trade. During the eighteenth century, however, an alliance between British commercial and political interests led to the emergence of a British territorial empire in the Indian Ocean region, centred upon South Asia. In the nineteenth century British commercial domination developed into British capital domination, which led to the overwhelming of indigenous economies and their subjugation by a core European industrial economy.

In the telling of this story I have become increasingly aware of the questions which still have to be answered. There are great gaps in our knowledge of Indian Ocean maritime peoples and in our understanding of the technology and mechanics of early maritime trade. I have outlined in very broad terms the workings of the earliest maritime trade, but I am acutely conscious of the critical need for historians, archaeologists and anthropologists to reveal the histories of the earliest fishing and coastal agricultural communities, if we are to understand the driving forces behind the first maritime enterprises. Similar gaps exist in our knowledge of the first ports and mercantile communities *and* the cargoes they dealt in. Too frequently, non-European maritime trade has been dismissed as a peddling trade posited upon luxuries, yet there are now sufficient clues to indicate that this was not the case. It was a complex and sophisticated economic system which, from the fifteenth to the eighteenth century, held its own against European commerce in the Indian Ocean region.

In addition, we know very little about production processes associated with trade. At least 5000 years ago there were industrial sites in Egypt, Mesopotamia and the Indus valley which produced goods—

ceramics, beads, worked shells and ivory, copper ingots and jewellery, faience objects, and cotton textiles—intended for distant markets. But as yet we have only the faintest clues to enable us to fix these sites and processes in a specific human environment. Who controlled and financed these operations, and what relationship did they have with ruling groups? There is a temptation to apply nineteenth and twentieth century political theories (particularly those of Wallerstein) to such economic activity, but, given our limited knowledge, it is a temptation to be avoided.

When writing about the people who used the Indian Ocean there are many problems. The main one is that most of these people are without a written history. Few left behind any intimate details of their existence and one is forced into generalizations, based on the specific details left by a handful of travellers over the millennia. We have some stimulating histories based on the memoirs of medieval travellers such as Ibn Battuta and Marco Polo, and an emerging body of literature relating to the hajj, but there still remains much to be done by anthropologists and historians in the area of oral history, and in the great body of official and non-official literature left by Europeans active in the region from 1498 to the twentieth century. Other problems relate to pre-conceptions of modern scholars. The civilizations of the Indian Ocean region have been great and magnificent, providing a bottomless mine for archaeologists, anthropologists and historians who have burrowed down into the interstices of particular civilizations, with only a few making links between these civilizations. None of these civilizations were discrete entities, but too often they have been treated as such.

In the nineteenth and twentieth centuries this problem was compounded by the rise of spectacular and enormously pov. erful European colonial empires, whose magnificent facades bemused, and continue to bemuse, many historians who have concentrated upon the structure of empires rather than upon their foundations. By inspecting the foundations one gains a novel view of the origins of European empires in the Indian Ocean region. What is clear, is that such empires were constructed on the basis of indigenous economic collaboration. The establishment of empires did not mark the passing of indigenous economic enterprise, but rather was frequently the result of intimate economic collaboration between local and foreign interests.

I have discussed this in greater detail in the main body of this book, but recently read the *Memoirs of Seth Naomul Hotchand 1804–1878*, which confirmed my belief that the growth of European colonies cannot be simplistically dismissed as the triumph of European capitalism and the destruction of indigenous economic enterprise, but was rather based on ancient human and economic continuities.[1] The author of the memoirs belonged to a Hindu Sindhi family which had been engaged in maritime trade across the Arabian Sea for several generations. The family flourished in an area beyond European rule, bounded by Karachi, Muscat, Bahrain and Basra, but it also benefited from the commercial activities of Europeans, linking its operations into British Indian ports such as Bombay and Calcutta, from where they established branches, ran European ships with European officers and followed the British flag to Hong Kong. In time, the author became one of the agents for the British conquest of Sind in 1843, and helped finance that conquest.

The importance of his story for me was the portrayal of a vigorous and dynamic indigenous commercial system which existed at the time when the British were constructing their Indian empire. The construction of that empire stimulated the fortunes of Seth Hotchand's family which eventually found a niche within it. Hotchand's success story was compounded by the establishment of a European colonial empire which initially opened up new opportunities for indigenous economic activity. I write 'initially' quite deliberately, because once the empire was fully established and industrial capitalism began to work upon indigenous economies, the economic role of merchant families such as Hotchand's changed dramatically.

The spread of European-controlled technologies (particularly relating to shipbuilding) and new forms of commercial activity undermined the range of economic activities open to indigenous merchant groups. Hotchand's family owned European vessels in the early decades of the nineteenth century, but within a lifetime such ownership was a rarity, as European shipping companies came to hold a monopo-

[1] Seth Naomul Hotchand, 1982.

ly of new shipping technologies. Hotchand's family survived, but as landowners and members of the imperial bureaucracy. Other indigenous mercantile families fared better as capitalists, but in general within a much more restricted arena of economic activity than had existed up to the early nineteenth century.

This last point deserves greater consideration. Until the nineteenth century many indigenous élites were active partners in trade. For example, along the Malabar coast of southern India and in the Malay peninsula and the Indonesian archipelago rulers of small coastal states were intimately associated with the workings of maritime trade, taxing, arbitrating and extending patronage to secure a share of the profits of that trade. Indigenous merchants worked closely with such rulers, extending the range and nature of their economic activities wherever possible. With the creation of the colonial state, all this changed. Many indigenous courts vanished, but even where they survived—as in British Malaya—the old élites lost their control over trade and associated technology. The rules of the game had been altered and were now set by the foreigners who created new economic relationships and loyalties. The scale and complexity of maritime trade had changed, and it was now beyond many old ruling élites and indigenous mercantile groups.[2] Some of these mercantile groups did find a niche in the new order, but most found that they needed the services of new middlemen to negotiate the new system. From being rivals and partners in commerce with Europeans, indigenous merchants now became servants of a system determined by extra-regional imperatives.

Opposed to Hotchand and other indigenous groups who found a niche in the new political and economic system are the victims of European imperialism whose lives, cultures and futures were stunted by colonial rule. But what has to be borne in mind is that the processes of imperialism cannot be readily categorized according to one theory or another, or based on a divide between 'them' and 'us'. The historian of the Indian Ocean region has much to contribute to world history, by a closer examination of the fortunes of the indigenous people who worked the sea, and the precise nature of their relationship with Europeans from 1498.

[2] Edwin Lee, 1978, 25–37.

Much of this history has been concerned with the linkage between maritime trade and cultural diffusion and interaction. I have argued that maritime trade provided the means, and often was the stimulus, for interaction between various indigenous civilizations of the Indian Ocean region. To understand processes of cultural diffusion and interaction in the Indian Ocean region one has to understand the processes of maritime trade, for it was maritime trade which gave the Indian Ocean its distinctive human identity in the pre-modern world. By the eighteenth century European intrusion had begun to disrupt ancient patterns of maritime activity and this, in association with the establishment of European territorial empires in the region, fatally disrupted equally ancient patterns of cultural diffusion and interaction. Culturally and economically, Europeans fragmented the ancient 'world' of the Indian Ocean, reducing it to a dependent region of a worldwide economic and cultural system dominated by the industrialized nations of the northern hemisphere.

As an inhabitant of the Indian Ocean region I find it impossible to end the story I have written. During the twentieth century there has obviously been a fundamental change in the relationship between people and the Ocean. Fewer people now use the Ocean as fishermen, sailors or travellers, but more people than ever are conscious of the Ocean as a determining factor in our future: as a major influence upon our physical environment and a source of food and raw materials. The modern states which border the Ocean carry with them a vital legacy from the past, in that the cultures and religions of all but a handful have been shaped by ancient processes of interaction between peoples around the Ocean. The experience of European colonialism has left behind it a preoccupation with extra-regional influences, but the realities of the present are such that we must consider the pre-European past if we are to understand the region we live in.

In the 1990s political and economic orientations based upon either the colonial past or the political doctrines which underpinned the Cold War have begun to dissolve. The Cold War was in many ways a diversion which drew attention away from very real local problems to the global struggle between the USA and the USSR (and their allies). Former colonies were drawn into this struggle as they sought assistance to resolve their pressing problems, and in doing so they were rarely free to make self-interested national decisions about the shape of their future. However, in the wake of the Cold War there is an opportunity to tackle problems associated with economic development, population growth and national rivalries outside the arena of Great Power politics. These changes in the international climate have encouraged many of the modern states of the Indian Ocean region to focus their attention on the region, particularly as the two great imperial patrons of the twentieth century—the Soviet Union and the United States of America—have resolved their differences, and the great ideological divide which separated them and their clients from one another has, for all practical purposes, vanished.

The extra-regional powers who exercised so much influence on the politics of Indian Ocean states during the twentieth century have now withdrawn from direct intimate participation in the affairs of the region, except where they perceive an immediate threat to their interests, as was the case in the Iraq–Kuwait conflict. This has left a power vacuum in the region, with the Super Powers less inclined to intervene, except in special circumstances, and has forced regional states to a new assessment of their relations with one another in the absence of direct imperial patronage. Even in Australia, new sensibilities concerning its place in the world, and new patterns of migration and trade (most particularly with Indonesia, Singapore, Malaysia, India, Sri Lanka, the Persian Gulf states, Lebanon, Egypt, Mauritius and South Africa) have led to stronger links with Asia and Africa, and have broken the ancient insularity of that continent from its neighbours, with whom it must now learn to share the past and the future of the Indian Ocean, and dissolve the divide between 'them' and 'us'.

Bibliography

1. Unpublished sources

PALAT, R.A., 1988 'From World-Empire to World-Economy: Southeastern India and the Emergence of the Indian Ocean World Economy (1350–1650)', (Ph.D. thesis, Binghampton).

REEVES, P., 1992 'The Koli and the British at Bombay: the structure of their relations in the mid-19th century', paper for the 9th Biennial Conference of the Association for Asian Studies of Australia, Armidale.

SIRISENA, W.M., 1969 'Ceylon and South-East Asia: Political, Religious and Cultural Relations from AD c. 1000 to c. 1500', (Ph.D. thesis, ANU).

VILLIERS, J., 1983 'One of the especiallest flowers in our garden: the English factory at Makassar 1613–1667', paper, XXXIst International Congress of Human Sciences in Asia and North Africa, Tokyo and Kyoto.

WINIUS, G.D., 1989 'The "Secret People" in their several dimensions', paper, Fifth International Seminar on Indo-Portuguese History, Cochin.

2. Published sources

BOS   Broeze. F. (ed.) *Brides of the Sea. Port Cities of Asia from the 16th–20th Centuries* (Sydney, 1989).

JMBRAS   *The Journal of the Malaya Branch of the Royal Asiatic Society.*

IESHR   *The Indian Economic and Social History Review.*

ICIOS   *International Conference on Indian Ocean Studies.*

ION   *Indian Ocean Newsletter*, 1980–87, (Centre for Indian Ocean Regional Studies, Curtin University, Western Australia).

IOR   *The Indian Ocean Review*, 1987, (Centre for Indian Ocean Regional Studies & Indian Ocean Centre for Peace Studies, Curtin University & The University of Western Australia, Western Australia).

JSAS   *Journal of Southeast Asian Studies.*

MAS   *Modern Asian Studies.*

MBRAS   *Malaysian Branch of the Royal Asiatic Society.*

SA   *South Asia* (Journal of the South Asian Studies Association of Australia and New Zealand).

UGHA   *UNESCO History of Africa.*

A relation of the voyage to Siam performed by six Jesuits sent by the French King, to the Indies and China in the year 1685 (Bangkok, 1981: orig. published 1688).

ABDULLAH, T., 1989 'Islam and the Formation of Tradition in Indonesia: A Comparative Perspective', *Itinerario*, 1, XII, 17–36.

ABEYASEKERE, S., 1987 *Jakarta. A History* (Singapore).

ABRAHAM, M., 1988 *Two Medieval Merchant Guilds of South India* (Delhi).

ABU-LUGHOD, J., 1989 *Before European Hegemony: The World System AD 1250–1350* (New York).

ADAM, P., 1979 'Le Peuplement de Madagascar et le Probleme des Grandes Migrations Maritimes', 349–53, *Mouvements de Populations dans l'Ocean Indien* (Paris).

ALAM, M., 1989 'Competition and Co-Existence: Indo-Islamic Interaction in Medieval North India', *Itinerario*, 1, XIII, 37–60.

AL-QASIMI, M., 1988 *The myth of Arab piracy in the Gulf* (London).

ALPERS, E.A., 1975 *Ivory and Slaves in East Central Africa* (London).

ANFRAY, F., 1981 'The civilisation of Aksum from the first to the seventh century', *Ancient Civilisations of Africa*, UGHA, II (Berkeley), ed. G. Mokhtar.

ANSTEY, V., 1929 *The Trade of the Indian Ocean* (Cambridge).

ARASARATNAM, S., 1978 'Indian commercial groups and European traders, 1600–1800: changing relationships in southeastern India', *SA*, NS 1, 2, September, 42–53.

—— 1983 (a) 'Indian merchants and the decline of Indian mercantile activity: the Coromandel case', *The Calcutta Historical Journal*, VII, 2, 27–42.

—— 1983 (b) 'Mare Clausum the Dutch and Regional Trade in the Indian Ocean 1650–1740', *Journal of Indian History*, LXI, Parts 1–3, April–December, 73–91.

—— 1984 'The Coromandel-Southeast Asia Trade 1650–1740', *Journal of Asian History*, 18, 2, 113–35.

—— 1986 *Merchants, Companies and Commerce on the Coromandel Coast 1650–1740* (Delhi).

—— 1988 'The Rice Trade in East India 1650–1740', *MAS*, 22, 531–49.

—— 'European port-settlements in the Coromandel commercial system 1650–1740', *BOS*, 75–96.

—— 1989 (a) 'Islamic Merchant Communities of the Indian Subcontinent in Southeast Asia', *Sixth Sri Lanka Endowment Fund Lecture, University of Malaya*, 11 October 1989 (Kuala Lumpur).

ARASARATNAM, S., 1989 (b) 'Coromandel revisited: problems and issues in Indian maritime history', *IESHR,* XXVI, 1, January–March, 1989, 101–10.

ASHTOR, E., 1980 'The Volume of Medieval Spice Trade', *The Journal of European Economic History,* 9, 3 (Winter).

AXELSON, E., 1969 *Portuguese in South-East Africa 1600–1700* (Johannesberg).

BANDARANAYAKE, S., *et al.,* 1990 *Sri Lanka and the Silk Road of the Sea* (Colombo).

BASSETT, D.K., 1958 'English Trade in Celebes, 1616–67', *JMBRAS,* XXXI, 1, May, 1–39.

—— 1971 *British Trade and Policy in Indonesia and Malaysia in the Late Eighteenth Century* (Hull).

BAYLY, C.A., 1989 *Imperial Meridian: The British Empire and the World 1780–1830* (London).

BAYLY, S., 1989 *Saints, Goddesses and Kings. Muslims and Christians in South Indian Society, 1700–1900* (Cambridge).

BEACH, D.N., 1980 *The Shona & Zimbabwe 900–1850* (Marshalltown, USA).

BERNARD, J., 1972 'Trade and Finance in the Middle Ages', *The Middle Ages, The Fontana Economic History of Europe,* vol. 1, (London), 274–338, ed. Carlo M. Cipolla.

BIBBY, G., 1969 *Looking for Dilmun* (New York).

BLUSSÉ, L., 1986 *Strange Company: Chinese settlers, mestizo women and the Dutch in VOC Batavia* (Dordrecht).

—— 1988 'The Run to the Coast: Comparative Notes on Early Dutch and English Expansion and State Formation in Asia', *Itinerario,* XII, (1), 195–214.

BORSA, G., (ed.), 1990 *Trade and Politics in the Indian Ocean* (New Delhi).

BOUCHON, G., 1988 *'Regent of the Sea'. Cannanore's Response to Portuguese Expansion, 1507–1528* (Delhi).

BOUCHON, G. and L.F.F.R. THOMAZ (eds.), 1988 *Voyage dans les deltas du Gange et de l'Irraouaddy 1521* (Paris).

BOUCHON, G. and D. LOMBARD, 1987 'The Indian Ocean in the Fifteenth Century', *India and the Indian Ocean 1500–1800* (Oxford), 46–70, (eds.) Ashin Das Gupta and M.N. Pearson.

BOXER, C.R., 1965 *The Dutch Seaborne Empire 1600–1800* (London)

—— 1967 *Francisco Vieira de Fiqueiredo: A Portuguese Merchant-Adventurer in Southeast Asia, 1624–1667* (The Hague).

BOXER, C.R., 1969 *The Portuguese Seaborne Empire* (London).

—— 1985 *Portuguese Conquest and Commerce in Southern Asia, 1500–1750* (London).

BRADDELL, Dato Sir R., 1956 'Malayadvipa: A Study in Early Indianization', *The Malayan Journal of Tropical Geography*, 9, December, 1–20.

BRAUDEL, F., 1986 *The Structures of Everyday Life*, vol. 1, *The Wheels of Commerce*, vol. 2, *The Perspective of the World*, vol. 3 (New York), Civilisation & Capitalism 15th–18th Century.

BRAUDEL, F., 1972/73 *The Mediterranean and the Mediterranean World in the Age of Philip II*, vol. I (New York), vol. II (New York).

BROCKWAY, L., 1983 'Plant Imperialism', *History Today*, 33, July, 31–6.

BROEZE, F.J.A., 1978 'The merchant fleet of Java 1820–1850', *Archipel*, 251–69.

—— 1981 'The Muscles of Empire. Indian Seamen under the Raj, 1919–1939', *IESHR*, 18, 43–67.

—— 1984 'Underdevelopment and Dependency: Maritime India during the Raj', *MAS*, 18, 432–41.

BROEZE, F.J.A., K.I. MCPHERSON and P.D. REEVES, 1987 'Engineering and Empire: The Making of the Modern Indian Ocean Ports' in *The Indian Ocean: Explorations in History, Commerce and Politics* (New Delhi), ed. Satish Chandra.

CARSWELL, J. and M. PRICKETT, 1984 'Mantai 1980: A Preliminary Investigation', *Ancient Ceylon*, 5, 3–80.

CHANDRA, M., 1977 *Trade and Trade Routes in Ancient India* (New Delhi).

CHANG, P., 1989 'The Evolution of Chinese Thought on Maritime Foreign Trade from the Sixteenth to the Eighteenth Century', *International Journal of Maritime History*, 1, 1, June, 51–64.

CHAUDHURI, K.N., 1978 *The Trading World of Asia and the English East India Company 1660–1760* (Cambridge).

—— 1985 *Trade and Civilisation in the Indian Ocean. An Economic History from the Rise of Islam to 1750* (Cambridge).

—— 1990 *Asia Before Europe: Economy and Civilisation of the Indian Ocean from the Rise of Islam to 1750* (Cambridge).

CHAUDHURI, S., 1975 *Trade and Commercial Organisation in Bengal 1650–1720* (Calcutta).

CHITTICK, N., 1979 'Sewn Boats in the Western Indian Ocean and Survival in Somalia', *The History of Commercial Exchange & Maritime Transport*, Section III, ICIOS I (Perth).

CLARENCE-SMITH, G., 1989 (a) 'Indian Business Communities in the Western Indian Ocean', *IOR*, 2, 4, December.

CLARENCE-SMITH, G., 1989 (b) (ed.), *The Economics of the Indian Ocean Slave Trade in the Nineteenth Century* (London).

COATES, W.H., 1911 *The Old 'Country Trade' of the East Indies* (London).

COLLESS, B.E., 1969 'The early western ports of the Malay peninsula', *The Journal of Tropical Geography*, 29, December, 1–9.

CONNAH, G., 1987 *African civilisations: Pre-colonial cities and states in tropical Africa: an archaeological perspective* (Cambridge).

CONTENSON, H. DE., 1981 'Pre-Aksumite culture', *Ancient Civilisations of Africa*, UGHA, II (Berkeley), ed. G. Mokhtar.

CORREIA-AFONSO, J., 1991 'The Second Jesuit Mission to Akbar (1591)', *Indica*, 28, 2, September, 73–93.

CURTIN, P.D., 1984 *Cross-Cultural Trade in World History* (Cambridge).

CURTIN, P., *et al.*, 1982 *African History* (London).

DAS GUPTA, A., 1967 *Malabar in Asian Trade: 1740–1800* (Cambridge).

—— 1974 'Presidential Address: 'The Maritime Merchant, 1500–1800', *Proceedings of the Indian History Congress*, 35th Session, Jadavpur, 99–111.

—— 1979 *Indian Merchants and the Decline of Surat c. 1700–1750* (Wiesbaden).

DAS GUPTA, A. and M.N. PEARSON (eds.), 1987 *India and the Indian Ocean 1500–1800* (Delhi).

DE SILVA, C.R., 1978 'The Portuguese and Pearl Fishing off South India and Sri Lanka', *SA*, NS 1, 1, March, 14–28.

—— 1989 'The Portuguese Impact on the Production and Trade in Sri Lanka Cinnamon in Asia in the Sixteenth and Seventeenth Centuries', *Indica*, 26, 1 & 2, March–September, 25–38.

DHARMASENA, K., 1980 *The Port of Colombo 1860–1939* (Colombo).

—— 'Colombo: gateway and oceanic hub of shipping', *BOS*, 152–172.

DHAVALIKAR, M.K., 1991 '4000 Year Old Merchant Traders of Western India', *IOR*, 4, 4, December, 10–13, 20.

DIGBY, S., 1984 'The Maritime Trade of India', in *The Cambridge Economic History of India*, v. 1, (Delhi), 125–62, eds. Tapan Raychaudhuri and Irfan Habib.

DISKUL, M.C.S., (ed.), 1980 *The Art of Srivijaya* (Unesco).

DISNEY, A., 1978 *Twilight of the Pepper Empire, Portuguese Trade in Southwest India in the Early Seventeenth Century* (Cambridge, Mass.).

—— 1989 'Smugglers and smuggling in the western half of the Estado da India', *Indica*, 26, 1 & 2, March–September, 57–75.

DIXON, C., 1980 'Lascars: The Forgotten Seamen', *Working Men who Got Cold* (St John's, Newfoundland), 265–81, eds. R. Ommer & G. Pantma.

DOMENICHINI-RAMIARAMANANA, B., 1988 'Madagascar' *Africa from the Seventh to the Eleventh Century*, UGHA, III, (Berkeley), ed. M. El Fasi.

DUNN, R.E., 1989 *The Adventures of Ibn Battuta: A Muslim Trader of the 14th Century* (Berkeley).

EARLE, T.F. and VILLIERS, J., (eds. & trans.), 1990 *Albuquerque. Caesar of the East* (Warminster, England).

FAGAN, B.M., 1970 'Early Trade and Raw Materials in South Central Africa' in *Pre-Colonial African Trade: Essays on Trade in Central and Eastern Africa before 1900* (London), 24–38, eds. R. Gray and D. Birmingham.

FAIRBANK, J.K., 1969 *Trade and Diplomacy on the China Coast: The Opening of the Treaty Ports 1842–1854* (Harvard).

FAROQHI, S., 1990 *Herrscher Uber Mekka. Die Geschichte der Pilgerfahrt* (München).

FELDBAEK, O., 1969 *India Trade Under the Danish Flag 1772–1808* (Copenhagen).

FLORES, J.M., 1990 'The Straits of Ceylon and the Maritime Trade in Early Sixteenth Century India: Commodities, Merchants and Trading Networks', *Moyen Orient & Ocean Indien*, VII, 27–58.

FLORES, J.M., (ed.), 1991 'The Asian Seas 1500–1800. Local Societies, European Expansion and the Portuguese', special issue of *Revista de Cultura* (Macau), 13/14, January/June.

FORBES, A.D.W., 1979 'Southern Arabia and the Islamicisation of the Central Indian Ocean Archipelagoes', *Cultural Exchanges & Influences*, Section V, ICIOS I (Perth).

—— 1982 'Tenasserim: The Thai Kingdom of Ayutthaya's Link with the Indian Ocean', *ION*, 3, 1, June, 1–3.

FURBER, H., 1948 *John Company at Work* (Harvard).

—— 1976 *Rival Empires of Trade in the Orient* (Minneapolis).

GABRIEL, T.P.C., 1989 *Lakshadweep: History, Religion and Society* (New Delhi).

GALLA, A., 1987 (a) 'Comments on the writing of the early history of the Indian Ocean region', *ION*, VIII, 2, July, 16–18.

—— 1987 (b) 'Towards a reinterpretation of the early history of the regions of the Indian Ocean', *Review* (Asian Studies Association of Australia), 11, 1, July, 15–22.

GEERTZ, C., 1971 *Islam Observed: Religious Development in Morocco and Indonesia* (Chicago).

GERBEAU, H., 1979 'The Slave Trade in the Indian Ocean', *The African Slave Trade from the Fifteenth to the Nineteenth Century* (Unesco).

GIBSON-HILL, C.A., 1950 'The Indonesian Trading Boats Reaching Singapore', *JMBRAS*, XXIII, 1, February, 108–38.

GLAMANN, K., 1958 *Dutch Asiatic Trade 1620–1750* (Copenhagen).

—— 1974 'European Trade 1500–1750', *The Sixteenth and Seventeenth Centuries, The Fontana Economic History of Europe*, vol. 2 (London), 427–526, ed. Carlo M. Cipolla.

GLOVER, I.C., 1990 *Early Trade between India and South-East Asia: A Link in the Development of a World Trading System* (Centre for Southeast Asian Studies, Hull, 2nd edition).

GREEN, J., 1990 'Maritime Archaeology in Southeast and East Asia', *Antiquity*, 64, 243, June, 347–63.

GROOM, N., 1981 *Frankincense and Myrrh: A Study of the Arabian Incense Trade* (London).

GUNAWARDANA, R.A.L.H., 1987 'Changing Patterns of Navigation in the Indian Ocean and their Impact on Pre-colonial Sri Lanka', *The Indian Ocean. Explorations in History, Commerce & Politics* (New Delhi), ed. Satish Chandra.

GUY, J.S., 1988–89 'The Vietnamese Wall Tiles of Majapahit', *Transactions of the Oriental Ceramic Society*, 3, 28–46.

—— 1989 ' "Sarasa" and "Patola": Indian Textiles in Indonesia', *Orientations*, 2, 2, January, 48–60.

—— 1990 *Oriental Trade Ceramics in South-East Asia: Ninth to Sixteenth Centuries* (Singapore).

HALL, K.R., 1980 *Trade and Statecraft in the Age of the Colas* (New Delhi).

—— 1982 'The Indianization of Funnan: An Economic History of Southeast Asia's First State', *JSAS*, XIII, 1, 81–106.

—— 1985 *Maritime Trade and State Development in Early Southeast Asia* (Sydney).

HASAN, M., 1977 'Tipu Sultan's Commercial Activities in the Persian Gulf (1783–1799)', *Aspects of Deccan History* (Hyderabad), 40–51, ed. V.K. Bawa.

HAWKINS, C.W., 1977 *The Dhow* (London).

—— 1980 *Argosy of Sail* (Auckland).

—— 1982 *Praus of Indonesia* (London).

HEESTERMAN, J.C., 1989 'The "Hindu Frontier"', *Itinerario*, XIII, 1, 1–16.

—— 1991 'Warriors and Merchants', *Itinerario*, XV, 1, 37–50.

HEIMANN, J., 1980 'Small Change and Ballast: Cowry Trade and Usage as an Example of Indian Ocean Economic History', *SA*, NS, vol. II, I, June, 48–69.

HERCHELHEIM, F.M., 1960 Review. *Journal of Economic and Social History of the Orient*, 111, 108–10. See Polanyi, *et al.*

HOGENDORN, J. and M. JOHNSON, 1986 *The Shellmoney of the Slave Trade* (Cambridge).

HORRIDGE, A., 1978 *The design of planked boats of the Moluccas* (Greenwich).

—— 1981 *The Prahu: Traditional Sailing Boat of Indonesia* (Kuala Lumpur).

—— 1987 *Outrigger Canoes of Bali and Madura, Indonesia* (Honolulu).

HOTCHAND, S.N., 1982 *Memoirs of Seth Naomul Hotchand 1804–1878* (Karachi, original published, 1915).

HOURANI, G.F., 1951 *Arab seafaring in the Indian Ocean in ancient and early medieval times* (Princeton).

HOYLE, B.S., 'Maritime perspectives on ports and port systems: the case of East Africa', *BOS*, 188–206.

HUNTINGFORD, G., (ed.), 1980 *The Periplus of the Erythraean Sea* (London).

IRELAND, J. de C., 1986 'Chinese voyaging in the Indian Ocean before the European influx', *ION*, VII, 3, November, 6–7.

JOHNSTONE, P., 1980 *The Sea-craft of Prehistory* (London).

JUMSAI, S., 1989 *Naga: Cultural Origins in Siam and the West Pacific* (Singapore).

KAEMPFER, E., 1987 *A Description of the Kingdom of Siam 1690* (Bangkok, original published, 1727).

KAY, G., 1975 *Development & Underdevelopment: A Marxist Analysis* (London).

KENNEDY, K.A.R., 1975 *The physical anthropology of the megalith-builders of South India and Sri Lanka* (Canberra).

KENT, R.K., 1979 'The Possibilities of Indonesian Colonies in Africa with Special Reference to Madagascar' in *Mouvements de Populations dans l'Ocean Indien*, 93–105, (Paris).

KESTEVEN, G.L., 1949 *Malayan Fisheries* (Singapore).

KIDWAI, A.H., 'Port cities in a national system of ports and cities: a geographical analysis of Indian ports in the twentieth century', *BOS*, 207–22.

KIENIEWICZ, J., 1986 'Pepper gardens and market in precolonial Malabar', *Moyen Orient & Ocean Indien*, 3, 1–36.

KING, B.B. and M.N. PEARSON (eds.), 1979 *The Age of Partnership: Europeans in Asia Before Dominion* (Honolulu).

KOBISHANOV, Y.M., 1981 'Aksum: political system, economics and culture, first to fourth century', *Ancient Civilisations of Africa*, UGHA, II (Berkeley), ed. G. Mokhtar.

KUCZYNSKI, R.R., 1949 *Demographic Survey of the British Empire* (London), vol. II.

LAHIRI, N., 1990 'Harappa as a Centre of Trade and Trade Routes: A Case-Study of the Resource-Use, Resource-Access and Lines of Communication in the Indus Civilisation', *IESHR*, 27, 405–44.

LEE, E., 1978 'Trade and Migration in the Malay World', *Berita Anthroplogi*, X, 35, June, 25–37.

LEUR, J.V. van, 1955 *Indonesian Trade and Society* (The Hague).

LIMA CRUZ, M.A., 1986 'Exiles and renegades in early sixteenth century Portuguese India', *IESHR*, 23, 249–62.

LY-TIO-FANE, M., 1970 *The Triumph of Jean Nicolas Cere: Mauritius and the Spice Trade* (Paris).

—— 1976 *Pierre Sonnerat* (Mauritius).

MACADAM, H.I., 1990 'Dilmun Revisited', *Arabian Archaeology and Epigraphy*, 1, 2/3, December.

MACKNIGHT, C.C., 1976 *The Voyage to Marege: Macassan trepangers in northern Australia* (Melbourne).

MANDEL, E., 1968 *Marxist Economic Theory* (London).

MANGUIN, P.Y., 1980 'The Southeast Asian Ship: An Historical Approach', *JSAS*, XI, 2, 136–71.

—— 1984 'Sewn-Plank Craft of South-East Asia. A Preliminary Study', *Maritime Studies*, vol. E, ICIOS, II (Perth).

—— 1985 'Late Medieval Asian Shipbuilding in the Indian Ocean', *Moyen Orient et Ocean Indien*, 2, 2, 13–15.

—— 1986 'Shipshape Societies: Boat Symbolism and Political Systems in Insular Southeast Asia' in *Southeast Asia in the 9th and 14th centuries* (Singapore & Canberra), 187–214, eds. D.G. Marr and A.C. Milner.

MARR, D.G. and A.C. MILNER (eds.), 1986 *Southeast Asia in the 9th and 14th centuries* (Singapore & Canberra).

MARSHALL, P.J., 1976 *East Indian Fortunes: The British in Bengal in the Eighteenth Century* (Oxford).

MARTIN, E.B., 1979 'The geography of present-day smuggling in the western Indian Ocean: the case of the dhow', *The History of Commercial Exchange & Maritime Transport*, Section III, ICIOS, I (Perth).

MARTIN, R.M., 1839 *Statistics of the Colonies of the British Empire . . .* , (London).

MASAO, F.T. and H.W. MUTORO, 1988 'The East African coast and the

Comoro Islands' in *Africa from the Seventh to the Eleventh Century*, UGHA, III (Berkeley), ed. M. El Fasi.

MATHESON, V., 1975 'Concepts of State in the "Tuhfat Al-Nafis"', *Pre-Colonial State Systems of Southeast Asia*, Monograph of MBRAS, no. 6 (Kuala Lumpur), 12–21, eds. A. Reid and L. Castles.

MCNEILL, W.H., 1976 *Plagues and Peoples* (New York).

MCPHERSON, K., 1984 'Processes of Cultural Interaction in the Indian Ocean: An Historical Perspective', *The Great Circle*, 6, 2, 78–92.

MCPHERSON, K., F.J.A. BROEZE and P.D. REEVES, 1986 'Imperial ports in the modern world economy: the case of the Indian Ocean', *Journal of Transport History*, 3rd serv., 7, 2, 1–20.

MCPHERSON, K., 1987 (a) 'A Secret People of South Asia. The Origins, Evolution and Role of the Luso-Indian Goan Community from the Sixteenth to the Twentieth Centuries', *Itinerario*, XI, 2, 72–85.

MCPHERSON, K., 1987 (b) with F.J. BROEZE, P.D. REEVES and J. WARDROP, 'The Social Experience of the Maritime World of the Indian Ocean; Passenger Traffic and Community Building, *c.* 1815–1939' in *Maritime Aspects of Migration* (Cologne), 427–40, ed. Klaus Friedland.

MCPHERSON, K., 1988 (a) 'Maritime Passenger Traffic in the Indian Ocean Region', *The Great Circle*, 10, 1, April, 49–61.

—— 1988 (b) with F.J. BROEZE and P.D. REEVES, 'Maritime Peoples of the Indian Ocean: Changing Occupations and Industries Since *c.* 1800', *Mariners Mirror*, 74, 3, August, 241–54.

—— 1990 'Chulias and Klings: Indigenous Trade Diasporas and European Penetration of the Indian Ocean Littoral' in Giorgio Borsa (ed.) *Trade and Politics in the Indian Ocean* (New Delhi), 33–46.

MEILINK-ROELOFSZ, M.A.P., 'The structure of trade in Asia in the sixteenth and seventeenth centuries', *Mare Luso-Indicum*, IV, 1–43.

MEKOURIA, T.T., 1988 'The Horn of Africa', *Africa from the Seventh to the Eleventh Century*, UGHA, III (Berkeley), ed. M. El Fasi.

MICHALOWSKI, K., 1981 'The Spreading of Christianity in Nubia', *Ancient Civilisations of Africa*, UGHA, II (Berkeley), ed. G. Mokhtar.

MINCHINTON, W., 1990 'Corporate Ship Operation from the Late Sixteenth to the Late Eighteenth Century', *International Journal of Maritime History*, II, 1, June, 117–54.

MOOKERJI, R., 1912 *Indian Shipping: A History of the Sea-Borne Trade and Maritime Activity of the Indians From the Earliest Times* (London).

MORAIS, J., 1988 *The Early Farming Communities of Southern Mozambique*, Studies in African Archaeology 3 (Maputo & Stockholm).

MUNRO-HAY, S., 1979 'The foreign trade of the Aksumite port of Adulis', *The History of Commercial Exchange and Maritime Transport,* Section III, ICIOS, I (Perth).

—— 1984 'An African Monetarised Economy in Ancient Times', *Maritime Studies,* vol. E, ICIOS, II (Perth).

MURPHEY, R., 'On the evolution of the port city', *BOS,* 223–46.

NIGHTINGALE, P., 1970 *Trade and Empire in Western India 1784–1806* (Cambridge).

OLIVER, R. and ATMORE, A., 1981 *The African Middle Ages 1400–1800* (New York).

OTTINO, P., 1979 'Mythe et Histoire: Les Andriambahoaka Malagaches et l'Heritage Indonesien', *Cultural Exchanges & Influences,* Section V, ICIOS, I (Perth).

PAGE, W.J., 1987 'The Lakato hypothesis: summary of a recent inquiry into the origins of the Fijians', *ION,* VIII, I, March, 8–11.

PAGE, W.J., 1989 'Afro-Indonesian Contacts', *IOR,* 2, 2, June, 6–8.

PARKER, G., 1988 *The Military Revolution* (Cambridge).

PEARSON, M.N., 1976 *Merchants and Rulers in Gujarat* (Los Angeles).

—— 1979 'Corruption and Corsairs in Sixteenth-Century Western India: A Functional Analysis', *The Age of Partnership. Europeans in Asia Before Dominion* (Honolulu), 15–42, eds. Blair B. Kling and M.N. Pearson.

—— 1985 'Littoral Society: The Case for the Coast', *The Great Circle,* 7, 1, April, 1–8.

—— 1987 (a) *The Portuguese in India* (Cambridge).

—— 1987 (b) 'Maritime History Theory and Empirical Testing', *Review* (Asian Studies Association of Australia), 11, 1, July, 23–31.

—— 1988 'Brokers in Western Indian Port Cities their Role in Servicing Foreign Merchants', *MAS,* 22, 455–72.

PINA-CABRAL, J. de., 1989 'The Mediterranean as a Category of Regional Comparison: A Critical View', *Current Anthropology,* 30, 3, June, 399–406.

POLANYI, K., 1981 *The Livelihood of Man* (New York), ed. Harry W. Pearson.

POLANYI, K., C.M. ARENSBERG and H.W. PEARSON, 1957 *Trade and Market in Early Empires* (Glencoe, Illinois). See F.M. Herchelheim.

POUWELS, R.L., 1987 *Horn and Crescent. Cultural Change and Traditional Islam on the East African Coast, 800–1900* (Cambridge).

PRAKASH, OM, 1988 *The Dutch East India Company and the Economy of Bengal 1630–1720* (Delhi).

PRASAD, P.C., 1977 *Foreign Trade and Commerce in Ancient India* (New Delhi).

PTAK, R., (ed.), 1987 *Portuguese Asia: Aspects in History and Economic History* (Wiesbaden).

PTAK, R. and ROTHERMUND, D., (eds.), 1991 *Emporia, Commodities and Entrepreneurs in Asian Maritime Trade, c. 1400–1750* (Wiesbaden).

PUTNAM, G.G., 1924–1930 *Salem Vessels and their Voyages*, Series I–IV (Salem).

QUIASON, S.D., 1966 *English 'Country Trade' with the Philippines 1644–1765* (Quezon City).

RATNAGAR, S., 1981 *Encounters. The Westerly Trade of the Harappa Civilisation* (Delhi).

RAY, ASIM, 1984 *The Islamic Syncretistic Tradition in Bengal* (Princeton).

RAY, H.P., 1986 *Monastery and Guild. Commerce Under the Satavahanas* (Delhi).

—— 1989 (a) 'Early Maritime Contacts between South and Southeast Asia', *JSAS*, XX, 1, 42–54.

—— 1989 (b) 'Early Historical Trade: An Overview', *IESHR*, 26, (1989), 437–58.

RAY, H., 1987 'China and the 'Western Ocean' in the Fifteenth Century' in *The Indian Ocean. Explorations in History, Commerce and Politics* (Delhi), 109–124, ed. Satish Chandra.

RAYCHAUDHURI, T., 1962 *Jan Company in Coromandel 1605–1690* (s'Gravenhage).

—— 1984 'Inland Trade' in *The Cambridge Economic History of India*, v. 1 (New Delhi), 325–59, eds. Tapan Raychaudhuri and Irfan Habib.

REEVES, P.D., 1985 'The past of our future: Indian Ocean influences in Australian History' (The Peter Eldershaw Memorial Lecture, 1985) in Tasmanian Historical Research Association, *Papers and Proceedings*, 32, 3, 82–94. Reprinted in *ION*, 7, 1, 1986, 1–5 and 16.

REEVES, P., BROEZE, F.J.A. and MCPHERSON, K., 'Studying the Asian port city', *BOS*, 29–53.

REID, A., 1980 'The Structure of Cities in Southeast Asia, Fifteenth to Seventeenth Centuries', *JSAS*, XI, 2, 235–50.

REID, A., (ed.), 1983 *Slavery, Bondage and Dependency in Southeast Asia* (St Lucia).

REID, A., 1988 *Southeast Asia in the Age of Commerce 1450–1680* (Yale).

—— 'The organisation of production in the pre-colonial Southeast Asian port city', *BOS*, 54–74.

RICHARDS, J., (ed.), 1983 *Precious Metals in the Later Medieval and Early Modern Worlds* (Durham, North Carolina).

ROONEY, D.F., 1987 *Folk Pottery in South-East Asia* (Singapore).

SAID, E., 1985 *Orientalism* (Melbourne).

SANDHU, K.S. and WHEATLEY, P., 1983 *Melaka* (Kuala Lumpur), 2 vols.

SCAMMEL, G.V., 1988 'The Pillars of Empire: Indigenous Assistance and the Survival of the "Estado da India", 1600–1700', *MAS*, 22, 473–89.

SCHRIEKE, B., 1966 *Indonesian Sociological Studies* (The Hague).

SEDLAR, J.W., 1980 *India and the Greek World* (New Jersey).

SENTANCE, D., 1979 'Ships and their significance in the re-appraising of Indian Ocean history', *The History of Commercial Exchange & Maritime Transport*, Section III, ICIOS, I (Perth).

SHEPHERD, G., 1982 'The Making of The Swahili', *Paideuma*, 28, 129–47.

SHERIFF, A.M.H., 1981 'The East African coast and its role in maritime trade', *Ancient Civilisations of Africa*, UGHA, II (Berkeley), ed. G. Mokhtar.

SILVER, M., 1985 *Economic Structures of the Ancient Near East* (London).

SINGH, M.P., 1985 *Town, Market, Mint and Port in the Mughal Empire 1556–1707* (Delhi).

SITWELL, N.H.H., 1986 *Outside the Empire: The World the Romans Knew* (London).

SPENCER, G.W., 1983 *The Politics of Expansion: The Chola Conquest of Sri Lanka and Sri Vijaya* (Madras).

STEENSGARD, N., 1970 'European Shipping to Asia, 1497–1700', *Scandinavian Economic History Review*, XVIII, 9.

—— 1972 *Carracks, Caravans and Companies: The Structural Crisis in the European-Asian Trade in the Early Seventeenth Century* (Copenhagen).

STEIN, B., 1989 *Vijayanagara* (Cambridge).

SUBRAHMANYAM, S., 1984 'The Portuguese, the port of Basrur, and the rice trade, 1600–50', *IESHR*, 21, 4, 433–62.

—— 1985 'Staying on: the Portuguese of southern Coromandel in the late seventeenth century', *IESHR*, 22, 446–63.

—— 1986 'The Portuguese Response to the Rise of Masulipatnam 1570–1600', *The Great Circle*, 8, 2, October, 127–31.

—— 1988 (a) 'Persians, Pilgrims and Portuguese: The Travails of Masulipatnam Shipping in the Western Indian Ocean, 1590–1665', *MAS*, 22, 503–30.

—— 1988 (b) Review. 'Asian Trade and European Affluence? Coromandel, 1650–1740', *MAS*, 22, 179–88.

—— 1988 (c) 'The Tail Wags the Dog or Some Aspects of the External

Relations of the Estado da India, 1570–1600', *Moyen Orient & Océan Indien*, 5, 131–60.

SUBRAHMANYAM, S., 1989 (a) Review. ' "World Economies" and South Asia, 1600–1750: A Sceptical Note', *Review*, (Fernand Braudel Centre), XII, 1, Winter, 141–48.

—— 1990 (a) *The Political Economy of Commerce: Southern India 1500–1650* (Cambridge).

—— 1990 (b) 'Rural Industry and Commercial Agriculture in Late Seventeenth Century South Eastern India', *Past & Present*, 26, February, 76–114.

—— 1990 (c) *Improvising Empire: Portuguese Trade and Settlement in the Bay of Bengal 1500–1700* (Delhi).

—— 1990 (d) Rural Industry and Commercial Agriculture in Late Seventeenth-Century South Eastern India', *Past & Present*, 125, February, 76–114.

SUBRAHMANYAM, S. and L.F.F.R. THOMAZ, 'Evolution of Empire: The Portuguese in the India Ocean During the 16th Century', *The Economics of Merchant Empires* (New York, forthcoming), ed. James Tracy.

SUBRAHMANYAM, S. and C.A. BAYLY, 1988 'Portfolio Capitalists and the Political Economy of Early Modern India', *IESHR*, 25, 401–24.

SUTHERLAND, H., 'Eastern emporium and company town: trade and society in eighteenth-century Makassar', *BOS*, 97–128.

SUTTON, J., 1981 *Lords of the East. The East India Company and its Ships* (London).

TALIB, Y., 1988 'The African diaspora in Asia', *Africa from the Seventh to the Eleventh Century*, UGHA, III (Berkeley), ed. M. El Fasi.

THOMAZ, L.F.F.R., 1991 'Factions, Interests and Messianism; The Politics of Portuguese Expansions in the East, 1500–21', *IESHR*, 28, 97–110.

—— *In the Shadow of Melaka: Essays on the Portuguese in 16th Century Asia* (forthcoming).

TIBBETTS, G.R., 1979 *A Study of the Arabic Texts Containing Material on South-East Asia* (Leiden & London).

—— 1981 *Arab Navigation in the Indian Ocean before the Coming of the Portuguese* (Oriental Translation Fund, New Series vol. XLII) (London).

TOUSSAINT, A., 1968 *A History of the Indian Ocean* (London).

—— 1977 *A History of Mauritius* (London).

TREGONNING, K.G.P., 1953 'The Elimination of Slavery in North Borneo', *JMBRAS*, XXVI, 1, July, 24–36.

VERIN, P., 1981 'Madagascar' in *Ancient Civilisations of Africa*, UGHA, II (Berkeley), ed. G. Mokhtar.

VILLIERS, A., 1952 *The Indian Ocean* (London).

—— 1958 *Give Me a Ship to Sail* (London).

—— 1969 *Sons of Sinbad: The Great Tradition of Arab Seamanship in the Indian Ocean* (New York).

VILLIERS, J., 1981 'Trade and Society in the Banda Islands in the Sixteenth Century', *MAS*, 15, 723–50.

—— 1982 'De um caminho ganhar almas e fazenda: motives of Portuguese expansion in eastern Indonesia in the sixteenth century', *Terrae Incognitae*, 23–39.

—— 1986 'Caravels, Carracks and Coracoras: Notes on Portuguese Shipping in the Indian Ocean, the Malay Archipelago and the South China Sea in the Sixteenth and Seventeenth Centuries', *Kapal dan Harta Karam (Ships and Sunken Treasure)*, (Kuala Lumpur), 40–52.

VITHARANA, V., 1992 *The Oru & The Yatra: Traditional Out-Rigger Water Craft of Sri Lanka* (Dehiwela).

WAGSTAFF, J.M., 1985 *The Evolution of Middle Eastern Landscapes. An Outline to AD 1840* (London).

WAKE, C.H.H., 1979 'The Changing Pattern of Europe's Pepper and Spice Imports, *ca.* 1400–1700', *The Journal of European Economic History*, 8, 2, Fall, 361–403.

WALLERSTEIN, I., 1974 *The Modern World-System*, 1 (New York).

—— 1979 *The Capitalist World Economy* (New York).

—— 1987 'The Incorporation of the Indian Subcontinent into the Capitalist World-Economy', *The Indian Ocean: Explorations in History, Commerce and Politics*, (Delhi), 222–53, ed. Satish Chandra.

WARMINGTON, E.H., 1974 *The Commerce between the Roman Empire and India* (London, rev. edn).

WARREN, J.F., 1981 *The Sulu Zone 1768–1898. The Dynamics of External Trade, Slaver, and Ethnicity in the Transformation of a Southeast Asian Maritime State* (Singapore).

WATSON, A.M., 1977 'The Rise and Spread of Old World Cotton' in *Studies in Textile History. In Memory of Harold B. Burham* (Toronto), ed. Veronica Geevers.

—— 1981 'A Medieval Green Revolution: New Crops and Farming Techniques in the Early Islamic World', *The Islamic Middle East 700–1900. Studies in Economic and Social History* (New Jersey), 29–58, ed. A.L. Udovitch.

WATSON, I.B., 1980 *Foundation for Empire: English Private Trade in India 1659–1760* (New Delhi).

WHEATLEY, P., 1980 *The Golden Khersonese* (Kuala Lumpur).

WHITE, W.G., 1922 *The Sea Gypsies of Malaya* (London).

WILDING, R., 1987 *The Shorefolk: Aspects of the Early Development of Swahili Communities*, Fort Jesus Occasional Papers No. 2 (Mombasa).

WILLS, J.E., 1974 *Pepper, Guns & Parleys: The Dutch East India Company and China, 1662–1681* (Cambridge, Mass.).

WINIUS, G.D., 1985 *The Black Legend of Portuguese India* (New Delhi).

WINK, A., 1987 'The Jewish Diaspora in India: Eighth to Thirteenth Centuries', *IESHR*, 24, 4, October–December, 349–66.

——— 1990 *Al-Hind. The Making of the Indo-Islamic World*, vol. 1 (Leiden).

WOLF, E.R., 1982 *Europe and the People Without History* (Berkeley).

WOLTERS, O.W., 1967 *Early Indonesian Commerce: A Study of the Origins of Srivijaya* (Ithaca: Cornell University).

WOLTERS, O.W., 1970 *The Fall of Srivijaya in Malay History* (Ithaca: Cornell University).

WONG, L.K., 1960 'The Trade of Singapore 1819–1869', *JMBRAS*, XXXIII, 4, December, 5–315.

Index